A Guide to
RISC Microprocessors

A Guide to
RISC
Microprocessors

Edited by

Michael Slater
Microprocessor Report
Sebastopol, California

Academic Press, Inc.
Harcourt Brace Jovanovich, Publishers

San Diego   New York   Boston   London   Sydney   Tokyo   Toronto

This book is printed on acid-free paper. ∞

Academic Press, Inc.
San Diego, California 92101

United Kingdom Edition published by
Academic Press Limited
24–28 Oval Road, London NW1 7DX

Library of Congress Cataloging-in-Publication Data

A Guide to RISC microprocessors / [edited] by Michael Slater.
       p.   cm.
    Includes index.
    ISBN 0-12-649140-2
    1. RISC microprocessors.   I. Slater, Michael.
  TK7895.M5G85   1992
  621.39'16--dc20   91-34192
                                                                         CIP

PRINTED IN THE UNITED STATES OF AMERICA
92 93 94 95 96 QW 9 8 7 6 5 4 3 2 1

Contents

Part III.   MIPS

Part IV.   Motorola 88000

Part V.   Intel 860

Part VI.   Intel 960

Part VII.   AMD 29000

Preface

This book is composed of articles from *Microprocessor Report,* an industry newsletter that began publication in the fall of 1987. Coincidentally, RISC microprocessors were just emerging from research labs into the commercial marketplace at that time. RISC microprocessors, which weren't even mentioned in the newsletter for the first six months of its publication, have become one of its key subjects.

Articles in the newsletter, written by myself and several contributing editors, have covered every major RISC microprocessor family in depth. By focusing on microprocessors, we provide a comprehensiveness of coverage that is unmatched.

Making sense out of all the different microprocessors on the market is a challenging task. Each vendor promotes the value of its unique features and denigrates those of its competitors, and independent appraisals are rare. Articles about microprocessors are often written by the companies selling them. The articles in *Microprocessor Report,* on the other hand, are written by independent reviewers with extensive technical backgrounds. As a result, each article provides a critical perspective, exploring weaknesses as well as strengths.

The RISC microprocessor market now has half a dozen major architectures and twice that many vendors. The articles presented here cover every major commercially available RISC microprocessor family: SPARC, MIPS, Intel's 860 and 960, Motorola's 88000, AMD's 29000, and HP's PA-RISC. No other volume combines as much information about all the latest RISC microprocessors.

Thanks to the generous efforts of the contributing editors to *Microprocessor Report,* these articles represent a broader perspective and greater expertise than any one person could provide. The contributions of John Wharton, Brian Case, and Nick Tredennick have been especially valuable in assembling this book. Many others helped make the newsletter possible and contributed valuable suggestions and insight, including Dennis Allison, Rich Belgard, Roger King, Bruce Koball, George Morrow, Andy Rappaport, David Schwartz, and John Wakerly. The newsletter truly would not have been possible were it not for the support of my wife Irene Stratton, who not only put up with a publication that ruled our personal lives for several years but also helped run the business.

Michael Slater
Editor and Publisher, *Microprocessor Report*
Sebastopol, California

Contributors

The following contributing editors to *Microprocessor Report* have authored pieces that are included in this book.

Brian Case, Tim Olson, Michael Slater, Mark Thorson, John H. Wharton

Note: For information on subscribing to *Microprocessor Report,* send your name and address to *Microprocessor Report,* P.O. Box 2438, Sebastopol, CA 96472; phone (707) 823-4004; fax (707) 823-0504; or send email to mslater@cup.portal.com.

I

Perspective

1

RISC Architectures

Michael Slater

Beginning in the late 1980s, RISC architectures (Reduced Instruction Set Computer) quickly became the dominant CPU design philosophy. Although new implementations of the two major CISC architectures (Complex Instruction Set Computer) appeared—i.e., Intel's i486 and Motorola's MC68040—all of the investment in new architectures went toward RISCs such as Sun Microsystems' SPARC, MIPS Computer Systems' R2000/R3000/R4000, Advanced Micro Devices' 29000, and Intel's i860.

In this chapter, we present a perspective on RISC architecture intended to help you understand the technical details and the significance of the new chips.

The Search for Speed

A new generation of microprocessors following the RISC design philosophy has taken over the high end of the microprocessor market. This new high end, however, is beyond what have been microprocessor-class applications in performance, price, and complexity. At present RISC processors are the province of workstations, computers, and very high-end embedded controls.

Performance is the driving force behind RISC architectures, and RISC processors today are aimed exclusively at high-end applications. In time, however, the lessons from RISC designs will impact all microprocessor

3

systems. Scaled-down RISC designs optimized for embedded control applications with lower performance levels and lower costs have appeared. The issues involved are thus of importance to all microprocessor system designers, not just those working on workstations and other high-performance applications.

A Break from the Past

Since the introduction of the 8008 and 8080, compatibility with existing architectures has been a major issue in microprocessor design. Intel has maintained some degree of compatibility in their architectures from the 8008 up through the 386 (80386); and while compatibility with the 8086 is essential to the success of the 386, it has also made the architecture more awkward and complex than it would otherwise have been.

Motorola, on the other hand, chose to break completely from its existing architectures when it introduced the 68000. As a result, the 68000 has a much cleaner, simpler design than the 8086, and has had a much easier time maintaining compatibility as the addressing range has been increased and other features have been added in the 68020, 68030, and 68040.

RISC processors give everyone a chance to make a clean break from existing architectures and start anew. Freed from the constraints of compatibility with earlier architectures, chip designers can produce more streamlined, consistent, and efficient processors.

RISC Origins

While early microprocessor designs were the product of semiconductor companies and logic designers, RISC designs have emerged from the universities and research labs. IBM began work on their 801 computer design in 1975; although the term RISC was not used, the 801 processor incorporated may RISC concepts. The term RISC was coined by David Patterson of UC Berkeley in 1980.

Professor Patterson led the design of the Berkeley RISC chips, which were developed as academic explorations and not as commercial products. Patterson then worked with Sun Microsystems to define the SPARC (Scalable Performance Architecture), which can be viewed as a commercial outgrowth of the Berkeley RISC design.

A group at Stanford, led by Professor John Hennessy, designed a somewhat different RISC processor called the MIPS machine. Like the Berkeley RISC chip, the first MIPS chip was an academic exercise. Hennessey, along with John Moussouris (who worked on VLSI RISC chips at IBM) and Skip Stritter (chief architect of the 68000), then founded MIPS Computer Systems, Inc. to commercialize the technology.

RISC processors are simpler to design than CISC (Complex Instruction Set Computer) processors. This has made it more attractive for many systems vendors, including Sun, Apollo, IBM, HP, Pyramid, and Ridge, to develop their own processors. RISC makes it feasible for every computer architect to have a shot at designing his own processor. The inevitable NIH (not invented here) syndrome, combined with the relative ease of implementation, has led to a large number of RISC designs in a relatively short period of time.

CISC Processor Development

To understand the motivations behind RISC architectures, it is useful to first look at how CISC processors evolved. CISC processors are the result of an evolutionary process. Early microprocessors were severely constrained by the limits of what could be implemented on a single piece of silicon. Ease of programming was not high on the priority list. With each successive generation, increased chip design capabilities have been used to provide higher performance, simpler hardware implementations, and more complex instructions. Processor complexity is used to simplify the programming task by matching machine-level instructions to high-level constructs.

For example, the 68030 (Figure 1) includes support for array indexing with array elements of different sizes, parameter range checking, and complex operations such as bit field insertion and extraction. Seven data types and 18 addressing modes are supported. As a result, the 030 is a very complex chip—approximately 300,000 transistors. Simple instructions execute in as little as two cycles if there is a cache hit, but complex instructions require dozens of cycles.

The RISC Alternative

RISC architects challenged whether this increasing complexity was the right approach. The guiding principle of RISC designs is to achieve the highest performance system possible, where "the system" includes not only the processor and memory but also the compiler.

System performance, in terms of the time required to perform a given task, can be viewed as the product of three factors:

- number of instructions required to perform a task (I)
- number of clock cycles required per instruction (clocks per instructions, or CPI)
- the length of a clock cycle (T)

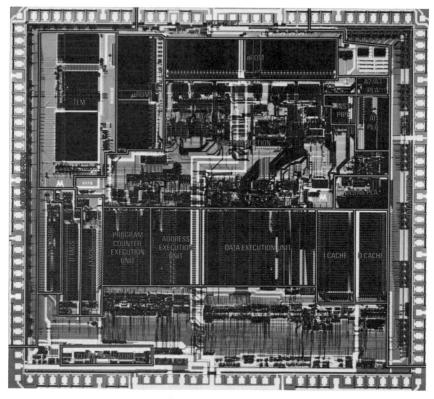

Figure 1. Motorola's 68030 Microprocessor. Approximately 300,000 transistors, it includes not only the CPU but also instruction and data caches and memory management unit.

CISC designs attempt to minimize the first factor by providing powerful instructions. However, as a result of the instruction complexity, the second factor (CPI) becomes larger. Both RISC and CISC designs attempt to maximize the third factor, clock rate. In principle, RISC designs should be able to achieve higher clock rates due to their shorter internal delay paths. Existing RISC and high-end CISC processors both typically operate at 25 to 50 MHz. RISC processors typically have three to five times CISC processor performance at the same clock rate. Typical RISC and CISC characteristics are shown in Table 1.

RISC designs place their emphasis on reducing the second factor, CPI. Most current architectures have an inherent minimum of one cycle per instruction, and RISC processors strive to come as close to this value as possible. In the latest designs, a CPI of less than one will be possible through the use of concurrent instruction execution.

The number of instructions to perform a task (I) is certain to increase,

Table 1. Typical RISC and CISC Characteristics

	RISC	CISC
Number of Instructions	under 100	over 200
Number of Address Modes	1–2	5–20
Instruction Formats	1–2	3+
Average Cycles per Instruction	near 1	3-10
Memory Access	load/store only	most CPU ops
Registers	32+	2–16
Control Unit	Hardwired	Microcoded
Instruction Decode Area	10%	over 50%

however, as the instruction set is simplified. The RISC gamble is that the drastic reduction in CPI will more than outweigh the increase in ''I.'' Existing implementations have shown that this gamble has paid off, and that instruction count is increased by only a modest amount—only 10% by some estimates.

In a CISC processor, microcode generates sequences of simple operations to execute complex instructions. RISC processors have no microcode. Rather than having microcode provide fixed, hopefully useful sequences of low-level operations, RISC processors provide the low-level operations directly and depend on the compiler to string them together to provide more complex functions.

The simplified instruction set of RISC processors drastically reduces the amount of silicon area needed for instruction decoding. The silicon area saved can be used for pipeline control, memory management, floating point, a large register file, or just to make the chip smaller.

The Compiler Connection

The original RISC concepts emerged not from groups working on CPU design, but from optimizing compiler projects. As compiler technology advanced, it became clear that there was a poor match between existing instruction sets and compiler technology. The powerful, complex instructions that high-end processors provided are difficult for compilers to take advantage of, and compiler-generated code tends to make frequent use of a relatively small number of simple instructions.

RISC processors are not intended to be programmed in assembly language. They provide an instruction set that is designed for an optimizing compiler—not for a human coder. The goal is not to provide a rich, high-level instruction set, but to provide a set of very fast, basic instructions that are well matched to what an optimizing compiler can make use of. The compiler produces instruction sequences as needed by more complex operations. Most RISC architectures also place additional demands on the compiler, as described later in this article. The idea is to provide streamlined pipelines.

Streamlined Pipelines

The term RISC is somewhat misleading, since reducing the instruction set is not its central concept. Reducing the instruction set is a byproduct of the desire to make the instructions execute as quickly as possible—ideally, in one clock cycle.

Conventional microprocessors have a variable instruction length and variable instruction execution times. In one sense, this makes efficient use of resources, since each instruction is given just the amount of memory and processor time that it needs. However, there is one problem with this approach—it makes pipelined processors difficult to implement. While high-end CISC processors are pipelined, they cannot take advantage of the same degree of pipelining that is possible on a RISC processor, and the logic required is very complex.

In a simple, nonpipelined processor, each instruction executes to completion before the next one can begin. In this type of processor, the instruction rate is simply the inverse of the average instruction execution time.

In contrast, a pipelined processor executes several instructions concurrently. Ideally, one new instruction is begun and one new instruction is completed each clock cycle. Thus, even though each instruction may require four clocks to execute (Figure 2), the overall rate at which instructions are executed can approach one per clock cycle.

Avoiding Pipeline Stalls

If the data needed by an instruction is not yet available, the pipeline must be *stalled;* progress on one or more instructions must stop while other instructions catch up. For example, if a load instruction is immediately followed by an instruction that acts on the data fetched by the load, the data from memory will not be ready in time. Delay cycles are introduced into the instruction that is waiting for data. Most RISC designs reduce the delay required to one clock cycle; this is called the *load delay slot*.

Branches pose a similar problem. Until the branch condition is evaluated and, if the branch is to be taken, the new instruction is fetched, the

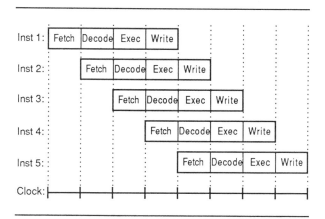

Figure 2.   Four-stage pipeline

processor doesn't know whether or not to execute the instruction immediately following the branch. Thus, unless some trick is used, the pipeline must be stalled (and potentially flushed) each time a branch occurs.

Because branches are very common in most programs, it is important to speed up their execution as much as possible. To make use of the delay slot following the initiation of a branch instruction, most RISC processors use a *delayed branch*. This means that the first instruction after a branch is *always* executed—even if the branch is taken.

It is up to the compiler to create code that deals effectively with these situations. Load delay slots can often be filled by simply rearranging the instruction sequence. Delayed branches are a little trickier. The compiler first places a "no-op" instruction after every branch instruction. Its optimizer then attempts to replace each no-op with a "safe" instruction—one that is OK to execute whether the branch is taken or not. Good compilers are able to fill the great majority of delay slots with useful instructions.

Various hardware mechanisms, such as register scoreboarding, can be used to ensure that the pipeline is stalled when necessary. Another alternative is to place all of this burden on the compiler, letting it insert no-ops as needed to guarantee that no hardware pipeline stall is ever needed.

Load/Store Architecture

Variable-length instructions make trouble for pipeline designers. A major reason for variable-length instructions is to allow many different instructions to access memory. On the 68000 family processors, for example, most ALU (Arithmetic Logic Unit) instructions can access either the destination or source operand in memory; the 68030 provides indirect memory referencing, which requires two memory reads just to determine the address of the operand.

One feature of nearly all RISC architectures is that the only instructions that access memory are the load and store instructions. All other instructions operate on registers. RISC architectures typically have large numbers of registers—at least 32, and as many as 192 in current designs. Compilers for RISC machines place great emphasis on efficient use of the register file to reduce memory accesses, and the load/store architecture supports this approach well.

Register Windows

Many different techniques have been used to streamline the passing of parameters between procedures and minimize the number of memory accesses required. The most common is called *register windows*. Register windows was first used in the Berkeley RISC design and is one of the more controversial aspects of the SPARC architecture.

In most processors, the register file is directly addressed. In processors with register windows, only a "window" into a larger register file is accessible. Each time a procedure call occurs, the window is shifted down, but overlaps the previous window location. The overlapping region is used to pass parameters between the two procedures.

Many architects argue that the large register file implied by register windows takes up more silicon than it is worth. Proponents of highly optimizing compilers argue that intelligent use of a single, smaller register file can provide nearly the same performance.

High-Bandwidth Memory

All RISC processors rely on a high-bandwidth memory. A processor that can execute one instruction per clock cycle is of little use unless it has a memory system that can feed it instructions at that rate. With processor cycle times of 40 to 60 ns now common, a standard dynamic RAM array isn't going to work.

Most RISC systems use cache memory to provide the memory bandwidth required for high performance without causing the entire main memory to be unreasonably fast. A few, however, offer lower-cost alternatives, such as use of static-column DRAM or video RAMs without cache. These designs incur a several-clock delay on the first access to a new page, but provide single-clock memory cycles on successive accesses.

Many RISC systems use separate instruction and data caches to achieve higher performance.

Applications

The current success of RISC is tied closely to UNIX. Because UNIX itself and most UNIX software is written in C, a new microprocessor architecture does not represent much of a problem. In the MS-DOS and Macintosh worlds, on the other hand, processor compatibility is everything.

Another major area for RISC processors is high-end embedded control. Such applications could use the CPU without memory management and without cache to reduce the system cost. Typical applications include laser printer controllers, communications processors, and military systems. AMD is making a strong push in this area with their 29000, and Intel is doing likewise with their i960.

Another possibility is emulation of existing instruction sets. RISC architectures are quite efficient for emulating other processors. Because RISC processors are often several times faster than CISC processors, a comparable-speed emulation may be possible. This would throw away much of the RISC performance gains, but would allow old software to run on the new machines. The "native" instruction set would give new software access to the full performance of the machine. If RISC processors succeed in outdistancing CISC performance by a sufficient margin, this path will become attractive for companies such as Apple and IBM.

What Lies Ahead?

RISC architecture is here to stay. Many of the architectural features associated with RISC will influence CISC processor design as well. CISC processors will be around for a long time, for several reasons. First, of course, is the massive existing software base. RISC today is limited to high-end applications.

Ironically, the "complex" CISC chips are much easier to build systems with today. Not only do RISC chips typically require external cache controllers and cache memory chips, but the entire system design is made complex and expensive by the short cycle time.

In time, RISC chips will be improved to make system designs simpler. Memory will get faster, and cache controllers will get better. RISC is truly in its infancy, and the next year will see many major product introductions and dramatic increases in performance. RISC will also migrate downward, in versions designed to operate at slower clock speeds and without cache memory support. Some of the silicon saved by the simpler instruction decoder can be used to simplify the system-level hardware design, making RISC chips more attractive for embedded control.

2

Instruction Set Design

Brian Case

"Marketing hoopla" behind the promotion of RISC architectures has been criticized, and it may seem that most of the popular press radiates more heat than light. The key issues in the RISC versus CISC comparison are the interactions between computer architecture, computer implementation, and compiler technology, and the astonishing synergy that can result from good design. RISC is both hardware and software.

While it is true that RISC stands for Reduced Instruction Set Computer, the point of the RISC philosophy is *not* simply the reduction of the number of instructions. "RISC" was chosen because it is a catchy name and because one of the most apparent attributes of the first publicized RISC instruction sets was the dramatically smaller number of instructions. Having a small number of instructions is not important, however; what *is* important is the *nature* of the instructions.

RISC Instructions Allow Uniform Pipelines

The people who promote RISC architectures apparently believe that the instruction set is fundamental to improved performance. I, personally, want you to believe it because it is the truth. The instruction set has a *first-order* impact on performance simply because *hardware must somehow implement the semantics of the instructions.*

Everyone knows the two ways to improve the performance of a computer: (1) speed up the clock[1] and (2) use parallelism. A *uniform pipeline* is the most fundamental characteristic of RISC hardware because it *both* increases cycle time (the processor hardware is distributed among several pipe stages) and increases parallelism (several instructions are processed simultaneously). Sadly, I have never seen the idea of a uniform pipeline associated with RISC in the trade press. No wonder everyone misunderstands RISC.

A RISC instruction set is one in which every instruction can flow through a processor pipeline in exactly the same way. This is the distinguishing characteristic between RISC and CISC instruction sets: it is impossible to construct a simple, uniform pipeline for every instruction in a CISC instruction set (except the degenerate, one-stage pipe). This is why the VAX architecture has no really high-performance implementations. A uniform pipeline allows each of the major functional units of a general-purpose processor—instruction memory (cache), instruction decoder, register file, ALU, TLB, data memory (cache), and register write-back—to reside in its own pipe stage (if so desired). The cycle time of the machine is then determined by the functional unit with the longest propagation delay.[2]

Compilers Are Part of RISC

The second half of the RISC story is software. The most important piece of software is the compiler for your favorite language. Happily, a simple instruction set is exactly what the compiler writer ordered. A simple instruction set is important for several reasons.

An optimizing compiler is ultimately written by an overworked human being. If the human being can't figure out how to make the compiler profitably use a given instruction, then his compiler is not going to emit it. Thus, the answer to a compiler writer's prayer is an instruction set that satisfies the following constraints: (1) the size of each instruction is easy to calculate, and (2) the execution time of each instruction is easy to calculate. A very important consequence of these two constraints is that *either there be no interactions between any two instructions or that the interactions be very simple to figure out.*

---

[1] Actually, this is not sufficient: The memory must also get faster. It is possible to decrease performance by speeding up the processor clock only slightly; e.g., compare a 60-ns processor where a load takes 3 cycles and a 59-ns processor where a load now takes 4 cycles (180 ns versus 236 ns for a load).

[2] Many people say that large register files are detrimental for this reason; however, it is most likely that one of the caches (instruction, data, or TLB) will be the slowest.

Remember, the optimizing compiler writer must code algorithms that will figure out the fastest and/or smallest code sequence to implement the semantics of the HLL program. "Features" such as many addressing modes, special-purpose ("typed") registers, variable length instructions, and memory-to-memory *plus* memory-to-register *plus* register-to-register instruction variants cause a mind-boggling combinatorial explosion that can be handled by a compiler writer in only one way: completely ignoring all but a few of the simpler combinations. This is one of the reasons that optimizing compilers have historically used only a subset of a CISC instruction set.

[Exercise for the reader (10 points): Look at the VAX instruction set. Consider the 11/780 implementation. How long does each instruction take to execute? Consider the 8700 implementation. Now how long does each instruction take to execute? Now write a compiler that produces good code for both implementations. Do the same for the 68000, 68020/30, and forthcoming 68040. What is the best way to allocate the separate data/address registers? Take as much time as you need, not to exceed your lifetime. Good luck.]

Simplicity is good by itself, but there are some instruction set details that further help the compiler writer. An accumulator machine is simple, but what good is a fast cycle if the processor must access data memory on every cycle?

Three-address instructions (which specify the location of two operands and the destination for the result) allow the results of intermediate computations to be saved for later use without accessing memory. Of course, more registers are needed to keep these intermediate values around long enough to be reused. Three-address instructions also allow computations to be done without overwriting one of the source operands. A result is fewer register-to-register moves.

Register Files versus Cache

A large number of registers is crucial to a fast machine: the register file has the highest performance of all the levels in the memory hierarchy. Indeed, once a proper instruction set has been chosen, the major challenge in implementing a RISC machine is in the memory hierarchy design. Thus, it is correct to emphasize a Harvard architecture and I/O concurrency. To evaluate a separate memory and bus for a cached "stack space," let's compare the performance attributes (bandwidth and latency) of a data cache and a register file (see Table 1).

Most people don't think about the facts that: (1) in one cycle, a register file can read two operands and write a third; this is *three times* the band-

Table 1.   Register File versus Cache

	Register File	Data Cache
Bandwidth	3 words/cycle	1 word/cycle
Place in Pipe	Early (first or second stage)	Late (after ALU or TLB)
Access Method	Direct	Tag compare

width of a single-cycle cache; if the cache takes more cycles, the bandwidth advantage is even greater; (2) a register file is early in the pipeline; this makes the pipeline latency to its access short; (3) access to a register file is direct while a tag compare is required for a cache; and (4) fewer bits are needed to specify a register address.

To be fair, register files are less dense than caches. However, there is no substitute for a register file. If high performance is a goal, keeping as many values as possible in a large (but not *too* large) register file is of paramount importance. Good register allocation algorithms exist, but their effective application requires the registers to be plentiful and fully general purpose.

Another instruction set detail is the exposure of underlying hardware parallelism. Exposing low-level parallelism is the source of the by-now-familiar delayed branch and overlapped loads and stores. Exposing such parallelism leads to both simpler hardware and faster execution since the job of reorganizing instruction sequences can be handled by a compiler. Once again, the reorganization is made tractable by the fact that the interactions between instructions are easily predictable.

RISC Techniques for CISC Designs

So what is a CISC designer to do? The same thing that compiler writers have done: subset the architecture. The subset of the instruction set that will fit into a uniform pipeline is made to go fast by implementing that pipeline; the other instructions are emulated either by trapping to software routines or by microcode routines that take over the processor pipeline for a few cycles. This is exactly the technique used in one of the early "single-chip" VAX implementations. Compilers are written to take advantage of the fast instruction subset. The slower, "CISCy" instructions must be supported, but they will become more and more vestigial.

It is possible that the RISC subset of a CISC architecture can be made to run as fast as a pure RISC instruction set. However, the design of such a machine can be a nightmare. RISC maintains an advantage in design simplicity. Personally, I look forward to the day when the processor architecture is inconsequential.

Conclusion

RISC is *not* simply fewer instructions. The instruction set design is crucial to a high-performance implementation. Proper design tradeoffs result in both faster hardware and more effective software; in particular, optimizing compilers become more effective. The impact on performance can be more than simply additive; synergism results from good design.

3

Design Issues for Next-Generation Processors

Brian Case

In the mid-1980s, the RISC philosophy allowed semiconductor manufacturers to deliver microprocessors with high-performance pipelined implementations—not just a small amount of simple overlap between instruction prefetch and on-chip execution, as in the 8086. Silicon technology was just dense enough to permit the implementation of a chip with a 32-bit architecture and a four- or five-stage pipeline. If the designers chose a gate array implementation, as was the case with the original SPARC chip, little more than the bare pipeline could be implemented. With a custom layout implementation, a pipeline plus a TLB and perhaps a small cache would fit on the die, as evidenced by MIPS' R3000 and AMD's 29000. Other design points were possible, such as Motorola's 88000 with its integer and floating-point pipelines on the same die, but these were not in the mainstream.

In the 1990s, half-micron technologies will allow so much to be integrated on a single die that the choice of a design point for a microprocessor will become much more difficult. In the technology area alone there will be dense CMOS, BiCMOS, and ECL processes. Once a technology has been chosen, it will be necessary to decide on a microarchitecture approach and select which features to integrate on the chip. Given 2 to 10 million transistors, features that might be included are

- Large caches, register files, or on-chip RAM
- Instruction queues or write-back buffers

- Translation look-aside buffers (TLBs)
- Branch prediction and/or branch target caching
- Superscalar integer and/or floating-point pipelines
- Superpipelined integer and/or FP pipelines
- Multiple execution units
- A vector floating-point unit
- A VLIW integer/floating-point pipeline
- System functions such as DMA and I/O interfaces
- Microcode ROM

Most of these features have been incorporated into at least one 1980s microprocessor.

One implementation technique that has not yet been seen is superpipelining of the integer unit. Like superscalar, superpipelining is an implementation technique available to all microprocessor designers because object-code compatibility can be maintained. The same cannot be said of VLIW or vector processors, although it is possible to simply ignore (or not purchase) the vector facility of a new processor.

Super Basics

The point of superscalar and superpipelined implementations is improved performance through the exploitation of instruction-level parallelism. RISC has exactly the same justification: by restricting the instruction set to those instructions that "fit" into a uniform, lock-step pipeline, the implementation of a RISC can easily exploit the natural parallelism that exists between the five or so distinct phases of instruction completion (fetch, decode/register read, execute, memory access, and register writeback). Superscalar and superpipelined implementations are proposed as answers to the question: "What comes next?"

Another part of the RISC justification is that by selecting the right instructions, the processor implementation can both have a fast cycle time and be simple. While superscalar and superpipelined processors share with RISC the goal of exploiting parallelism, they may not share the side-effect of a relatively simple implementation.

Pipelining can, of course, also be applied to CISC architectures, as Intel's 486 and Motorola's 68040 demonstrate. The pipeline is much more complex and less natural, however, because of the variable length of instructions and the complexity of decoding and executing each instruction. Superpipelining and superscalar implementations of CISC processors are possible but will be significantly more difficult than for RISC processors.

Before we begin an earnest analysis of superscalar and superpipelined implementations, we need to understand each implementation technique on an intuitive level.

Basic RISC Processor

The heart of a basic RISC processor is a single, very natural pipeline in which each stage consists of one fundamental piece of hardware. For example, the classic four-stage pipeline has an instruction cache in the fetch stage, register file read ports and some simple decoding hardware in the decode/read stage, an ALU in the execute stage, and a register file write port in the write-back stage. In some RISC pipelines, a data cache is given its own "mem" stage that sits between the execute and write-back stages.

Superscalar Processor

The heart of a superscalar processor is, at least conceptually, multiple pipelines where each pipeline is not significantly different from a basic RISC pipeline. An equally important part of a superscalar processor is the instruction dispatcher that attempts to issue multiple instructions per cycle, one into each pipeline. Since the pipelines are the same as basic RISC pipelines, the cycle time of the superscalar processor is not improved, but its performance is improved by the ability to issue and execute more than one instruction per cycle.

While at least two examples of superscalar processors exist, the i960CA from Intel and the RS/6000 from IBM, forthcoming superscalar processors are likely to be more general in their "superscalarness" (i.e., their ability to dispatch and execute multiple instructions at the same time). The i960CA has many constraints on what instructions can be issued and executed simultaneously, and the RS/6000 mostly exploits parallelism between integer and floating-point instructions.

Superpipelined Processor

Like a basic RISC processor, the heart of a superpipelined processor is a single pipeline but the pipeline has more stages. Extra stages are added solely to reduce the cycle time of the processor. Instructions are issued into the superpipeline in the same way that instructions are issued into the basic RISC pipeline: at a maximum rate of one per cycle. At least one of the fundamental hardware blocks (the slowest) in a basic RISC processor is split into two or more pipeline stages, and the latency (in clock cycles) of at least some instructions is increased.

Superpipelining is, in many ways, just the 90's name for 60's-style mainframe pipelining. What we now call RISC pipelining can be viewed as simple instruction overlap, and what we now call superpipelining was once called pipelining.

To help quantify the differences between processors in each class, three implementation metrics can be defined. (For the discussion in this analysis, I take my lead from a paper by Jouppi and Wall [1]). These metrics are

- Instructions issued per cycle
- Cycles of latency per simple operation
- Degree of parallelism required for full utilization

For a basic RISC processor, each of these metrics has a value of one. A RISC processor can issue one instruction per cycle (with perfect memory); most simple operations (add, xor, jump, etc.) take one cycle, and a degree of instruction-level parallelism of one is all that is necessary to get maximum performance out of the processor.

For a basic RISC processor, the third metric (degree of parallelism required) simply means that each instruction can depend on the previous one without limiting performance. (In reality, there are exceptions to this rule in every RISC processor.) In contrast, a processor that requires parallelism of degree two can achieve maximum processor utilization (i.e., performance) only if every pair of instructions consists of two independent instructions.

Figure 1 illustrates the degree of parallelism metric. In Figure 1(a), all three instructions are independent and, given a suitable processor, could be executed in parallel. In Figure 1(b), the three instructions are all dependent: the first instruction must execute before the second because the second uses the result of the first, and the second must execute before the third because the third uses the result of the second. The three dependent instructions cannot be executed in parallel, but they can still be executed at a rate of one per cycle by a basic RISC.

Figure 2 shows instructions executing in a basic RISC pipeline. This graphically illustrates the first two metrics: one instruction is issued into

---

load	r1←(r2)	add	r3←r3+1
add	r3←r3+1	add	r4←r3+r2
fpadd	r5←r6+r7	store	(r4)←r0

| (a) parallelism = 3 | (b) parallelism = 1 |

Figure 1. Two code segments showing levels of parallelism

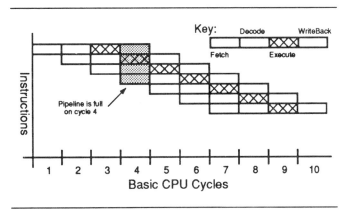

Figure 2.   Operation of a basic RISC pipeline

the pipe on each cycle and the execute stage takes one cycle (i.e., simple operations have one cycle of latency).

At processor startup, the pipeline becomes full (completely busy) on cycle 4 when four instructions are in various stages of completion. If a branch in this processor caused a complete pipeline flush, then the diagram would also illustrate what happens after a taken branch.

Superscalar Characteristics

A superscalar implementation of degree n is characterized by the following values for the three metrics:

- Issue rate $= n$
- Operation latency $= 1$
- Parallelism required $= n$

Figure 3 puts these numbers in graphical form for a superscalar processor of degree two.

It is clear from the metrics that what distinguishes a superscalar processor from a basic RISC processor is the ability of the former to issue more than one instruction per cycle. Since all instructions issued in a given cycle must be independent (as indicated by the simultaneous execution phases in Figure 3), the degree of parallelism required for full utilization is equal to the issue rate.

The cycle time of a superscalar processor is conceptually no longer than that of a basic RISC processor. This is true because the cycle time of a RISC processor is determined (according to RISC lore) by the time for the

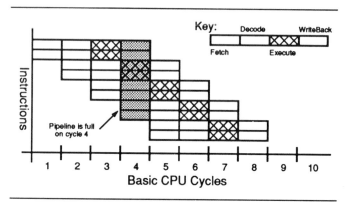

Figure 3. A superscalar pipeline

execute stage. This is the delay of the ALU plus the forwarding multi-plexers, which is likely to be the critical path in the superscalar processor as well.

Just as with the basic pipeline, the superscalar pipeline becomes full on cycle 4, but notice that it now takes eight instructions to fill the pipe.

Superpipelined Characteristics

A superpipelined implementation of degree m is characterized by the following values for the three metrics:

- Issue rate = 1
- Operation latency = m
- Parallelism required = m

Figure 4 shows the operation of a superpipelined processor of degree two.

The metrics say that a superpipelined processor is just like a basic RISC processor except that operations have m cycles of latency instead of one. Since each operation takes m cycles to complete, there must be m independent instructions following each instruction to be able to fully utilize the processor.

This dependency is illustrated in Figure 4 by the overlapping (occupying the same column) of the second execute phase of one instruction with the first execute phase of the following instruction. If the second execute phase of one instruction is just beginning, the result of that phase is not available for input to the first execute phase of the immediate successor instruction.

Figure 4 also shows that the cycle time of the superpipelined processor is, conceptually, only $1/m$ (1/2 in this case) that of a basic CPU cycle. This is a corollary of the first two metrics: the reason the operation latency is m times as long is that there are m pipeline stages in the execution unit. Assuming good logic and circuit design, this should result in a cycle time nearly m times faster than the base processor. (It is not quite m times faster because the additional pipeline stages introduce some overhead.)

Notice that the pipeline in Figure 4 becomes full on cycle 4.5, which is actually cycle 8 if measured in terms of the superpipeline clock.

Superduper

In theory, an implementation can be both superscalar and superpipelined. Such a processor would have the following three metrics:

- Issue rate $= n$
- Operation latency $= m$
- Parallelism required $= m \times n$

Looking only at the first two metrics would lead one to believe that this is an incredibly fast processor: it can issue n instructions per cycle and has a cycle time m times as fast as those outdated RISCs. Unfortunately, the third metric indicates that such a processor would be drastically underutilized when running most programs. Even for the smallest interesting case when $m = n = 2$, full utilization requires instruction-level parallelism of degree four. Most parallel processors are justified on the strength of the first two metrics and fail in the market because of the last metric.

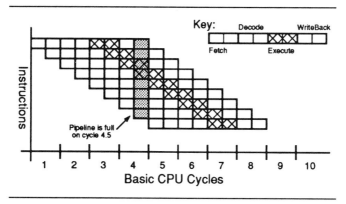

Figure 4. A superpipelined pipeline

Super Comparison

As Jouppi and Wall conjecture and then demonstrate through simulation, a superscalar processor and a superpipelined processor of the same degree will have roughly the same performance. This is true because they issue and complete the same number of instructions per basic CPU cycle.

One difference is in the time it takes to fill the pipeline in each processor. With plenty of available parallelism, a superscalar processor of degree two fills its pipeline after three basic CPU cycles while a superpipelined processor fills its pipeline after 3.5 basic CPU cycles. Thus, at system startup, the superpipelined processor gets behind a little. Assuming enough parallelism is available to keep each pipeline full after startup, the difference between the two processors will be only the initial 0.5 basic CPU cycle lost at the beginning.

If enough parallelism is not available, the longer startup cost of the superpipelined processor will also affect performance at each branch target. Consider a branch to two independent instructions, such as the first two instructions in Figures 3 and 4. The superscalar processor will complete execution of these two instructions at the end of cycle 3, and their results will be available for use by any subsequent instructions. The superpipelined processor will complete execution of the first and second instructions at the end of cycle 3 and the end of cycle 3.5, respectively.

Thus, in the superpipelined processor, the result of the second instruction is available one-half base cycle later. In some cases the two instructions at the branch target can simply be reordered to remove a subsequent dependency, but there will be cases where there is no way to recover the extra half-cycle of latency.

A superpipelined processor does have some possible advantages over a superscalar processor of the same degree. The finer granularity in a superpipelined processor may be a benefit, especially in the execute stage. In a basic RISC processor, the cycle time is set by the latency of the ALU when it is performing a subtract operation, which consists of inverting an operand, propagating a carry across all bits, and possibly bypassing the register file through a multiplexer. Unfortunately, this latency is longer than the time needed to perform the really simple ALU-type operations. The prime examples are logical operations and register-register moves.

In a superpipelined processor, these faster operations can be processed in fewer than m execute cycles (where m is the degree of superpipelining). This means that when subsequent instructions depend on the results of these faster operations, the superpipelined processor is likely to be able to issue them sooner than the superscalar processor. The finer granularity may also be advantageous in handling cache misses. The pipeline diagrams in Figures 3 and 4 illustrate this effect graphically: the edge of the super-pipelined diagram approximates a straight line more closely (fewer jaggies) than the superscalar diagram.

Superpipelined processors are also likely to have fewer issue restrictions than superscalar processors. To keep the design complexity to a manageable level, most superscalar implementations will be able to issue multiple instructions only if they meet a relatively constraining set of criteria.

In practice, the advantages of superscalar and superpipelined implementations roughly cancel, and they perform roughly equally, with a slight advantage for superscalar. As the degree of superpipelining and superscalar increases, the difference between the two decreases.

Superpipelined processors may, however, have an important edge in the amount of hardware required. A superpipelined processor requires only slightly more circuitry than a basic RISC processor. A superscalar processor with multiple pipelines, complex dependency-checking logic, and multiple execution units will require much more circuitry.

Architectural Divergence

It is interesting to note that the delayed branches and delayed loads incorporated into early RISC architectures are a nuisance for designers of superscalar implementations. Consider delayed branches, for example. In a superscalar processor, it is quite likely that the best implementation technique is to process branches entirely in the instruction dispatcher, which means the main pipelines never see branch instructions.

In a superscalar processor, a delayed branch does not provide enough parallelism to keep the processor busy while the target is fetched, so additional techniques (branch history tables and other branch prediction techniques) must be used. Thus, the delayed branch gets in the way, instead of helping as in a basic RISC, by providing additional special cases that must be checked by the dispatching hardware. This is perhaps the reason IBM's RS/6000 and Intel's 960 do not have delayed branches [2].

For superpipelined processors, as with basic RISC processors, delayed branches and loads probably still do make sense. Thus, if total architectural freedom were available, there would probably be some divergence between architectures aimed specifically for superscalar implementations and those aimed for superpipelined implementations. The RS/6000, claimed to be tailored for superscalar implementation, supports this conjecture.

From Super to Microsuper

Although it may seem that superpipelining represents a new and more aggressive design style, most high-performance machines have some degree of superpipelining already. Jouppi and Wall develop a metric they call the "average degree of superpipelining" to express the amount of super-pipelining present in an implementation. (For readers of the Jouppi and Wall paper, note that their computation of the degree of superpipelining is incomplete: the cycles of latency for an operation must be divided by the issue rate for that operation.) Not suprisingly, supercomputers were the first venue for superpipelining, but all RISCs use superpipelining to accommodate the realities of implementation technology and memory systems.

Superpipelining is present whenever an operation has an issue rate that is faster than the operation's latency. For example, if a processor can issue an integer ADD on every cycle but each ADD takes two cycles to complete, the ADD functional unit is superpipelined. This would have been called a "pipelined functional unit" in the old days. (Note that the second ADD instruction must not depend on the result of the first.)

With this definition in mind, the instruction-fetch and memory-reference units of modern RISC processors, such as the R3000, are superpipelined: the processor is allowed to issue a branch or a load on every cycle, but branches and loads take two cycles to complete (two-cycle latency).

It is perhaps surprising at first that basic RISC processors are so advanced, but the "single-cycle instruction execution" RISC tenet can be bought only through superpipelining with its attendant multicycle latency. In the case of basic RISC processors, the multicycle latency is exposed only in places where instruction-level parallelism is likely to cover the latency: delayed branches and loads.

Now that we better understand the super techniques, a couple of critical questions arise. First, what are the issues involved in designing and building super microprocessors? Second, how soon will super microprocessors be available? Answering these questions is important because system designers need to know whether and when superprocessors will be among their choices. Third, what will the performance impact of these processors be, and what will be required to take advantage of the improved performance?

Hardware Comparison

In comparing superscalar and superpipelined implementations, it is clear that the demands placed on semiconductor manufacturers and microprocessor designers are similar in some ways and quite different in others. The most obvious difference is in cycle time: a superscalar processor can achieve performance gains even with yesterday's cycle time while a super-pipelined processor must decrease processor cycle time by a significant factor to achieve a performance gain. Since even a basic RISC implementation using next generation technology would have an improved cycle time as a result of process technology improvements, a superpipelined processor must have a dramatically shorter cycle time.

On the other side of the coin is the logic-design effort required. A superpipelined implementation will certainly be more complicated than a basic RISC implementation, but the complication will be mostly of a linear nature; that is, the complexity of adding extra pipeline stages does not explode geometrically with the number of stages. Greater than linear expansion of logical complexity will occur in some areas. For example, taking advantage of short-latency operations in the execute stage will require more complex pipeline control, but the job is largely "more of the same."

A big problem for superpipelined implementors is how to segment conceptually indivisible structures such as caches and TLBs. One goal of RISC is a balanced pipeline in which each stage takes the same amount of time. In practice, it turns out that the fundamental hardware elements, ALUs, TLBs, etc., are roughly the same speed. To build a superpipeline, it is easy to see how to put a pipe stage in the middle of an ALU, but it is less clear how to divide an instruction cache or TLB in half.

In stark contrast, a full-blown superscalar implementation in which all functional units, all data paths, all register file ports, etc., are duplicated to the degree of the superscalarness will have complexity growth proportional to the cross-product of all possible combinations of concurrent operations. For a superscalar processor of degree four, the complexity of checking all dependencies is roughly the number of possible operations raised to the fourth power. Even for a RISC architecture with a simple instruction set, this can be a daunting problem. Sufficient design tools are not yet available to make the problems associated with high-degree superscalar implementations solvable by the average design team. The key word here is average: some design teams will surely succeed.

Considering the size of the combinatorial dependence-checking problem, it is easy to see how the result could be a large block of complex, slow logic. Thus, a real danger for superscalar implementations is a sacrifice in clock speed, from both logic complexity and the diversion of talent from the job of critical path tuning to the even more important job of just making it work.

The differences in the problems associated with the two super implementation techniques leads to the generalization that superscalar imple-

mentations stress the logic designers and microarchitects while superpipelined implementations stress the circuit and process designers.

Software Comparison

Another issue with super implementation techniques is whether the processors perform up to their potential. Even assuming that a high-degree
super processor can be built, sufficient instruction-level parallelism in
major applications must exist; otherwise, potential performance will remain just that. This syndrome is quite well known in the supercomputer
world where fantastic peak performances are claimed but real performances are either a small fraction of the claims or are realized only by a
few handcrafted programs (constructed at the cost of millions of taxpayer
dollars).

Thus, this question is really about the characteristics of software, both
compilers and applications. Certain types of applications, such as the
analysis of weather satellite data, are highly parallel. It has been shown
that these types of applications profit from almost any kind of parallel
processor architecture or implementation. It is also known, at least by
some, that more common applications, compilers, editors, and databases,
have limited instruction-level parallelism, at least the way they are coded
in current languages.

In the end, the presence of parallelism in applications and either the
ability of compilers to express that parallelism or the ability of hardware to
detect it will determine the performance gain of high-degree super microprocessors. Microprocessor vendors and system designers must confront
the fact that the majority of their customers' applications are not highly
parallel.

Super Realities

In the press for ever-improving performance and, it is sad to say, the
need to keep up with the Jones' marketing, all serious vendors of
high-performance microprocessors will try one or the other of these techniques. The complexity problems and lack of instruction-level parallelism associated with super implementations of high degree will mean that
levelheaded designers will aim fairly low on the super scale, at least at
first.

Thus, the first super microprocessors are likely to be either superscalar or superpipelined implementations of degree two or three. Intel's i960CA and IBM's RS/6000 are examples in point.

For most superscalar designs, there will likely be restrictions so that certain combinations of operations will not be able to operate in parallel. The restrictions will be based on analysis of existing program behavior and issues of design complexity. These first superscalar implementations will be skewed in favor of the most frequent parallel constructs and/or the ones easiest to implement, and they will have clock rates between 1.5 and 2 times current basic RISC clock rates.

For superpipelined designs, the degree will be limited by available parallelism, determined by analysis of current program behavior and the ability to segment the fundamental logic blocks. These processors will be recognizable by their high clock rates, if not external then internal. The MIPS R4000 operates internally at 100 MHz from an external 50-MHz clock. If the R4000 represents a trend, then we can expect superpipelined implementations to run at clock speeds anywhere from 3 to 3.5 times the current basic RISC clock rates.

All serious high-end microprocessor vendors will at least attempt a super implementation. Some vendors, such as LSI Logic with its Lightning SPARC implementation, will attempt to use even more aggressive techniques, such as out-of-order execution, by fetching a large number of instructions into "holding tanks." Instructions will then be taken from the tanks when all of their operands are available and control dependencies have been resolved. These processors will use advanced techniques, such as register renaming, and will be very complex.

When the clock rates are multiplied by the issue rates that are achieved on real code, it is quite likely that the performance realized by super microprocessors of each type will be roughly equal, just as Jouppi and Wall claim.

For example, assume a previous RISC processor has an average issue rate of 1.25 cycles per instruction (0.8 instructions per cycle). If a superscalar processor issues 25% more instructions per cycle, 1.0 IPC (or 1.0 CPI), and has a clock rate 1.5 times faster than a previous processor, its speed-up will be about 1.9. (A 25% improvement in issue rate for a superscalar processor may seem dismally small, but it is probably typical without out-of-order execution or aggressive, new compiler tricks. And if you want to run those old binaries, you cannot take advantage of new compilers.) If a superpipelined processor has a clock rate three times faster than a previous processor and an issue rate about 80% of the previous processor, say 0.64 IPC (or 1.56 CPI), its speed-up will also be about 1.9. The real difference will be in cost and time to market.

References

[1] Jouppi, N. P., and Wall, D. W. "Available Instruction-Level Parallelism for Superscalar and Superpipelined Machines." *ASPLOS-III Proceedings*, Boston, April 1989.

[2] Cocke, J., and Markstein, V. "The evolution of RISC technology at IBM." *IBM Journal of Research and Development*, Vol. 4, No. 1, January 1990.

II

SPARC

4

SPARC Architecture

Brian Case

In the early 1980s, when "RISC" was still mostly a concept and the first arguments for simple architectures were being made, simplicity of implementation was seen as perhaps the most important goal of RISC. This led the Berkeley architects, who coined the term "RISC," to define a very simple architecture with as few instructions as possible. The small number of instructions led to simple and fast instruction-decode logic. According to the arguments, the small decode logic left room for functions that were more important to overall performance than complex instructions such as memory-to-memory operations. The Berkeley team concluded that data cache was the next item to be integrated on-chip. To avoid wasting space with cache tags and to directly speed up procedure calls, they implemented the data cache as a large register file with overlapping "windows."

The SPARC architecture bears a significant resemblance to the Berkeley RISC architectures because the goals of the two efforts were compatible and because some members of the Berkeley team were also part of Sun's architecture team. Sun wanted a simple architecture that could be built in a gate array and that would reduce loads and stores as much as possible.

Register Windows

The concept of register windows is not the only resemblance between the Berkeley RISC architectures and SPARC, but it is the most striking. As for the Berkeley RISC architectures, there were several justifications for including register windows in SPARC:

- To reduce the register-allocation burden on compiler writers.
- To reduce the number of loads and stores in code generated by simple compilers.
- To exploit on-chip RAM in current and future implementations.

Reducing the number of loads and stores was a primary concern in the formative stages of SPARC because the first implementations would not have separate instruction and data buses. The use of a combined instruction and data bus was probably influenced by cost considerations: A combined bus can mean a cheaper processor package and implies a single external cache, which is cheaper than two external caches.

Run-Time Stacks

To see how register windows can reduce the number of loads and stores, an understanding of the basics of run-time stack management is needed. Figure 1 shows a representation of a run-time stack in memory. As is typical, the stack grows from higher addresses to lower addresses, and a "stack pointer" (whose value is maintained in a processor register) marks the lowest location in the stack that is currently active. Stack locations are addressed by specifying a positive offset from the stack pointer.

The run-time stack is used to support procedure calls in languages such as C. A compiler generates code for a procedure according to simple rules. At the start of a procedure, it generates code that allocates a "stack frame" for the private use of the procedure (by decrementing the stack pointer). Following the code for the procedure itself, the compiler generates code that deallocates the procedure's stack frame (by incrementing the stack pointer).

A compiler generates code to pass parameters using a procedure "calling convention." In a typical calling convention, each stack frame consists of three areas: incoming parameters, private local variables, and outgoing parameters. In Figure 1, the shaded area shows how parameters and results are passed between a calling procedure and a called procedure: the stack frames of the procedures involved are allocated so that they overlap. The overlap area is where outgoing parameters are placed by the calling procedure ("Previous Frame" in Figure 1) and accessed by the called procedure ("Current Frame").

By using this calling convention, the compiler can compile each of the two procedures completely independently. It generates code to reference the variables on the stack using the appropriate offsets for the procedure being compiled. To reference the first parameter, an offset of +9 would be used by the called procedure ("Current Frame"), while an offset of +0 would be used by the calling procedure ("Previous Frame").

Stack In Registers

Register windows mimic this stack structure, with two differences: the structure is implemented in on-chip registers, and the sizes of the three areas are fixed. (For a memory-based run-time stack, the compiler decides the size of each area.)

The "stack-in-registers" approach has two major advantages over the run-time stack in memory. First, no memory references are needed to access the stacked data; and second, the data is resident in the register file, which means two operands can be read and a third written in every cycle.

Figure 2 illustrates the operation of register windows. Each window has three sets of registers—ins, locals, and outs—that correspond directly to areas in a run-time stack frame. At any one time, a single window is active or "current."

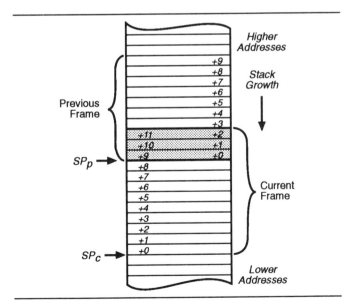

Figure 1. Run-time stack. SP$_c$ is the current stack pointer, and SP$_p$ is the previous stack pointer.

In the SPARC architecture, each window contains 24 registers—eight of each of the three kinds. In addition, there are eight "globals" that are always active regardless of which window is active. Thus, at any one time, 32 registers are directly addressable. Gr0 always reads as zero, and writing to it has no effect. The SPARC architecture allows implementations to provide any number of register windows from 1 to 32.

The register file is generally implemented as a big block of registers; the overlapping effect is produced by the register-address decoding hardware. To decide what physical register to address, the decoding circuits use both the register number from an instruction and the "window number" supplied by a special processor register. The outs and ins that overlap actually map to the same physical registers in the file.

The register file is circular; that is, the "last" window overlaps with the "first" window. For example, consider an implementation with three windows, as in Figure 2. The outs of the window labeled "Next Window" would overlap with the ins of the window labeled "Previous Window."

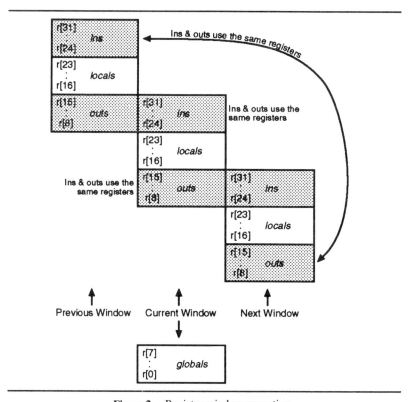

Figure 2.   Register window operation

Register File Management

To manage the register windows, SPARC has three special instructions and two special registers. The instructions are SAVE, RESTORE, and RETT (return from trap). The registers are the CWP (current window pointer) and the WIM (window invalid mask).

The CWP serves the same purpose for the register windows that the stack pointer serves for memory-based stack frames. The CWP determines which window is current (and, by implication, which windows are previous and next).

The WIM determines which of the windows in the register file are "valid" or available. For the register windows scheme to function properly, there must always be one invalid window so that overflow and underflow can be detected. Overflow (trying to allocate a new window when the register file is "full") and underflow (trying to deallocate a window when the register file is "empty") can occur because there are only a few windows on-chip (typically seven or so) that are trying to contain an arbitrarily long run-time stack.

By always having at least one window marked invalid, a program is guaranteed to bump into the invalid window as the CWP wraps around the circular window file. When a program tries to use the window marked as invalid, a hardware trap is taken to a routine that either flushes some of the register file contents to memory or restores some of the register file contents from memory. In essence, only a portion of the top of the memory-based run-time stack is always contained in the register file.

Another reason to always have one window marked invalid is to support fast trap processing. SPARC traps automatically decrement the CWP. In the case when all but one of the windows is valid, the trap-handling routine will be guaranteed free access to the window marked as invalid; there is no danger of the trap routine clobbering valid data in the register file. The RETT instruction automatically increments the CWP.

The SAVE and RESTORE instructions perform the basic allocation and deallocation of windows (stack frames) in the register file. SAVE decrements the CWP and checks the appropriate bit in the WIM to see if overflow has occurred. RESTORE increments the CWP and checks the appropriate bit in the WIM to see if underflow has occurred.

One drawback of register windows is the large processor context. When a task switch occurs, all valid register windows—including any that have been written to memory—must be saved. This is not particularly significant in a Unix system because of the other system overhead associated with a context switch, but in a real-time multitasking system it can be a serious problem. Switching of windows is performed by a separate instruction, not by the CALL instruction, so it is possible for a compiler to generate code that does not use register windows within a task. In this case, register windows can be used instead on a one-per-task basis to provide fast context switching. Existing SPARC compilers do not support this mode of operation, however.

Instruction Set

Partially because of register windows, the SPARC instruction set is similar to the Berkeley RISC instruction set. Table 1 shows the SPARC instruction set as of version 7 of the architecture manual. Some slight modifications are expected in version 8, such as full multiply and divide instructions.

SPARC includes an abundance of load and store instructions. The usual byte, halfword, and word operations are provided, and loads of byte and halfword data can zero or sign-extend as desired. In addition, SPARC can move a double-word operand (64 bits) with one instruction.

As compared to MIPS and the 29000, SPARC has a fairly rich set of memory addressing modes. An address can be any of the following: register, register-plus-register, register-plus-signed constant, and signed constant. Figure 3 shows the three encoding formats for SPARC instructions. The first two cases under format 3 show the encoding of loads and stores.

Table 1. SPARC Instruction Set

LDSB	A	Load Signed Byte
LDSH	A	Load Signed Halfword
LDUB	A	Load Unsigned Byte
LDUH	A	Load Unsigned Halfword
LD	A	Load Word
LDD	A	Load Doubleword
LDF		Load Floating-point
LDDF		Load Double Floating-point
LDFSR		Load Floating-point State Reg.
LDC		Load Coprocessor
LDDC		Load Double Coprocessor
LDCSR		Load Coprocessor State Reg.
STB	A	Store Byte
STH	A	Store Halfword
ST	A	Store Word
STD	A	Store Doubleword
STF		Store Floating-point
STDF		Store Double Floating-point
STFSR		Store Floating-point State Reg.
STDFQ	P	Store Double Floating-point Queue
STC		Store Coprocessor
STDC		Store Double Coprocessor
STCSR		Store Coprocessor State Reg.
STDCQ	P	Store Double Coprocessor Queue
LDSTUB	A	Atomic Load-Store Unsigned Byte
SWAP	A	Swap Register with Memory

Table 1. (*Continued*)

ADD	cc	Add
ADDX	cc	Add with Carry
TADDcc	tv	Tagged Add and modify icc
SUB	cc	Subtract
SUBX	cc	Subtract with Carry
TSUBcc	tv	Tagged Subtract and modify icc
MULScc		Multiply Step and modify icc
AND	cc	And
ANDN	cc	And Not
OR	cc	Inclusive-Or
ORN	cc	Inclusive-Or Not
XOR	cc	Exclusive-Or
XNOR	cc	Exclusive-Nor
SLL		Shift Left Logical
SRL		Shift Right Logical
SRA		Shift Right Arithmetic
SETHI		Set High 22 bits of register
SAVE		Save caller's window
RESTORE		Restore caller's window
Bicc		Branch on integer condition codes
FBfcc		Branch on floating-point condition codes
CBccc		Branch on coprocessor condition codes
CALL		Call
JMPL		Jump and Link
RETT	P	Return from Trap
Ticc		Trap on integer condition codes
RDY		Read Y register
RDPSR	P	Read Processor Status Register
RDWIM	P	Read Window Invalid Mask register
RDTBR	P	Read Trap Base Register
WRY		Write Y register
WRPSR	P	Write Processor State Register
WRWIM	P	Write Window Invalid Mask Register
WRTBR	P	Write Trap Base Register
UNIMP		Unimplemented instruction
IFLUSH		Instruction cache Flush
FPop		Floating-point operate: FiTO(s,d,x), F(s,d,x)TOi FsTOd,FsTOx,FdTOs,FdTOx,FxTOs,FxTOd,FMOVs, FNEGs,FABSs,FSQRT(s,d,x),FADD(s,d,x),FSUB(s,d,x), FMUL(s,d,x),FDIV(s,d,x),FCMP(s,d,x),FCMPE(s,d,x)
CPop		Coprocessor operate

"A" indicates instructions that can provide an address space identifier (asi); "cc" indicates that the condition codes may optionally be set; "tv" indicates that the instruction can optionally trap on overflow; and "P" indicates that the instruction is privileged.

The "i" bit must be set to "1" to choose register-plus-signed constant (case 2). Otherwise, register-plus-register (case 1) is chosen. The other two modes are implemented by setting the rs1 field to select gr0 (which always reads as zero). Note that the signed constant is only 13 bits long, but that is sufficient for the most frequent uses, such as addressing an operand in a structure or stack frame.

Loads and stores for byte, halfword, word, and double-word operands can access either "normal" main memory or any of 256 "alternate address spaces." (Actually, four of the 256 "alternate" spaces are the normal address space, as described below.) The alternate address space is speci-

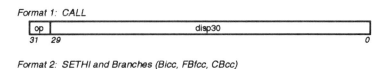

Figure 3. SPARC instruction formats

fied by the "asi" field in case 1 of format 3. The versions of these instructions that use the asi field are privileged, so they cause a trap if executed in user mode.

The processor always generates an asi. Four of the asi's are reserved to indicate the mode and type of access that is being performed: asi 8 is user instruction space, asi 9 is supervisor instruction space, asi 10 is user data space, and asi 11 is supervisor data space. All other asi's are implementation definable. Thus, they could be used to control I/O devices or implement communication protocols in multiprocessor systems. Alternate address spaces are used to access the memory management unit in designs using the "reference" MMU, and are also used for the control registers of the on-chip peripherals in Fujitsu's SPARClite.

The SPARC architecture defines load and store instructions that transfer data between memory and a dedicated floating-point register file. These instructions can move either a single-precision (32-bit) operand or a double-precision (64-bit) operand. The load and store floating-point state and queue instructions are provided to allow an operating system to handle floating-point exceptions and sharing of the floating-point unit under multitasking.

SPARC also defines load and store instructions for a user-defined coprocessor. These instructions assume the coprocessor is structured like the floating-point unit: It has a separate register file and an instruction queue of pending operations.

Rounding out the set of loads and stores are the LDSTUB and SWAP instructions. These instructions are mutual-exclusion primitives used in multitasking and multiprocessing operating systems.

The SPARC arithmetic and logical instructions are typical for a RISC processor. The set includes the usual add and subtract with and without carry, left and right logical shifts and an arithmetic right shift, and the logical ops AND, OR, and XOR in plain versions and versions with the second operand complemented.

The add, subtract, and logical instructions are available in two versions: one that modifies the condition codes (indicated by ''cc'') and one that leaves them unchanged. The ability to specify arithmetic instructions that do not modify the condition codes is helpful to compiler optimizations that reorganize instruction sequences, since it can prevent condition codes from being modified by instructions between the ones calculating the desired condition and a conditional branch.

All arithmetic, shift, and logical instructions are three-address register-to-register operations. Each instruction specifies either three registers (two sources and a destination) or two registers and a signed constant (one source register, one source constant, and one destination register). Arithmetic instructions use case 2 of format 3.

The SETHI instruction is used in combination with a regular arithmetic instruction to form a full 32-bit constant in a register. First, an ADD or OR instruction that operates on gr0 and a small constant places the lower 13 bits of the 32-bit constant in a register. Then, a SETHI sets the upper bits of the register.

One unique feature of the SPARC architecture is its support for tagged data types. The support is minimal at best since it consists of only two instructions: TADDcc and TSUBcc. These instructions work just like the ADDcc instruction except that the V (overflow) condition code is determined differently: an overflow occurs if a regular arithmetic overflow is generated or if either of the two least-significant bits is set in either source operand. As indicated in Table 1, these two instructions come in a variant (indicated by ''tv'') that traps if an overflow is generated.

The least-significant two bits of integer operands are treated as a two-bit tag by these instructions. The tag can have four values, and the architecture defines the value ''00'' to mean''30-bit integer.'' Since the other three values are not directly implemented by the architecture, a trap is generated. The trap handler can then implement whatever function is appropriate. This capability was intended for use by AI-oriented languages such as LISP, but has been rarely used.

The current SPARC architecture has no integer multiply or divide instructions. The low frequency of such operations combined with the difficulty of implementation in the original SPARC gate array probably explains the absence. Since multiply is much more frequent than divide, a multiply step instruction was included. Had the SPARC architects had a bit more foresight, they could have defined multiply and divide instructions that caused a trap, with the trap handler emulating the instructions. This is the approach used by AMD's 29000, and it allows a full multiply to be added to the implementation without requiring software changes to take advantage of it.

The SPARC architecture manual gives several examples of how multiplication and division can be performed. Using MULScc, a 32×32 multiplication with a 64-bit result can be done in roughly 40 instructions, which, assuming cache hits, is not much less efficient than microprocessors that use microcode. Division, on the other hand, must be implemented with a subroutine that executes a few instructions per bit.

Some users have reported that multiply- and divide-intensive programs run faster on Sun-3's (68000-based machines) than on Sun's SPARC-based machines. Version 8 of the SPARC architecture will include multiply and divide instructions. SPARClite adds a multiply instruction and divide step.

Branch instructions in the SPARC architecture are fairly typical. There is a single unconditional CALL, a slightly more general jump-and-link, a return-from-trap, and three sets of conditional branch instructions, each of which tests a different set of condition codes. The trap-conditionally instruction is also technically a branch instruction.

CALL is the only instruction that uses format 1. The 30-bit displacement is shifted left two bits so CALL can jump to a subroutine anywhere in the 32-bit address space. Also, CALL writes the value of the PC, which is the address of the CALL itself, into out register r[15]. A routine that has been CALLed must return to the address "r[15]+8." (The offset of 8 is required because an offset of 4 would point to next instruction, which is the branch delay slot.) Nested subroutines don't have to save the return address, since the register window's mechanism provides a "new" r[15] for each procedure.

Jump-and-link (JMPL) uses case 2 of format 3. JMPL is more general than CALL because the return address is written to the register specified in the rd field; thus, the return address can be saved in any general register. Also, JMPL branches to the address specified by the sum of register rs1 plus either the register rs2 or the 13-bit constant simm13. Thus, JMPL can perform an indirect call. Also, by specifying gr0 in the rd field, JMPL can implement the return from a subroutine: rs1 specifies r[15] (actually r[31] in the new window) and simm13 specifies the integer "+8."

The return-from-trap (RETT) is used only to return from the implicit subroutine call that is made whenever a trap is taken by the processor. RETT takes care of returning to the interrupted instruction stream, switching processor state if necessary, incrementing the CWP, etc. RETT is privileged, as indicated by the "P" in Table 1.

SPARC defines three sets of condition codes: the integer condition codes (icc), the floating-point condition codes (fcc), and the coprocessor condition codes (ccc). A separate group of conditional branch instructions is defined for each set of condition codes. All the usual conditional branches are possible, e.g., branch-not-equal, branch-greater-than, etc.

Conditional branches are always PC-relative and use case 2 of format 2 in Figure 3. This gives them a generous 22-bit relative displacement.

The 1-bit "a" field in the format is the "annual" bit. For conditional branches, setting "a" to zero yields the familiar delayed branch: the instruction immediately following the branch (the delay instruction) is always executed regardless of the outcome of the branch.

When "a" is set to one, the behavior changes. When the branch is not taken, the delay instruction is not executed. When the branch is taken, the delay instruction is executed. Thus, annulling conditional branches are optimized for use at the bottom of loops: the annulling action removes a restriction on what instructions can be placed in the delay slot because the delay instruction will not execute when the loop exits.

The trap-on-integer-condition-code (Ticc) instruction can test for all the usual conditions. If the test is true, a trap is taken. This instruction can be used to implement system calls in a protected operating system or to perform bounds checking on array accesses.

As discussed previously, the SAVE and RESTORE instructions change the CWP and perform a check against the WIM to see if an overflow or underflow has occurred. In addition, SAVE and RESTORE act like regular ADD instructions. These instructions use case 2 of format 3 in Figure 3 just like the ADD instruction and can therefore specify registers and a constant to be added. The one twist is that the source registers are read from the old window (the one addressed by CWP before the SAVE or RESTORE changed it) while the result is written into the new window (the one addressed by the new CWP).

This allows SAVE and RESTORE to simultaneously allocate a new window in the on-chip register file and allocate a new stack frame in main memory. A subroutine would need to allocate both if it needed more local storage than is available in a single window.

The RD and WR instructions are used to read and write special-purpose processor state registers. These include the Y register, which is used to capture the high word of a 32-by-32-bit multiplication performed using the multiply-step instruction; the PSR (processor status register); the WIM (window invalid mask) register; and the TBR (Trap Base Register), which contains the base address of a table of addresses of exception handling routines.

The IFLUSH instruction is provided to permit a program to flush the instruction cache.

The FPop instruction encodes all of the floating-point operations. This instruction uses case 3 of format 3 in Figure 3. The "opf" field encodes the various operations. As with the integer arithmetic instructions, this format encodes three-address register-to-register operations. FPop encodes a large number of operations including conversions (F?TO?, where the question marks are replaced by "i" for integer, "s" for single, "d" for double, and "x" for extended) and all the usual arithmetic.

SPARC is the only major RISC architecture to support extended-precision (128-bit) operands. So far, however, SPARC hardware has only implemented single- and double-precision operations.

The CPop instruction is like the FPop instruction except that no operations are predefined. The semantics of the CPop instruction are dependent on specific coprocessor implementations.

Bus Implementations

SPARC implementations have been criticized because the processor chips have only a single 32-bit data bus. Other chips, such as the 29000 and 88000, have separate buses, and the MIPS chips use a single bus twice per cycle to get the effect of two buses. The single bus means that loads and stores take at least one additional cycle when compared to chips with separate or time-multiplexed buses (instruction fetching must be suspended while the bus is used for data). This is one reason the SPARC-based machines have yielded less performance than competing machines (notably MIPS) at equal clock rates.

Despite this deficiency, SPARC-based systems are some of the cheapest Unix machines available. Cost is one place where a single bus is an advantage: it allows the easy implementation of single, unified external cache. Also, SPARC-based systems are starting to overcome the performance degradation of the single bus with sheer clock speed. The 40-MHz SPARCstation-2 compares favorably to other workstations based on processors with separate buses.

The lack of separate buses is turning out to be a temporary deficiency as chip densities increase. Even the inexpensive SPARClite has separate on-chip buses and caches, and future high-end implementations are likely to use a similar implementation.

Conclusions

The "S" in SPARC ostensibly stands for scalable (though rumors are that it originally stood for "Sun"). While SPARC is probably no more scalable than any other architecture in most respects, it is truly scalable in one sense: the register file can be scaled up or down as technology permits. The only software affected by the register file size is part of the operating system. For most other architectures, the register file size is fixed for all implementations. In practice, however, this scalability has not been useful; all existing implementations use either seven or eight windows. Adding more windows is of no benefit unless the application makes frequent, deeply nested subroutine calls.

SPARC is not technically better than other RISC architectures. If an application really needs a large register file, the 29000 is probably a better choice since only 32 registers are addressable at any one time in SPARC. The 88000 has an extra addressing mode—base plus scaled index—and superior bit field support. MIPS has added the few features it lacks (but SPARC has) in the MIPS-2 architecture, which includes annulling branches, double-word memory reference instructions, and fully interlocked loads.

While SPARC is not an outstanding architecture, it is certainly viable (as tens of thousands of satisfied SPARC users will attest), and it will continue to build momentum because of Sun's success and the number of semiconductor vendors developed SPARC chips. Far more SPARC-based Unix systems have been sold than those based on any other RISC processor, and there are more new implementations of SPARC in progress than for any other architecture.

5

Cypress SPARC Chips

Michael Slater

Cypress Semiconductor has begun shipping their CY7C601, the long-planned full-custom CMOS implementation of the SPARC integer unit. The chip was designed in collaboration with Sun, which will use it in high-end Sun-4 workstations.

Previous SPARC chips have been made by Fujitsu. The first-generation chips, which are the heart of the existing Sun-4 systems, are a 16-MHz gate-array-based design. Only the R3000 from MIPS Computer Systems matches the 20 MIPS rating of Cypress' SPARC chip, although the 88000 and 29000 are close behind at 17 MIPS. (All ratings are VAX MIPS, meaning the performance relative to a VAX 11/780.)

The new CY7C601 integer unit improves on the Fujitsu devices' hardware interface in several ways. In the Fujitsu implementation, instructions for the floating-point coprocessor are fetched by the Integer Unit (IU) and then passed to the floating-point controller (FPC) via a dedicated bus called the F-bus. Cypress' implementation eliminates the F-bus by having the FPC watch the main processor buses and pick up its instructions directly. The 7C601 also has one more register window, for a total of eight overlapping windows of 24 registers each (136 registers total). The chip is packaged in a 207-pin PGA, is implemented in 0.8-micron CMOS, and consumes 3.3 W maximum.

A Different Approach

Cypress is taking a significantly different approach than that taken by Motorola's 88000 designers. The Cypress system is designed to have a much larger minimum cache size, and the cache RAM is thus not included on the MMU/Cache controller chip. The 7C603 provides a 256-entry MMU, following Sun's "Reference MMU" specification, plus control logic for the cache. It does not include the cache tags or the cache RAM.

The 7C181 cache tag chip provides the tag memory and comparators for a 32K-word direct-mapped cache. The 7C153 cache RAM is 32 K × 8, so four are needed for the minimum cache configuration of 128K bytes. A two-way set associative cache can be implemented by adding another cache tag chip, but with this large cache size, Cypress claims the direct-mapped approach is nearly as effective. Smaller caches are not supported.

The CPU/FPU/MMU/cache will require nine chips. The 88000 requires that same number of chips to match the 128K cache size. Cypress claims that their nine-chip set will cost much less, require less board area, and have higher performance. Motorola's minimum three-chip solution is two-thirds the price of the Cypress set, but has only 32K of cache; with 64K of cache, the 88000 chip set will be about the same price as the Cypress set with 128K.

This is an interesting comparison, but it is perhaps misleading. First of all, it assumes that 128K bytes of cache is a requirement; the 88000 is significantly cheaper with a smaller cache, while the cache size of the Cypress chip set cannot be reduced. The 88000's cache will also have a higher hit rate for a given size because of its 4-way set-associative design. Second, we expect that Motorola will reduce their prices significantly by the time Cypress is in production with the full chip set. Third, the 88000 offers more options; for example, using the same number of chips, a three-processor 88000 system with two CMMUs for each processor could be implemented. Finally, for embedded control applications that may get by without the MMU and cache, the Cypress CPU is three times Motorola's price. Thus, while Cypress may have a better solution for their targeted configuration, their ability to adapt to other applications is limited.

Focus on Uniprocessor Systems

While Motorola has gone to great lengths to provide multiprocessor capability for the 88000, Cypress has emphasized uniprocessors. They claim that the great majority of systems in the next few years will be uniprocessors, and that it makes more sense to emphasize this approach in this generation. Future generations will presumably address multiprocessor issues.

The Cypress design uses a virtual cache; that is, the cache is placed between the processor and the MMU. The advantage of this approach is that the MMU delay does not affect the cache access, so it is easier to speed up the processor clock and still have single-cycle cache access. This design follows the architecture that Sun has used in nearly all of their workstations; in fact, the entire Cypress chip set follows the Sun-4/200 architecture.

However, virtual caches have a drawback for shared-memory multi-processor systems—the snooping function required to maintain cache coherency is difficult to implement. Snooping requires monitoring the memory bus, which has physical addresses, and checking for matching cache entries. To do this with a virtual cache, it is necessary to either have a reverse translation buffer, which is complex and slow, or to maintain two sets of tags—one physical and one virtual. Cypress plans to implement the dual-tag approach in future designs.

For now, however, multiprocessor operation requires some com-promises. As long as programs are not modified while they are executing, it is possible to use multiple processors, each with its own instruction cache, without snooping. All processors would have to share a common data cache, which would introduce contention on loads and stores. Cypress claims that this configuration will allow a four-processor 55-VAX-MIPS system to be built; because of the data cache contention, performance is degraded from the 80 MIPS theoretical maximum (assuming 20 MIPS for each of the four processors). Motorola claims that a four-processor 88000 system will achieve 50 VAX MIPS.

Recent Developments

Since this introduction was written, the pinout of the Cypress 7C601 has become the standard for SPARC processors. Integer units that conform to this footprint are available from Cypress, TI, and LSI Logic. Fujitsu and Weitek produce chips compatible with this footprint that combine both an integer and floating-point unit.

The 88000 no longer seems to be a serious competitor in the Unix workstation market. Although Apple Computer once declared an intention to use the 88000 in future products, the change in course brought about by their partnership with IBM has ended any plans they may have had for 88000-based systems. Without this key customer, it would be difficult to justify the R&D expenditures needed to keep the 88000 family competitive with the state of the art.

6

SPARC Support

Michael Slater

The number of announced SPARC chips has essentially doubled (Figure 1), with LSI Logic and Texas Instruments both revealing plans to ship SPARC chip sets. Both companies will produce chip sets that are compatible with Cypress' recently announced set. While this gives Cypress a big boost by acknowledging the quality of their implementation, it also means that Cypress will have two powerful competitors that are known for aggressive price cutting.

As expected, LSI Logic announced that they will make a SPARC Integer Unit (IU) that is pin-compatible with Fujitsu's S-25, and also announced that they are sampling the two MIPS Computer Systems processors, the LR2000 and LR3000. More surprising was that LSI also announced a Cypress-compatible version.

This announcement illustrates LSI Logic's determination to be a player in the microprocessor business. Chairman Wilf Corrigan stated that he expects LSI's microprocessor revenue to grow from essentially zero to 50% of LSI's business within five years. With both SPARC and MIPS processors at very competitive prices, LSI stands an excellent chance of becoming an important microprocessor vendor. The processors will also be available as ASIC (Application Specific Integrated Circuit) cores for customization.

Texas Instruments is by far the largest U.S. semiconductor manufacturer to adopt SPARC, and thus provides a big boost to SPARC's credibility. Both TI and LSI Logic announced plans for future versions that will be faster and more highly integrated.

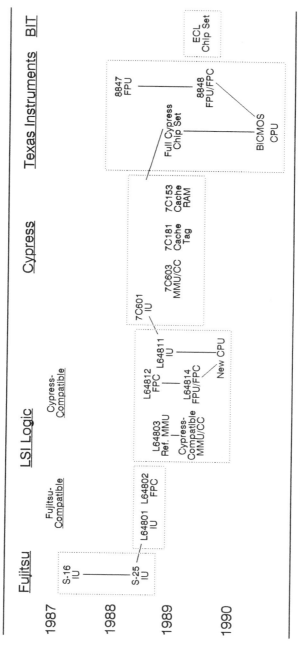

Figure 1. Announced and planned SPARC processors and support chips

Of course, TI did not have any other general-purpose high-performance microprocessor, and their choices for entering that business were limited. Introducing yet another proprietary architecture would have been foolhardy, and TI's experience with the 9900 and 99000 is likely to be sufficient to keep them from making such a mistake again.

The RISC microprocessor business seems to be moving into another phase, where the debate about which architecture is best gives way to issues of chip and software availability and pricing. Notable in both the LSI and Sun/TI announcements was a lack of any claim of architectural excellence; the points being stressed were availability from multiple sources, lower prices for the chips, and availability of operating systems and binary-compatible applications. Architecture and hardware details were ignored. Many would argue that other chips, such as MIPS' R3000, have a superior architecture, but this argument seems to be increasingly irrelevant. As Intel proved with 8086, having the best architecture is not a prerequisite to success.

Sun benefits from TI's and LSI's plans in several ways in addition to the obvious boost in credibility for SPARC. Sun is assured of an excellent selection of processors and support chips, all designed around their architecture, for future workstations. Their association with TI may help them get scarce memory chips, since TI is one of the few U.S. suppliers making DRAMs. The variety of new SPARC vendors also means that Sun will become much less dependent on Fujitsu.

Different Types of Deals

While at first glance it seems that LSI Logic and TI are involved in similar ventures (i.e., sourcing the Cypress SPARC chip set), they are in fact taking very different approaches. Both companies have agreements with Sun Microsystems, which is the ultimate source of expertise on the architecture.

TI has entered into a five-year alternate-source agreement with Cypress. The alternate-source pact covers a variety of levels of cooperation. At first, TI will label and sell Cypress-manufactured chips. However, TI expects soon to be manufacturing Cypress' Integer Unit on their own fab lines; Cypress will supply a full chip design database to TI.

TI's commitment to SPARC is more than just a chip-making venture— their computer group announced plans to use SPARC chips in future UNIX-based computer systems. They did not give any specifics, but referred to the future systems as a converging of their current AI workstations and commercial UNIX systems. The new machines are not expected for at least two years, and will most likely use TI's next-generation implementation of the CPU.

In return, Cypress gets the rights to TI's 74ACT8847 floating-point unit, which is the standard FPU for the Cypress chip set. Cypress will also receive rights to future SPARC family products designed by TI, including a new floating-point unit and future CPU designs.

LSI Logic, on the other hand, has no licensing agreement with either Cypress or Fujitsu. They have designed their own chips from the ground up, so the chip designs are new even though they are pin-compatible with existing chips. There seems to have been little, if any, cooperation between LSI Logic and the other vendors. All vendors, of course, have licenses from Sun. LSI Logic is covering all bases, with two flavors of SPARC chips and both MIPS chips. To LSI, it doesn't much matter which chip is most successful—as long as one of the four RISC chips they are producing is a winner.

The Floating-Point Connection

TI's 74ACT8847 floating-point unit (FPU) is used with both Fujitsu's and Cypress' SPARC chip sets. This chip was not, however, designed to be part of a SPARC chip set, and has a general-purpose interface. To use it with a SPARC processor, a floating-point controller (FPC) is required. The FPC has been implemented as a gate array by LSI Logic for both the Fujitsu and Cypress versions. The current Cypress chip set thus consists of the IU from Cypress, the FPU from TI, and the FPC from LSI Logic.

There is considerable inefficiency in this three-chip configuration, in terms of speed, pin count, and chip area. Both TI and LSI Logic are designing new FP/FPC combination chips. TI's will be based on their existing 8847 design, while LSI's will be a new design. Cypress will have rights to TI's new device. Both TI and LSI Logic will incorporate floating-point functions into future processor chips.

Cache and MMU Support

TI will supply the entire Cypress chip set, including the 7C603 MMU/cache controller, 7C153 cache RAM, and 7C181 cache tag, in addition to the 7C601 integer unit. LSI Logic will produce a similar chip set, and intends that their chips will be pin-compatible with those from Cypress and TI. However, as with the IU, LSI has no agreement with Cypress. Cypress has not released any details on their MMU/cache controller, so it seems rather speculative at this point for LSI to promise a pin-compatible device. Indeed, LSI officials hedged a bit, saying that their chips would be very similar but not necessarily identical.

All companies involved seem aware of the need for a complete SPARC chip set to help compete against Motorola's more highly integrated 88000 chip set. LSI Logic has much experience with "system-on-a-chip" sorts of products, particularly through their Headland subsidiary. They could well do for SPARC what they, and others, have already done for Intel's processors—make chip sets that implement a complete workstation in a minimum number of ICs. SPARC-based workstation design could become as simple as PC-compatible design.

Enough Vendors

Having lots of sources is good for systems builders, but the competition will make it tough for each of the IC vendors to make a profit. Apparently sensitive to this issue, Sun's Executive VP Bernie Lacroute stated "We don't see the need to license additional semiconductor partners, but would welcome existing vendors to solicit alternate sources." This is a shift in direction for Sun, and indicates that with the signing of TI they do not feel the need for more sources or more credibility.

The Future Is BiCMOS

Both TI and LSI Logic have stated that they are developing, with Sun, future implementations of the SPARC architecture in BiCMOS. Neither company is willing to provide any specifics. Future CPUs are certain to include on-chip floating-point, and some will include on-chip memory management and cache support.

An ECL SPARC implementation is underway at Bipolar Integrated Technology (BIT). Performance is expected to be about double that of the Cypress processor at 33 MHz, but Cypress expects to have parts at 50 MHz by the time BIT ships their chip set. BIT's version will have much higher power consumption than the CMOS implementations and will be significantly more expensive, so its market window seems to be shrinking.

Fujitsu, the first vendor to ship SPARC chips and still the only vendor whose chips appear in a Sun product, has not announced any support chips or plans for future processors. They have stated that they are working on cache and memory management support, and announcements are expected before the end of the year.

Where Is the Market?

The SPARC processor was designed as an engine for UNIX workstations, and that is likely to remain its primary application. In theory, SPARC could also be used in personal computers and in embedded control applications, but its chances for success in these areas is questionable.

It must surely be one of Sun's dreams, and one of Intel's nightmares, for SPARC to overtake the 386 as the processor of choice in personal computers. The cost of the chips won't be a barrier for long, nor will the level of integration. The real barrier is the software base. While the availability of SPARC-binary-compatible software is a strong advantage for SPARC in the workstation market, this software is not sufficient to compete in the personal computer market.

RISC processors have been intimately tied to UNIX because UNIX is the only popular operating system that is portable and carries with it a range of relatively portable applications. As personal computers move up the performance scale to the workstation level and workstations come down in price to the PC level, a merging of the two markets is inevitable.

The factor that will continue to differentiate the two markets is the software base. Personal computers are tied to the MS-DOS and Macintosh software bases, which are in turn tied to the Intel and Motorola CISC architectures. The only clear chance for RISC processors to achieve very high sales volumes is for UNIX to break into the personal computer market. This possibility has moved one step closer to reality with the "Open Look" user interface shell. The remaining piece of the puzzle is a large base of high-quality applications at competitive prices, which is a long way away.

Another possibility is the use of emulation or binary translation to allow existing software to be executed on new, incompatible processors. This is unlikely to be a long-term solution, but could serve as a bridge to a new processor platform.

SPARC is unlikely to have much success in embedded control. Chip count is often critical in embedded applications, and SPARC does not fare well in this regard, although it will do much better in the next generation. In-circuit emulators, which embedded control designers often insist upon, are unlikely to be available for the SPARC chips. But perhaps the biggest barrier is that both Intel and AMD have RISC processors aimed directly at that marketplace, with large, experienced sales and support organizations. The Sun-compatible software base, while a powerful asset for SPARC in workstation applications, is of little value for embedded control.

Recent Developments

Since this introduction was written, Cypress has redesigned its SPARC chip set as described in the following chapter. Cypress-compatible SPARC chip sets are in volume production at Cypress, TI, and LSI Logic. Fujitsu and Weitek are sampling chips that integrate the integer and floating-point units in a package pin-compatible with the 7C601.

Three companies offer system logic chip sets compatible with the SPARCstation 2: LSI Logic, Fujitsu, and Tera. All three companies have been licensed by Sun to sell the chip set developed for Sun by LSI Logic. However, all three also have proprietary designs that offer advantages over Sun's design. LSI's design has been plagued by delays, and they are initially promoting the Sun design. Fujitsu and Tera are promoting their own products and plan to offer the Sun design as an alternative for customers who desire multivendor compatibility.

7

Redesigned Cypress SPARC Chip Set

Michael Slater

In an unusual move, Cypress Semiconductor has redesigned the cache and memory management support chips for their SPARC processor, and will not produce the chips they originally announced. The new chip set will require fewer chips for a minimum system and will offer a number of features not present in the original design.

Earlier, Cypress announced their 7C601 33-MHz SPARC processor and a set of support chips. Both the processor itself and one of the support chips, the 7C608 floating-point controller, are now available. The cache and memory management chips were originally promised for sampling by the end of 1988 with production in the first quarter of '89.

In the meantime, however, Roger Ross (formerly head of the 88000 team) and several of his coworkers left Motorola to start Ross Technology, which is in the process of becoming a subsidiary of Cypress Semiconductor. After Ross and company reviewed the architecture of the support chips, they concluded that a redesign could offer significant advantages. Cypress bravely decided to redirect development of the original architecture and proceed with the new design.

Motorola sued Ross Technology, its founders, and Cypress shortly after they set up shop, alleging improper use of Motorola's proprietary information. The suit was subsequently settled out-of-court. Ross has, no doubt, kept its collective hands clean regarding use of Motorola's intellectual property. Nonetheless, they have provided many of the features of the

88200 CMMU design in the revised SPARC chip set and, with the benefit of hindsight, they have also improved on that design in several respects.

A Few Features Lost, Many Gained

The original design consisted of the 7C603 MMU and cache controller, 7C181 cache tag RAM, and 7C153 cache RAM. The minimum cache/MMU configuration required one 603, one 181, and four 153s, for a total of six chips. The new design replaces these with:

- 7C604 CMU (cache/memory management unit), which combines the functions of the 603 and 181
- 7C157 CRAM (cache RAM)

The basic configuration now consists of one CMU and two CRAMs, or half as many chips as the previous design. The reduction in the number of CRAMs was made possible by changing the organization of the CRAM chip from 32K × 8 to 16K × 16. While many improvements were made, a few things were given up:

- Cache size is now 64K bytes, rather than 128K
- MMU now has 64 TLB (translation look-aside buffer) entries, rather than 256

Among the improvements in the new design are

- MMU supports 4096 contexts, rather than 256
- TLB and cache locking capability
- New memory bus design with 64-bit data path
- Copy-back update policy supported, in addition to buffered write-through
- Multiple CMU-CRAM sets can be used to increase both cache size and number of TLBs (up to four sets, for 256K of cache and 256 TLBs)

The reduction in the number of chips is significant not only because of the obvious cost and space savings, but also because it reduces the capacitive load on the processor bus. This makes it more practical to increase the speed of the system. Cypress is planning a 40-MHz version of the chip set, to be followed by a 50-MHz version.

A key advantage of the Cypress design for real-time applications is the ability to lock entries in the TLBs and the cache. This is important when guaranteed minimum response times are needed; the cache and TLBs can be filled with the critical code sections, which will be sure to be there when they are needed. A group of any number of the TLBs can be locked by setting the lowest TLB number that is available for replacement. Cache entries cannot be selectively locked; the entire cache is locked by setting a control bit. No other RISC chip set yet announced provides these features.

No changes were announced for the basic processor, the CY7C601 Integer Unit (IU), or the floating-point strategy. Floating point is provided by TI's 8847 FPU (sold by Cypress as the 7C609), which requires the gate-array floating-point controller (FPC) to translate the FPU's native interface to that required by the SPARC architecture. Because of the amount of I/O required, this device is in a massive 299-pin PGA. It is made by LSI Logic as the L64812 and is also sold by Cypress as the 7C608. TI's 8848 FPU works directly with the 7C601 IU and eliminates the FPC. Cypress sells this part as the 7C602. LSI Logic has a similar device, called the L64814.

Multiprocessor Support Coming

When Cypress made their initial SPARC announcements, they down-played the importance of multiprocessor systems. Their virtual cache design makes bus snooping more difficult to implement, and no support for such snooping is provided in either the original or the revised chip set. However, Cypress has now announced a new multiprocessor cache/memory management unit (MP-CMU), the 7C605. This chip replaces the 7C604 for multiprocessor designs, and works with the same 7C157 CRAMs.

The 7C605 implements a sophisticated cache coherency protocol, which is modeled on the Futurebus. The virtual cache design is retained (meaning that the primary cache tags contain virtual, rather than physical, ad-dresses). These tags cannot be used for bus snooping, since the memory bus has physical addresses. To solve this problem, a second set of tags is added that stores the physical (translated) address. This set of tags is used by the bus snooping logic.

The second set of tags also provides another benefit: *aliases* can be detected by the hardware. Aliases are a problem that can occur in a virtual cache. In a multitasking system, each task can have a different mapping of virtual to physical addresses. Thus, it is possible for two different virtual addresses to map to the same physical address; these are called *aliases*. Aliases create a coherency problem, since one copy of the data may be modified, and the other will then be "stale."

The uniprocessor version of the CMU requires that operating system software ensure that the alias problem does not occur. Aliased virtual addresses must either be mapped to the same cache line, or must be made noncacheable.

Cache Coherency Protocol

Each cache line in the 7C605 MP-CMU has extra state bits for coherency support. Table 1 shows the five possible states for any cache line. The cache coherency protocol supports direct data intervention with or without reflection. An example will help clarify what these terms mean. Suppose we have a two-processor system. Each has its own cache; we'll call them A and B.

Suppose the following events take place:

- Processor A reads memory location X. The data in Cache A is marked as Private Clean.
- Processor B reads memory location X. Cache A observes the transaction, and asserts a special bus control line to tell Processor B that a copy of this data is present in another cache. Both caches now mark the data as Shared Clean.
- Processor A modifies memory location X, which is stored in its cache. Since it is marked as shared, Cache A executes a special "invalidate" bus transaction. This transaction has only an address phase (and no data phase), and thus is faster than a normal bus cycle. In response to the invalidate transaction, Cache B invalidates its copy of the data. Processor A now changes the state of the data to Private Dirty, since it knows that copies in other caches will have been invalidated but main memory is still out of date.
- Processor A again modifies memory location X. Now, since the data is marked as private, the cache does not need to write the data through to main memory.

Table 1. Possible States for Each Cache Line

State	Meaning
Invalid	Entry not valid
Private Clean	Entry in only one cache Same as copy in main memory
Private Dirty	Entry in only one cache Cache copy has been modified and not written to main memory
Shared Clean	Entry in two or more caches Same as copy in main memory
Shared Dirty	Entry in two or more caches Cache copy has been modified and not written to main memory

- Processor B reads memory location X. The main memory does not have the current version of the data; only Cache A has it. Cache A detects the read attempt and, seeing that the cached copy is dirty, it intervenes: *it inhibits the memory from providing the data, and provides the data itself.*

If the memory system is smart enough, it can detect the intervention of Cache A and capture the data as it is written from Cache A to Cache B. This is called a *reflective* memory system. If such a memory system is present, after the last step in the preceding example all copies of the data are up-to-date and can be marked as Shared Clean. The MP-CMU will also support nonreflective main memories; in this case, the main memory is left out of date after the last transaction, and the data must be marked as Shared Dirty in one of the caches.

Cypress versus Motorola

Of all the announced RISC chip sets, only Motorola's 88000 and the Cypress chip set provide integrated cache/memory management units that can be paralleled to increase the cache and TLB sizes. The 88200 and the recently announced 7C605 MP-CMU are also the only integrated cache/memory management units that include multiprocessor support.

Despite these similarities, the approaches taken in each chip set are significantly different. Table 2 summarizes the key differences. While Motorola has chosen to produce fully integrated CMMU chips with all memory on-chip, Cypress includes only the tags on-chip and requires external RAMs for the cached data and instructions. This gives Motorola the edge in chip count for a minimum system. The Cypress chips, on the other hand, will be easier to build, and the exclusion of the RAM for the cache controller chips provides more room for extra MMU and cache control functions, as well as more sophisticated multiprocessor support.

Motorola uses a physical cache, which allows them to get by without a separate set of tags for bus snooping. The downside of sharing the single set of tags is that the bus snooping contends for cache access, and can cause the processor to execute wait states even on a cache hit.

Motorola uses a 4-way set-associative cache structure, while Cypress uses the simpler direct-mapped approach. The direct-mapped cache is simpler to implement, and is faster for a given RAM technology. For small caches, the 4-way set-associative structure has a significantly higher hit rate. Cypress argues that as the cache size increases, the difference between the two approaches becomes insignificant.

Motorola has other reasons for using the set-associative structure. Since a physical cache depends on translated addresses to determine whether or

Table 2. Comparing Motorola's 88000 and Cypress' SPARC Cache Features

	Motorola 88100/88200	Cypress SPARC with MP-CMU
Cache addressing	Physical	Virtual
Instruction and data caches	Separate	Combined
Process technology	1.5 μ, moving to 1.2 μ	0.8 μ
Cache associativity	4-way set assoc.	Direct mapped
Cache line size	16 bytes	32 bytes
Cache-to-memory data bus width	32 bits	64 bits
Cache RAM	On CMMU chip	Two external RAM chips
Update policies	Write-through, write-once	Write-through, copy-back
Minimum cache size	32K	64K
Maximum cache size	128K	256K
Chip count for processor with floating-point and minimum cache	3	6 (5 when 8848 FPU available)
Chip count with 128K cache	9	9 (8 when 8848 FPU available)
Intervention	Indirect	Direct
Fully concurrent snooping	No	Yes
Cache and TLB Locking	No	Yes
Buffered write-through	No	Yes

not there is a cache hit, some technique must be used to "hide" the delay of the translation logic to allow zero-wait-state cache access. The technique used by Motorola is to overlap the cache access and the address translation by taking advantage of the set-associative structure.

Since the least-significant address bits are not translated, they are available without waiting for any translation delay. These address bits select one 4-line group of the cache. While these lines are being accessed from the cache, the high-order bits are translated. By the time the data are available, the translated high-order bits are also available, and these bits determine if there is a hit on one of the four lines. This technique hides the translation delay, but it limits the size of the cache to the MMU's page size times the number of sets in the cache. Motorola's 4K page size and 4-way set-associativity allows them to build a 16K cache chip.

Another architectural difference is Cypress' use of a single bus and unified cache for instructions and data, while Motorola uses a Harvard architecture with separate buses and caches. The SPARC ship suffers a pipeline stall whenever a load or store operation occurs, since data accesses contend for the same bus as instruction accesses. On the other hand, the unified cache is more flexible in that the partitioning between data and instructions in the cache is not fixed.

Motorola's 88200 uses a simpler but slower cache coherency protocol. When a cache's snooping logic detects that another processor is accessing a memory location whose copy in main memory is out of date, the cache causes the access to be aborted, updates main memory by writing the modified data, and then allows the access to be retried. This approach, called *indirect intervention*, is simpler to implement but has somewhat lower performance. Whether or not the difference is significant in a real system is hard to determine.

Conclusions

In retrospect, the decision to redesign the chip set turned out poorly. Although initially planned for availability in the third quarter of 1989, the 7C605 cache-controller/MMU chip took until mid-1991 to become available in sample quantity. Although the Sun-defined "reference MMU" and Mbus multiprocessing bus protocol implemented in the 7C605 have been around for years, neither appeared in a Sun product until the introduction of the SPARCserver 600MP series in late 1991. The original SRAM-based MMU has been used in all Sun desktop models through the SPARC-station 2.

With initial pricing at $1200 per chip in hundred-unit quantity (about $600 in high volume) for the 40-MHz version, the 7C605 is positioned at the high end of the market. The long delay in reaching silicon has given the competition time to develop more advanced designs that also use the reference MMU and Mbus, although none are as close to production availability as the Cypress chip set. TI has worked with Sun to create SuperSPARC, a single-chip implementation of a superscalar integer unit, floating-point unit, MMU, and instruction and data caches. LSI Logic and Metaflow are also known to be working on a superscalar design. With these powerful, integrated chips close at hand, it seems that the window for multichip solutions based on the 7C605 may soon begin to close.

First ECL Microprocessor

Michael Slater

Bipolar Integrated Technology (Beaverton, Oregon) has introduced their long-awaited ECL SPARC implementation. The 125,000-transistor B5000 SPARC integer unit is the most complex bipolar chip ever produced, and it is the first complete 32-bit microprocessor to be implemented in ECL (Emitter-Coupled Logic). The floating-point coprocessor, however, requires five additional chips.

BIT is aiming the chip set at high-end servers and workstations. It may also have applications in performance-critical embedded control applications for which bit-slice or custom controllers have been the only choice until now. Such systems could use the integer unit alone and use SRAM memory instead of a cache.

Figure 1 shows a block diagram of a complete BIT SPARC CPU. The B5100 floating-point controller, a 36,000-transistor chip, provides a floating-point interface compatible with the SPARC architecture specification. The floating-point registers are implemented in two B5210 register-file chips, and floating-point calculations are performed by the B5110 multiplier and B5120 ALU. The chips' I/O is ECL 10KH compatible.

Worst-case power consumption for the chip set is a staggering 80 W, although the typical value is a mere 50 W. While this is much higher than CMOS implementations, it is relatively low for an ECL system of this complexity. According to BIT, the special heat sink attached to the chips allows them to be cooled with forced room-temperature air.

BIT has been selling similar floating-point chips for use in a variety of high-performance CPUs, including Apollo's PRISM and HP's Precision

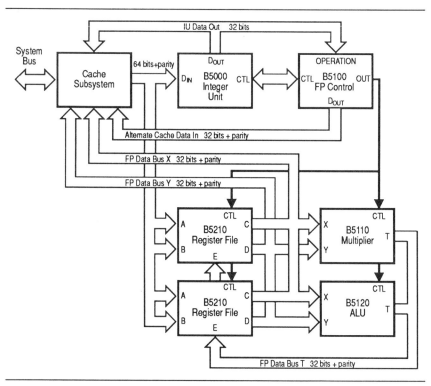

Figure 1. CPU based on BIT's ECL SPARC chip set

Architecture. The company was founded in 1983 by a team from Tektronix's IC design group, and shipped their first product in 1986. BIT has their own fabrication facility, and credits their proprietary "P111" process as the technology that has enabled this very high level of integration for a bipolar chip.

The SPARC IU and FPC were developed by a team of engineers from Sun and BIT. BIT also developed an ECL implementation of the MIPS microprocessor under contract to MIPS Computer Systems.

Operating at a clock frequency of 80 MHz, BIT rates their SPARC chip set at 65 native MIPS and 14 double-precision Linpack MFLOPS. The clock count improvements shown in Table 1 reduce the average number of clock cycles from 1.4–1.6 for existing SPARC implementations to about 1.2. This factor, combined with a clock rate that is 2.4 times higher, is claimed to make the chip almost three times as fast as Cypress' 33-MHz 7C601, which implies a rating of about 60 VAX MIPS. BIT says that chips are running in the lab at above 100 MHz, but no schedule has been announced for shipping chips rated above 80 MHz. Remarkably, BIT claims that the chips were 100% functional on first silicon.

Impressive as this achievement is, it falls short of providing a complete solution for building an ECL computer system. BIT is not providing any cache or memory management support. These are not simple functions to implement at this clock rate, and BIT concedes that a typical system will require two AISCs for the cache data path and another for cache and MMU control. The cache can be built with 7-to-8 ns ECL RAMs, which are available in a 16K × 4 configuration. A typical 128-Kbyte cache requires 24 RAM chips. Making a cache subsystem for a 100-MHz version would require sub-5-ns RAMs.

According to Jim Peterson, BIT's engineering manager for the SPARC project, each of their prospective customers has different requirements for the cache and MMU functions, and BIT concluded that whatever they implemented would not satisfy many of the customers. Peterson also pointed out that the sorts of customers at which these chips are aimed are used to designing custom chips for the entire CPU, so having to design chips for the cache and MMU functions is not such a hardship. Nevertheless, this points out that an ECL-based SPARC system will be much more difficult to design and build than a CMOS system.

Table 1. Comparing Cypress and BIT SPARC Chips

	Cypress 7C601	BIT B5000
Technology	0.8-micron CMOS	1.2-micron ECL
Clock Rate	33 MHz	80 MHz
Max. Power	3.3 W	20 W
Die Size	310 mils square	380 mils square
Transistors	72,000	125,000
Package	207-pin PGA	279-pin PGA
Buses	32-bit data in/out	32-bit data out and 64-bit data in
Floating-Point Unit	1-2 chips	5 chips
100-Piece Price	$557	$850
Integer ALU Operations	1 clock	1 clock
Branch	2 clocks	1 clock
32-bit Integer Load	3 clocks	1 clock
32-bit Integer Store	4 clocks	2 clocks
64-bit Integer Load	4 clocks	2 clocks
Double-Precision FP Load	3 clocks	1 clock
Double-Precision FP Store	4 clocks	1 clock
Double-Precision FP Add	8 clocks	2 clocks
Double-Precision FP Mult.	9 clocks	4 clocks

IU Design

The B5000 integer unit, while binary-compatible with CMOS SPARC chips, uses a considerably different implementation approach. ECL signals require low-impedance terminations, and bidirectional buses require termination at both ends; thus, they require stronger drivers and consume more power than unidirectional buses. For this reason, BIT's design uses two separate, unidirectional data buses: a 32-bit data output bus, and a 72-bit (64 bits plus parity) data input bus.

As with the initial CMOS SPARC implementation, there are seven register windows for a total of 120 registers. (To improve yield, there are actually 128 registers on the chip, and any block of eight can be disabled when the chip is tested.) Cypress's 7C601 has eight register windows, for a total of 135 registers, which will increase performance slightly for some applications.

The B5000 IU uses a five-stage pipeline similar to that used in the MIPS R3000, rather than the four-stage pipeline used in other SPARC designs. The first three stages are the fetch, decode, and execute, just as in other SPARC designs. The fourth stage is used for memory access, and results are written to the register file in the fifth stage. For ALU operations, the fourth stage is a one-cycle delay. This allows loads to be processed without a forced stall of one clock cycle in addition to the delay slot, as required by previous SPARC chips. Register bypass gates forward the data past idle stages, eliminating any unnecessary delays.

One design choice that is surprising, at first glance, is the use of a unified instruction/data cache, rather than the Harvard architecture usually associated with high-performance RISC implementations. BIT chose to use a unified 64-bit-wide cache, rather than two 32-bit-wide caches, for several reasons:

- Processor pin count is reduced, since only one address bus is required.
- Double-precision floating-point loads and stores can be performed in a single cycle.
- Two instructions can be fetched at a time.
- System implementation is simplified, since only one cache and one MMU are needed.

The IU includes a four-word prefetch buffer, which is a key to making efficient use of the cache. By prefetching two words at a time, the cache is needed for instruction fetching only every other cycle on average, allowing data accesses to occur without interfering with instruction fetches in most cases. This strategy is similar to that used by the 486.

The chip generally operates without stalls on both taken and untaken branches, while existing CMOS SPARC implementations require a stall cycle. This is made possible by the prefetch buffer and the 64-bit cache bus. The double-word bus guarantees that the branch instruction, the following instruction (in the delay slot), and the next instruction (executed if the branch is not taken) can be fetched in two cache accesses. The prefetcher then fetches the branch destination (in case the branch is taken), so by the time the instruction in the branch delay slot is executed, the next instructions for both the taken and the untaken cases are in the prefetch queue.

Double-word integer loads take two clock cycles; even though all 64 bits can be read in a single cycle, the port to the 32-bit-wide register file is not wide enough to allow both words to be written in a single cycle. Double-precision floating-point loads and stores, however, do execute in a single cycle, since the floating-point registers are in the external register file chips.

The BIT system provides parity throughout, including the register file in the IU and all external data paths. Parity is checked by the IU on data-in, but must be externally generated on data-out. The IU synchronously traps on parity errors before taking any action on the erroneous data, allowing accesses to be retried. If, for example, an error occurs in an unmodified cache line, the cache line can simply be invalidated and the data fetched from main memory.

ECL versus CMOS

BIT's ECL SPARC implementation not only runs at the highest clock rate of any commercially available microprocessor, but also averages fewer clocks per instruction than CMOS SPARC implementations. Next-generation CMOS processors, however, are likely to present a strong challenge. By 1992, single-chip CMOS designs with on-chip FPU, cache, memory management, and multiple functional units are expected. These designs will be a tough target for ECL chips that can't achieve the same density, though BIT expects to reach 500,000 transistors with their next-generation ECL process.

ECL processors have a window of opportunity for high-end servers and very-high-end workstations. In the long run, however, they will encounter serious competition from CMOS designs that will take advantage of CMOS's greater density to implement multiple functional units and on-chip caches, squeezing more performance out of every clock cycle.

9

LSI Logic Embedded Control SPARC Processor

Michael Slater

Barely a week after Cypress/ROSS's announcement of their 7C611 SPARC processor for embedded control, LSI Logic announced two new devices aimed at the same market. While Cypress/ROSS introduced only a pin-reduced, lower-cost integer unit, LSI has gone further by announcing an "Integrated System Controller" (ISC) that significantly reduces the number of chips required to make a complete system.

LSI Logic has previously announced two different SPARC integer units: the L64801, which is pin-compatible with Fujitsu's S-20 and S-25, and the L64811, which is pin-compatible with Cypress/ROSS's 7C601. The new integer unit is the L64901, which is derived from the Fujitsu-compatible L64801 design. The 801 has seven register windows, as compared to eight in the 811, and also has a simpler pipeline design, so the chip size is smaller. Thus, it was the natural choice for LSI to use as the base for the low-cost 901.

Both LSI Logic and Cypress/ROSS took similar approaches to developing a cost-reduced integer unit: take an existing design, remove some features to save pins, and package it in a PQFP. There are several differences, however. While Cypress/ROSS kept the floating-point interface but reduced the address bus to 24 bits, LSI kept a full 32-bit address bus but eliminated the floating-point coprocessor interface.

LSI Logic had a bit more flexibility than Cypress/ROSS, since the L64901 is a new design and not just a partial pin-out of an existing chip.

This allowed LSI to make some small changes, such as making the interrupt inputs active-low instead of active-high, and improving the bus timing. Such changes are much easier for LSI to make, since the processor is based on their standard-cell ASIC technology, while Cypress/ROSS's 7C601 is a full-custom design.

In addition to the higher clock speed, the Cypress/ROSS part should be slightly faster due to its more complex pipeline and, depending on the application, the additional register window. As both of these chips enter volume production, we expect that competition will drive them to very similar prices at equal clock rates.

Integrated System Controller

The L64951 Integrated System Controller (ISC) is the first integrated system support logic chip for embedded SPARC systems. Figure 1 shows the pin functions for this chip. The functions it provides include:

- Cache control logic for an 8-Kbyte, 32-Kbyte, or 128-Kbyte direct-mapped, write-through, unified cache.
- Eight programmable chip selects for memory or I/O devices, each of which can be programmed for the address range and number of wait states. Each address region also has two 4-bit protection fields, one for user mode and one for supervisor mode. For each region, data reads, data writes, and instruction fetches can be individually allowed or prohibited.
- Memory controller for up to four banks of DRAM, using either 1-Mbit or 4-Mbit chips for 1 Mbyte to 64 Mbytes of memory. Provides programmable RAS and CAS for each bank, and supports fast page mode.
- Eight memory protection or debug breakpoint registers, which cause a trap on access to selected address ranges. Each register can be used individually with any number of "don't care" bits for a 2^n size block, or two registers can be used in a pair to set high and low address limits for a block of arbitrary size.
- Clock buffers to provide minimum-skew clocks for the processor and other system logic.
- Schmitt-trigger reset circuit.
- Interrupt control logic for eight external and several internal interrupts, each of which can be individually masked.
- Three-channel DMA controller. Two channels are designed for use by I/O devices. The third channel is for use by the CPU to perform block moves.

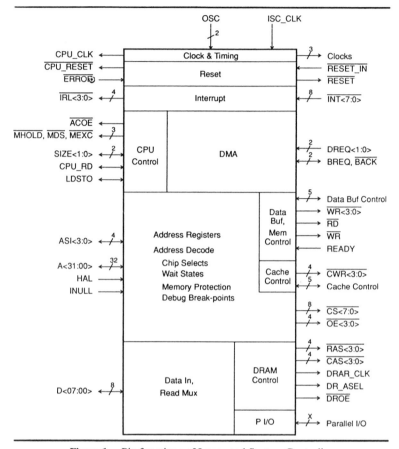

Figure 1. Pin functions of Integrated System Controller

The capabilities provided by the ISC go a long way toward making SPARC more suitable for embedded applications. While a traditional MMU is not provided, embedded systems generally don't need (or want) a Unix-style MMU. The simple protection functions provided by the ISC are more appropriate for embedded systems, and are especially useful when the system is being debugged.

System Configuration

Figure 2 shows a block diagram of a typical system with cache. All cache control logic is included in the ISC. Six standard SRAMs (2K × 8, 8K × 8,

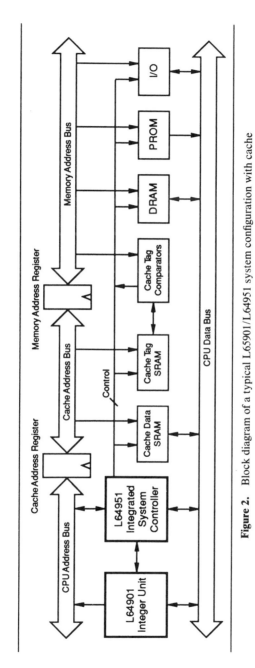

Figure 2. Block diagram of a typical L65901/L64951 system configuration with cache

or 32K × 8) provide the cache memory and tags. Four of the SRAMs are used for data, and two for tags. For 25-MHz operation, 25-ns RAMs are required; 35-ns RAMs can be used for 20-MHz operation. Because the cache access is built into the integer unit's pipeline, the tag RAMs do not need to be any faster than the data RAMs.

Two octal comparators (for comparing the processor address to the tags), two octal buffers, and two octal registers are also required. The cache architecture is quite simple: a write-through memory update policy, no write buffering, and a one-word line size.

The ISC provides RAS and CAS signals for each DRAM bank, along with an address multiplexer control signal. (An external address multiplexer is required.) The banks are not interleaved. At 20 MHz, 70- or 80-ns RAMs are required for zero-wait-state access on a page hit; the first access outside the page takes a total of four cycles (three wait states). The 80-ns DRAMs can be used in small systems with minimal bus loading, while larger systems will require 70-ns chips.

Using 256K × 4 DRAMs, a single bank requires only eight chips and provides 1 Mbyte of memory. A 4-Mbyte system can be built with 1-Mbit or 4-Mbit chips. Using 4M × 1 RAMs, a single bank provides 16 Mbytes, and the maximum four-bank system provides 64 Mbytes.

For minimum cost, the cache system can be eliminated. DRAM-only systems are possible, but will suffer in performance unless the number of page hits is very high. Systems that don't need much RAM might use all SRAM; the access time required is the same as for the cache RAMs. Another alternative is a mix of SRAM and DRAM, with the programmer allocating code and/or data to SRAM to optimize performance.

The Competition

The combination of the L64901 integer unit and L64951 ISC make SPARC competitive for a much broader range of embedded applications. Until recently, Motorola's 68020 was the leading processor for high-end embedded control, but the superior price/performance of RISC processors has steadily eroded the 68020's popularity for new designs. The two leading contenders are AMD's 29000 and Intel's 960 family, and LSI's new chip set compares quite favorably.

LSI rates the L64901 at 12.5 MIPS at 20 MHz, but does not specify what sort of MIPS these are or what memory system is assumed. Without benchmark data, it is difficult to evaluate how the performance will compare to the 29000 or the 960, but it should be in the same ball-park at the same clock frequency.

The 29000's MMU is much more sophisticated than the simple protection logic provided by the ISC. While most embedded applications don't need such an MMU, many designers have found it to be useful. Intel's 960 family has no MMU or protection logic at all, except in the mil-spec 960MC.

Intel's 960CA has the most similar set of functions to the LSI Logic chip pair. Both the 960CA and LSI chip pair have a programmable wait-state generator, DMA controller, and interrupt controller, and neither has any support for floating-point hardware. Because of its superscalar design, the 960CA should be significantly faster than the LSI Logic chip set.

The LSI Logic chip pair goes beyond the AMD and Intel solutions in providing integrated control logic for an external cache. On the other hand, the Intel and AMD chips both have some on-chip cache, so external cache is not as important. LSI's design is the only one to provide DRAM control.

Another advantage of the LSI Logic design is that both chips are implemented as ASICs, so they can be modified by high-volume users to meet their requirements. The integer unit is about 20,000 gates, while the ISC is about 15,000 gates. LSI is now producing gate arrays up to 50,000 gates, so in terms of complexity, it is feasible to combine the functions of the two chips. The problem in providing all the functions of both chips on a single device is that the number of pins becomes too large for low-cost packages, and the die itself could become pad-limited. For applications that need only some of the functions of the ISC or allow some address lines or other CPU signals to be deleted, combining the two chips into one may be feasible.

SPARC has the benefit of high-quality software development and debugging tools developed for workstations. Familiarity with the architecture is also an advantage; for an engineer who is comfortable developing code for his SPARCstation, being able to use the same processor architecture in an embedded application is appealing.

Intel and AMD, on the other hand, have a richer set of hardware development tools, including in-circuit emulators and logic analyzers with disassembly capability. Because the SPARC market is split among several different pin-outs, with more to come, developing an in-circuit emulator is impractical.

Conclusions

In the early stages of the evolution of RISC, all of the vendors targeted workstations and general-purpose computers. Because of the key importance of a wide variety of third-party applications, however, this market is difficult for new architectures to penetrate. Furthermore, given the dominance of the Intel/IBM standard for desktop business computers, the volumes in the RISC-based system area aren't exciting. As a result, some RISC architectures, such as AMD's 29000 and Intel's 960, are now marketed solely for embedded control applications.

Now that the SPARC and MIPS camps feel relatively secure in their positions in the general-purpose computing market, the chip vendors are pushing into embedded control in a search for more sockets. The cost-reduced integer units are uninteresting, except for their pricing. LSI Logic's ISC chip, on the other hand, will help make SPARC a viable competitor to the 29000 and 960 families for embedded applications.

The other key architecture in this battle is MIPS. LSI Logic is licensed to produce the MIPS chips as well as SPARC, and indeed is shipping the standard R3000 and R3010, in addition to a write-buffer chip designed for DEC. LSI appears to be focusing their initial development efforts on SPARC, however. The MIPS architecture is no less suitable for embedded control than is the SPARC architecture. In fact, IDT has taken a first step toward a version customized for embedded control with the R3001.

We expect to see more versions of MIPS and SPARC processors for embedded control. Fujitsu developed their own embedded SPARC line, and Philips announced that they would develop SPARC-based processors for embedded applications. IDT has led the MIPS push into embedded control, and other vendors are likely to follow. This flood of new devices is going to put pressure on Intel and AMD, which have so far been concentrating on battling each other for the high-end embedded control market.

10

Fujitsu Embedded SPARC Processor

Michael Slater

Fujitsu has announced the development of a new family of SPARC processors, called SPARClite, designed for embedded control applications. The first family member is the MB86930, which includes a new SPARC integer unit, data and instruction caches of 2 Kbytes each, programmable address decoder, wait-state generator, and 16-bit timer. While "embedded" SPARC processors have previously been announced by Cypress/ROSS, LSI Logic, and Fujitsu, those chips are simply workstation processors in low-cost packaging, generally with a few I/O signals deleted. The 86930 (Figure 1) is the first SPARC processor chip designed from the ground up for embedded applications, and significantly reduces the chip count for SPARC-based systems. Fujitsu claims it is also the first SPARC design implemented independently of Sun.

The 86930 is quite similar in concept to the embedded MIPS processors recently announced by LSI Logic and IDT. The most obvious difference, of course, is the use of the SPARC architecture instead of MIPS. Fujitsu's device includes more sophisticated caches, although the instruction cache is smaller than the cache on either the LSI or IDT chips. It also provides a more capable programmable address decoder and wait state generator. Like the LSI and IDT devices, it will be offered at clock rates from 20 to 40 MHz. (The lowest frequency LSI will offer is 25 MHz.)

The 86930 is implemented in 0.8-micron CMOS and includes 500,000 transistors on a 122,500-square-mil die (350 × 350 mils). Power consump-

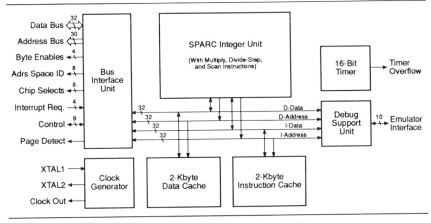

Figure 1. Block diagram of the 86930

tion ranges from under 1.4 W at 20 MHz to 3 W at 40 MHz. A 160-pin PQFP package will be used for the 20-MHz part, but because of power-dissipation limitations it cannot be used at higher clock rates. The 30-MHz version will be packaged in a ceramic QFP. The 40-MHz version requires a ceramic PGA.

Fujitsu is also developing a peripheral chip to work with the 86930. The MB86940 peripheral chip provides:

- Two 8251A-type USARTs operating up to 64 Kbaud synchronous or 19.2 Kbaud asynchronous.
- A 15-input interrupt controller.
- Four 16-bit counter/timers, each with a prescaler and compare/capture register.
- DRAM control logic.

This 120-pin chip is implemented in a gate array; it has been specifically designed to meet the needs of an unspecified high-volume customer.

New Processor Core

At the heart of the 86930 is a new SPARC processor core (integer unit, in SPARC parlance). Unlike Fujitsu's first SPARC processor, which was a gate array design, and its second implementation, which was a standard-cell design, the new integer unit is a full-custom, optimized design. This core will be the basis for the SPARClite family, of which the 86930 is just the first member. While the 86930 does not include a floating-point unit or support for an external FPU, future devices using the SPARClite core may include an on-chip FPU or an interface for an external FPU.

The SPARClite core, which is implemented in about 100,000 transistors, includes several new features. It is the first static SPARC processor design, which allows the clock to be slowed or stopped to reduce power consumption. It provides eight register windows, instead of seven as in Fujitsu's previous designs. (Cypress/ROSS's 7C601 also provides eight register windows.) Several instructions execute in fewer clock cycles than in previous implementations, as shown in Table 1. The clock counts for load and store instructions have been reduced by the addition of a fifth pipeline stage for memory access and the use of separate instruction and data caches. The 86930 uses a combined instruction/data external bus, like other SPARC implementations, but the on-chip caches are separate and each has its own 32-bit bus to the processor core. This allows the processor to fetch an instruction at the same time it is performing a load or store operation.

The SPARClite core implements three new instructions: multiply, divide-step, and scan. Table 2 shows the performance improvement that results from these instructions.

The current SPARC architecture definition, version 7, includes only a multiply-step instruction and no divide support. Version 8, which still has not been released, will include multiply and divide instructions. Fujitsu claims that SPARClite's multiply instruction conforms to the version 8 specification. It performs a 32×32 multiply with a 64-bit result in five clock cycles. Multiplications where one operand has 16 or fewer significant bits terminate early: a 32×16 multiply takes only three cycles, and a 32×8 multiply completes in two cycles.

The divide-step instruction allows a 32/32 division to be implemented in less than 40 clock cycles. Fujitsu argues that, for embedded applications, divide-step is a better solution than a full divide instruction. A full divide instruction, as included in version 8 of the SPARC specification, would be by far the longest instruction and would therefore increase interrupt la-

Table 1. Clock Counts for Instructions That Have Been Sped Up in the SPARClite Core. (Clock count assumes cache hit.)

Instruction	86901 Clocks	86930 Clocks
Single-Word Load	2	1
Double-Word Load	3	2
Single-Word Store	3	1
Double-Word Store	4	2
Untaken Branches	2	1

Table 2. Relative Execution Times for Code Sequences Using Version 7 SPARC
Instructions Compared to New SPARClite Instructions.

Instruction	Clock cycles using code sequence on 86901	Clock cycles using new instructions in 86930
32 × 32 Multiply	47	5
64/32 Division	330	52
Scan	43	1

tency. By using a series of divide-step instructions, an interrupt can be
processed at any point in the division process.

The scan instruction calculates the exclusive-OR of the two source
registers, finds the first one in the result, and then writes this bit number to
the destination register. If the two source registers have different data
values, this instruction finds the first bit that differs between the two
values. By setting one of the source registers to all zeros or all ones, the
instruction can be used to find the first one or first zero in the other source
register.

The scan instruction is useful for run-length encoding and floating-point
normalization. Combined with the fast multiply instruction, Fujitsu claims
that the scan instruction allows the 86930 to perform nearly 1 million
single-precision Linpack MFLOPS (at 40 MHz) using floating-point emulation software.

Cache Architecture

The 86930 includes separate 2-Kbyte caches for instructions and data.
Each cache is two-way set-associative and has a 4-word (16-byte) line size.
A least-recently used (LRU) algorithm determines which cache line is
replaced when a new line is allocated.

A separate "valid" bit is provided for each word, and only a single word
is filled when a cache miss occurs. As soon as the first word is passed to the
processor, prefetch logic reads the next word from memory, and if the
processor requests this word, it is stored in the cache and passed to the
processor. Because prefetching is overlapped with execution, when sequential words within a line are fetched the processor is only stalled for
one cycle with a two-cycle external memory access. If the processor
branches and does not request the successive words within the line, these
words are not filled. Fujitsu claims that the single-word refill, combined
with the prefetch mechanism, is more efficient than filling an entire line—

especially for typical embedded programs, which often have short loops and thus are likely not to need subsequent words within the line.

The 86930 caches include the most complete cache-locking capabilities yet offered in a single-chip device. The ability to lock entries in the cache is important in real-time systems, since worst-case response time to critical events often must be guaranteed. Unless the service routines for such events can be guaranteed to be present in the cache, the system designer cannot depend on the performance boost provided by the caches.

Two cache-locking mechanisms are provided: local and global. Two global cache-lock control bits allow the entire data and/or instruction cache to be locked. When the cache is locked, all valid entries in the cache are preserved. Invalid entries are still filled, so the cache is utilized to the maximum extent possible while guaranteeing that all information in the cache at the time it is locked is preserved.

Local cache locking can be performed manually or automatically. In the manual method, individual cache lines are locked by setting the lock bit in each cache tag. Cache lines can also be locked automatically by setting a local-lock-enable bit in the cache control register. All cache lines accessed while this bit is set are locked after they are filled. By setting this bit before executing a critical routine and then clearing it when the routine is done, all accesses performed by that routine are automatically locked in the cache. This locking mode is separately enabled for the instruction and data caches.

The two-way set-associative organization of the caches is important for the locked cache to perform efficiently. If lines in a direct-mapped cache are locked, then any access that maps to that line cannot be cached. In Fujitsu's design, the second set remains available even when one line in the set is locked. One entire set of cache lines could be locked, and the other set would continue to function as a direct-mapped cache.

The data cache normally uses a write-through memory update policy; all write cycles are propagated to main memory. A single-level write buffer provides some isolation from main memory write latency. When a write is performed to a locked cache line, however, the data is not written to main memory. This is similar to the operation of a copy-back cache, except that if the line is unlocked, memory will not be updated if the cache line is reallocated. This feature allows locked cache lines to be used as local scratchpad RAM. For example, the cache could be configured as a 1-Kbyte direct-mapped cache and a 1-Kbyte scratchpad RAM.

As compared to IDT's R3052 and LSI Logic's LR33000 embedded MIPS processors (Table 3), the 86930 has a small instruction cache— 2K versus 8K. Fujitsu's designers believe that larger caches are not a cost-effective way to improve performance, and have instead emphasized more optimized cache design. Embedded applications generally have rela-

Table 3.   Major Differences Among the Three embedded MIPS and SPARC Processors

	IDT R3051/52	LSI LR33000	Fujitsu MB86930
Instruction Set	MIPS	MIPS	SPARC with extensions
Instruction Cache	8K (3052) 4K (3051)	8K	2K
Data Cache	2K	1K	2K
Cache Organization	Direct-Mapped	Direct-Mapped	Two-Way Set-Associative
Snooping	No	Yes	No
Cache Locking	No	Limited	Yes
MMU	Yes (E versions)	No	No
Static Design	No	Yes	Yes
Write Buffer	4-Level	1-Level	1-Level
DRAM Control	No	Yes	Partial
Prog. Wait States	No	Yes	Yes
Prog. Chip Selects	None	2 (fixed)	8 (programmable)
Breakpoint Registers	None	Address Only	Address and Data
Counter/Timers	None	2 General-Purpose 1 Refresh	1 (Limited)
Address/Data Buses	Multiplexed	Non-Multiplexed	Non-Multiplexed
Price (25 MHz, 1000s, PQFP)	$54 (R3051) $81 (R3052)	$99.95	< $50 (20 MHz) < $80 (30 MHz)
Sample Availability	1Q91	12/90 (25 MHz) 1Q91 (33 MHz) 2Q91 (40 MHz)	late 1Q91
Production Availability	2Q91	2Q91 (PGA) 3Q91 (PQFP)	3Q91

tively small sections of code that are performance-critical, and Fujitsu correctly points out that cache models based on workstation applications may not be appropriate.

By allowing routines to be locked in the cache, the smaller cache may be just as effective as a larger one. LSI's MIPS-based embedded processor has a control input that allows limited cache locking to be implemented with external logic, and IDT's chip provides no cache locking capability at all. In this respect, Fujitsu's chip may have a significant advantage. The two-way set-associative cache design will also help Fujitsu's cache performance; IDT and LSI Logic both chose the simpler direct-mapped approach.

Bus Interface

The 86930 provides a nonmultiplexed bus interface with 32 bits each for address and data. (Actually, there are only 30 address lines. The two least-significant address bits specify a byte within a word, and this information is conveyed via the four byte-select signals.) The bus control signals are 68000-like, with address strobe, read/write control, and a ready signal to indicate when the addressed device is ready to complete the cycle. The bus can be granted to an external bus master via a typical request/grant handshake. The processor continues to execute from cache, if possible, while the bus is granted to another device. Cache snooping is not provided, so software must ensure that another bus master does not modify cached data or instructions.

To minimize external logic requirements, an on-chip address decoder provides eight chip-select outputs, each with a programmable wait-state generator. The upper 17 address bits and the eight address space identifier bits are compared against a programmed value for each chip-select output. A mask register allows any of the bits to be marked as a "don't care," so the address range decoded by each chip select output can be any power of two from 8 Kbytes to the full 4 Gbytes.

Unfortunately, the chip-select logic does not monitor the address bus when the bus has been granted to another device. Thus, in a system with a DMA controller or another processor that accesses the same memory or peripherals as the 86930, external address decoding logic for the alternate bus master and an OR gate for each chip select must be provided.

To facilitate page-mode DRAM operation, an on-chip comparator detects when a "page hit" occurs. Like the chip-select address range, the page size can be programmed to be any power of two from 8K to the entire 4-gigabyte address space. An output signal indicates when a page hit is detected.

The programmable wait-state generator also uses the page-hit detector. Two different wait-state values can be programmed for each address region: one that is used on page misses, and another for page hits. This allows a simple DRAM controller to provide faster access when a page hit occurs. The on-chip timer can be used as a refresh timer. External logic must provide RAS/CAS timing and address multiplexing.

Noncached external memory locations can be accessed in a single clock cycle, but most systems will require at least one wait state. Memory read access time for one-wait-state operation is 82 ns at 20 MHz, 48 ns at 30 MHz, and 32 ns at 40 MHz.

Development and Debug Support

The 86930 includes a dedicated 8-bit bus (plus two control signals) for emulation support. This bus has been defined in collaboration with Step Engineering, which is developing an in-circuit emulator to work with the processor.

By using a separate emulation bus, the emulator does not load the system address or data buses. This bus provides information for an external trace buffer to follow instruction fetches from the internal cache. While it is not wide enough to provide the full instruction stream, a complete address only needs to be output when a jump occurs. As long as jumps don't occur too frequently, the instruction fetch path can be fully traced.

The emulator interface provides access to four on-chip breakpoint registers: instruction data, instruction address, data data, and data address. It also allows the processor to be single-stepped.

Software development tools will be provided by Microtec Research. The tool set will include a C compiler with support for the SPARClite instruction extensions, assembler, libraries, linker, XRAY source-level debugger, an architectural simulator, and a ROM-based monitor program. Microtec tools are widely used by developers of 68000-family embedded applications, and the SPARClite tools will provide the same user interface. Both SPARC-based workstations and IBM PCs will be supported as hosts. Availability was promised for the first quarter of 1991.

Conclusions

Fujitsu's SPARClite processor will make SPARC a real competitor for mid-range embedded control applications for the first time. It is the only SPARC processor yet announced with on-chip cache, and it is significantly cheaper than existing SPARC processors. The lack of a floating-point or memory-management unit makes the chip unsuitable for Unix systems, but should not be much of an issue for most embedded control applications.

The only other SPARC design that offers a similar set of features is the two-chip set from LSI Logic: the L64901 processor and L64951 Integrated System Controller (ISC). The LSI processor is a basic SPARC integer unit with no on-chip cache. The ISC provides a cache controller, eight programmable chip selects, a DRAM controller, an eight-input interrupt controller, and a three-channel DMA controller. Six external SRAMs are required for the cache memory.

LSI's eight-chip solution is more capable than Fujitsu's two-chip set in some respects: it supports larger caches and provides a DMA controller. On the other hand, it does not include timers or UARTs, has fewer interrupt inputs, and requires substantially more board space. It also is available only at 20 and 25 MHz, and is significantly more expensive. The need for external SRAMs further increases the cost.

Fujitsu has funded the development of an in-circuit emulator from Step Engineering and software tools from Microtec. LSI Logic has contracted with Embedded Performance to provide an emulator for the LR33000, and IDT promises to have an R3051/52 emulator available but has not disclosed the source. It remains to be seen how the emulators from each of the vendors will compare. As for software tools, Fujitsu asserts that the Microtec compiler and debugger will be better suited to embedded system development than the MIPS software LSI and IDT are using.

Philips-Signetics announced its plans for embedded SPARC processors more than a year ago, but no products have been announced.

The Fujitsu chip is the third embedded RISC processor to be announced months in advance of silicon availability. These early announcements are presumably driven by the desire to lure design wins away from the entrenched Intel and AMD processors. Embedded SPARC and MIPS chips may provide significant competition for Intel and AMD by the end of 1991, but for the moment, the 960 and 29000 families have the considerable advantage of having parts ready to ship and large, experienced sales and application engineering staffs.

III

MIPS

11

MIPS Processor

Michael Slater

The three RISC processors most likely to make significant inroads in the Unix-based computing market are SPARC, RS/6000, and the MIPS processor. The MIPS chips are arguably the fastest of the bunch and are well ahead of SPARC in completeness of implementation.

With DEC's announcement of their MIPS-based DECstation 3100 workstation, the profile of the MIPS processor line was significantly raised. Despite their recent recognition, MIPS is no newcomer to the RISC business. In fact, MIPS was the first company to ship a commercial RISC processor—R2000 samples were shipped in the last week of 1985. Considering how long this chip has been in production, it is a remarkably sophisticated design. SPARC chips are only now beginning to be produced with comparable levels of integration.

Sun was concerned with getting their first SPARC chip into production as rapidly as possible, and thus designed the processor in a gate array. To keep the complexity down, they did not include any cache or MMU support. The MIPS approach, on the other hand, was to design their processor as a full custom chip. This allowed them to include both the MMU and cache control logic on the CPU chip. MIPS also makes their own floating-point coprocessor. This finely tuned implementation, combined with excellent compilers, puts MIPS ahead of the pack in both integer and floating-point performance.

Academic Origins

The MIPS and SPARC processors represent a major shift in the way commercial microprocessors have been designed. Until these two processors were introduced, commercial microprocessors were designed by semiconductor companies, which have a vested interest in maintaining compatibility with their existing architectures. The MIPS and SPARC designs emerged from the academic environment. Thus, their designers started with a clean slate and were willing to sacrifice binary compatibility with all existing software. Only after it became apparent that these upstart RISC processors were going to be significant competitors did established companies such as Intel, Motorola, and AMD introduce RISC architectures.

The MIPS processor design evolved from work done at Stanford University in the early 1980s under the direction of Professor John Hennessy. (The SPARC design is derived from the Berkeley RISC chip, designed by a group led by Professor David Patterson.) Several different designs have used the MIPS name, leading to some confusion about just what MIPS refers to. (Note that while the term MIPS usually stands for "millions of instructions per second," in this context it stands for "Microprocessor without Interlocked Pipeline Stages." We'll explain what this means later in this chapter.)

The original Stanford MIPS chip was completed in the spring of 1984. This project was intimately tied to compiler research, and one of the key contributions of this work was the demonstration that there is significant value in the compiler having intimate knowledge of the processor's pipeline, and optimizing accordingly.

The original MIPS project spawned three others:

- MIPS-X: A second-generation chip design, led by Stanford Professor Mark Horowitz, aimed at multiprocessor systems. It was the first RISC processor to include on-chip cache. A system was completed in the summer of 1987.
- Core-MIPS: A standard instruction set architecture, defined at Stanford for the Defense Advanced Research Projects Agency (DARPA) to provide a standard architecture that could be implemented in a variety of technologies for high-performance military computing applications.
- The R2000: A microprocessor designed at the newly formed MIPS Computer Systems. Like MIPS-X, this is a second-generation design, but was explicitly designed as a commercial product.

In early 1988, MIPS Computer Systems introduced the R3000, an enhancement of the R2000 with a higher clock rate, support for larger caches, and several enhancements in the cache operation, including better multiprocessor support. The instruction set architecture is identical to that of the R2000. Both chips include control logic for separate data and instruction caches using external SRAMs. A single set of address and data buses, which is cycled twice during a single clock period, is used to access both caches.

The result of the Stanford Core-MIPS effort was not a chip design or even a complete processor architecture, but rather an assembly language definition. This definition was then provided to a variety of DARPA contractors to develop high-performance microprocessors. The assembly language does not need to be directly implemented in hardware; macro expansion of instructions is allowed. Thus a variety of different chip designs can be viewed as a conforming to DARPA's Core-MIPS specification.

MIPS Architecture

The MIPS Computer Systems architecture defines both integer and floating-point instruction and register sets. Floating-point support is provided by a tightly coupled coprocessor.

The integer register set consists of thirty-two 32-bit general-purpose registers (r0–r31), plus two 32-bit registers (called HI and LO) used for the results of multiply and divide operations. Only 30 of the registers are truly general-purpose; r0 is a read-only register and is hardwired to provide the value 0, while r31 is the link register for branch-and-link instructions.

Unlike SPARC and the 29000, the MIPS architecture does not include register windows. The MIPS designers argue that with good compiler technology, the benefits of register windows are minor and the chip area used by large numbers of registers is not justified. Register windows (as they are commonly used) also slow down context switching. MIPS contends that a large register file will make it more difficult to increase the clock rate, but designers of SPARC and the 29000 don't agree.

In the existing MIPS implementation, the space that would have been consumed by a very large register file is better utilized for the memory management unit and cache control logic. While the lack of register windows prevents MIPS from increasing the size of the register file as chip density increases, they argue that on-chip cache memory will be a more effective use of chip real estate.

Table 1 summarizes the MIPS integer instruction set. In keeping with the purist RISC approach, the instruction set is quite spartan. Data types supported are signed and unsigned bytes, halfwords (16 bits), and words (32 bits). Either "little-endian" (least-significant byte first) or "big-endian" data ordering can be used, and is determined at power-up by the state of a control input. The only data addressing mode is base register plus 16-bit signed offset.

Table 1. R2000/R3000 Instruction Set

Load/Store Instructions	Multiply/Divide
Load Byte, Signed or Unsigned	Multiply, Signed or Unsigned
Load Halfword, Signed or Unsigned	Divide, Signed or Unsigned
Load Word	Move to/from HI
Load Word Left	Move to/from LO
Load Word Right	
Store Byte	**Jump and Branch Instructions**
Store Halfword	Jump
Store Word	Jump and Link
Store Word Left	Jump to Register
Store Word Right	Jump and Link Register
	Branch on Equal/Not Equal
Arithmetic Instructions	Branch on Less Than or Equal to Zero
(ALU Immediate)	Branch on Greater/Less than Zero
Add Immediate, Signed or Unsigned	Branch on Greater Than or Equal to Zero
Set on Less Than Immediate, Signed or Unsigned	Branch on Less Than Zero and Link
AND Immediate	Branch on Greater Than or Equal to Zero and Link
OR Immediate	
Exclusive OR Immediate	**Coprocessor Instructions**
Load Upper Immediate	Load Word from Coprocessor
	Store Word to Coprocessor
Arithemetic Instructions	Move to/from Coprocessor
(3-operand register operations)	Move control to/from Coprocessor
Add, Signed or Unsigned	Coprocessor Operation
Subtract, Signed or Unsigned	Branch on Coprocessor Z True/False
Set on Less Than, Signed or Unsigned	
AND, OR, Exclusive OR, NOR	**System Control Processor (CP0)**
	Instructions
Shift Instructions	Move to/from CP0
Shift Left/Right Logical	Read/Write Indexed TLB Entry
Shift Right Arithmetic	Write Random TLB Entry
Shift Left/Right Logical Variable	Probe TLB for Matching Entry
Shift Right Arithmetic Variable	Restore From Exception
	Special Instructions
	System Call
	Break

As with many RISC processors, there is no condition code register. Instructions such as "Set on Less Than" write a result of 1 or 0 to the specified destination register. A full set of single-cycle compare-and-branch instructions is also provided, which compare two registers and conditionally execute the jump depending on the relative values of the two registers.

Branches use a 16-bit program-counter-relative signed offset. Jump instructions use a 26-bit displacement, which is shifted left two places and then combined with the four most-significant bits of the program counter. "Jump to Register" (with the register holding the address) is the only way to jump to an arbitrary 32-bit address. Subroutine calls are implemented with "Branch and Link" instructions, which store the program counter in r31 before performing the branch.

Unlike SPARC, which includes only multiply-step and divide-step instructions, the MIPS design includes full integer multiply and divide instructions. In the current implementation, a multiply takes 12 clock cycles to complete and a divide requires 35 clock cycles. Multiplication and division are performed by an autonomous execution unit independent of the ALU. Other instructions can execute concurrently, and the pipeline is not stalled during a multiply or divide operation unless an instruction attempts to use the results of that operation before it is complete.

The MIPS architecture does not include an indivisible test-and-set or swap instruction, which is useful for multiprocessor support, but this function can be provided with additional hardware to lock or unlock the bus in response to writing to a "magic" location.

Some other RISC processors include richer instruction sets. Motorola's 88000, for example, provides bit testing and manipulation instructions, as well as indexed and scaled-indexed addressing modes.

Floating-Point Support

Table 2 summarizes the floating-point instruction set, which is implemented by the R3010 (or R2010) floating-point accelerator (FPA). The FPA has its own set of thirty-two 32-bit registers, which also can be accessed as sixteen 64-bit registers. Both single-precision (32-bit) and double-precision (64-bit) IEEE formats are supported; the extended (80-bit) format is not. Load and store instructions transfer data between the FPA registers and memory, while move instructions transfer data between the FPA and CPU registers.

Execution times for floating-point operations range from 1 to 19 clock cycles. The FPA includes a six-stage pipeline, and allows limited overlapping of floating-point instructions. For example, while a single-precision divide instruction requires 12 cycles, from the second to the ninth cycle other operations can be executed concurrently. Thus, two floating-point multiplies and two floating-point adds could all begin and complete execution while the divide was in progress.

Table 2. R2010/R3010 Floating-Point Instruction Set

Load/Store/Move Instructions	Computational Instructions
Load Word to FPA	Floating-Point Add
Store Word from FPA	Floating-Point Subtract
Move Move to FPA	Floating-Point Multiply
Move Word from FPA	Floating-Point Divide
Move Control Word to FPA	Floating-Point Absolute Value
Move Control Word from FPA	Floating-Point Move
	Floating-Point Negate
Conversion Instructions	
Floating-Point Convert to Single FP	**Compare Instructions**
Floating-Point Convert to Double FP	Floating-Point Compare
Floating-Point Convert to Fixed Point	

The MIPS architecture supports up to four coprocessors, with opcode space reserved for each. This provides a built-in mechanism for extending the instruction set for graphics or other specialized applications. So far, however, this capability has gone unused.

Pipeline Operation

Like all RISC processors, the MIPS machines rely on heavy pipelining to allow an instruction to be initiated (ideally) during every clock cycle. All integer instructions except multiply and divide execute in a single clock cycle. Latencies are kept to a minimum: there is only a single branch delay slot and a single load delay slot, as long as there is a cache hit. Memory writes are buffered externally, and do not cause any delay unless the buffers are full. If there is a cache miss, or if the write buffers are full, the pipeline is stalled until the memory access is completed.

(A *single load delay slot* means that the instruction immediately following a load instruction must not use the result of the load. The data resulting from a load instruction is available for the second instruction following the load. A *single branch delay slot* means that one instruction is executed following each branch instruction, whether the branch is taken or not.)

In contrast, the Cypress SPARC processor requires a two-clock delay after loads and stores. There is only a single delay slot, but there is also a one-clock pipeline stall after any load or store operation. This is due to the shared data and instruction cache, which makes it impossible to perform a data access in the same cycle as an instruction access. The extra clock cycle delay is not inherent in the SPARC architecture, but is merely a limitation of the current implementations. It will be eliminated in future Harvard-architecture versions.

In other RISC processors, a hardware interlock forces the pipeline to stall if an instruction attempts to use data being loaded by the immediately preceding instruction. The MIPS design does not include such hardware interlocks for loads; thus, the "Microprocessor without Interlocked Pipeline Stages" name. The compiler is required to arrange instructions so that one instruction will not attempt to use data loaded by the immediately preceding instruction. If it cannot do this, the compiler must place a no-op in the delay slot (the instruction following the load instruction). MIPS' compilers are able to fill load delay slots with a useful instruction an average of 70% of the time, and branch delay slots 50% of the time.

Eliminating the load interlock simplifies the design of the pipeline. However, it has some drawbacks. The instruction stream is scattered with no-ops, which occupy space on disk, in main memory, and, most important, in the cache. The lack of a load interlock may also be a weakness for future implementations. If a future implementation with on-chip cache is able to perform loads with no delay slot, existing code will still have no-ops following some load instructions and thus will not take full advantage of the new machine.

If the compilers are modified not to insert no-ops, then the new code will not work on the old processors that require a delay slot. Prof. Hennessy (who spends most of his time at Stanford but still holds the post of Chief Scientist at MIPS) contends that eliminating the load delay slot will never be the right design decision—''Show me a design without a load delay slot, and I'll show you a way to make the processor faster by redesigning it to have a delay slot.''

Future implementations designed to work with a lower-cost memory system may require more than one delay slot. In this case, hardware interlocks can be added so existing code will execute properly.

The MIPS design does include hardware interlocks for multiple-cycle instructions (multiply, divide, and floating-point). Thus, these instructions can be made faster (or slower) in future implementations without affecting compatibility. Despite the genesis of the company name, MIPS is not religiously committed to eliminating pipeline interlocks.

Memory Management

The R3000's on-chip translation look-aside buffer (TLB) consists of 64 fully associative entries. The memory management hardware and exception processing logic is called the ''System Control Coprocessor'' or co-processor 0 (CPO), even though it is part of the CPU chip. The processor has two modes of operation, termed User and Kernel. (These are similar to the User and Supervisor modes of the Motorola 68000 family.) All exceptions force the processor into kernel mode.

Figure 1 shows how the 4-gigabyte virtual address space is divided. User programs use the low 2 gigabytes; all addresses in this range are translated and cached. The upper 2 gigabytes are for kernel (system) access only. One-half of this kernel space is mapped normally through the TLB. The other half is further divided in two, with one part cached and the other noncached. Both of these ranges are mapped directly onto the low 512 Mbytes of physical address space. These regions are used for system initialization ROMs and I/O ports.

Including the TLB on the processor chip has significant advantages. The address translation delay is hidden by the pipeline, so a physical cache can be used without any access time penalty. Furthermore, all systems are guaranteed to have the same memory management hardware, providing a consistency that will not be present in SPARC-based systems.

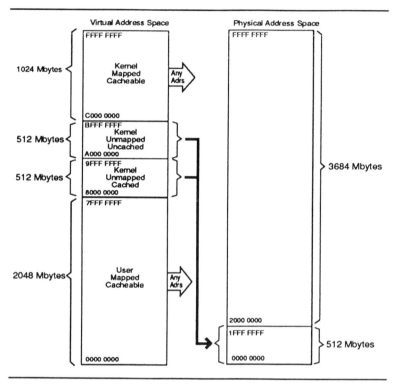

Figure 1. Mapping user and kernel addresses

On the other hand, the on-chip TLB in the R2000/R3000 has only 64 entries, and cannot be expanded. (Future implementations of the architecture may have larger TLBs without causing any application program incompatibility.) The Sun-4 SPARC-based workstations use a different memory management approach. Their MMU is built with SRAMs and PALs, and does not use a TLB; the entire page and segment table is stored in the MMU, rather than in main memory.

Motorola's 88000 design makes it possible, though expensive, to expand the size of the TLB. Motorola includes a 56-entry TLB (plus a 10-entry block address translation table) on the CMMU chip; up to four CMMU chips each can be used for instructions and data, providing up to 224 TLB entries for each.

The MIPS design provides no hardware support for handling TLB misses. When a TLB miss occurs, an exception is generated and the exception handler must access the page tables in memory and store a new entry in the TLB. AMD's 29000, the only other RISC processor with a TLB on the processor chip, also takes this approach. In Motorola's 88200

CMMU and the forthcoming CY7C604 CMU (for SPARC), on the other hand, TLB misses are handled entirely in hardware. This eliminates the need to provide software to handle this function. Handling the misses in software provides more flexibility, however, and MIPS claims that it is just as fast.

Interrupt Structure

In keeping with the purist RISC philosophy of moving complexity from hardware into software, the interrupt structure of the R3000 is primitive. There are six interrupt inputs, but there is no automatic vectoring and no mechanism for automatically fetching a vector from an I/O device. All interrupts cause a call to the "General Exception" handler. This same routine is also called for all exceptions other than reset and TLB misses, including address errors, bus errors, breakpoints, and illegal instructions. The software must test the "Cause" register to determine the source of the exception, and then vector to the appropriate routine. This is more awkward than the vectored interrupt structures designers have come to expect, but because of the rapid instruction execution rate, interrupt response is still faster than for most CISC processors.

Performance

MIPS rates their 25-MHz R3000 at 20 VAX MIPS. (VAX MIPS refers not to any actual instruction rate, but to the performance relative to a VAX 11/780.) The R2000 at 16 MHz is rated at 12 VAX MIPS. MIPS is especially strong in floating-point performance, which is also where the existing SPARC designs are especially weak. The 25-MHz R3000/R3010 pair is rated at 17.3 MWhetstones single-precision and 13.6 MWhetstones double-precision. The existing Sun-4 systems, which use Weitek floating-point chips, perform at about one-fourth of this level. Motorola's 88000 comes close in single-precision performance, but is much slower in double-precision.

Software Support

MIPS has implemented both Berkeley (4.3 BSD) and AT&T (System V.3) flavors of Unix. Their current operating system, which they call RISC/os, is System-V-based and includes some Berkeley features. The next release will fully merge the two.

From its inception, the MIPS project has been closely tied with highly optimizing compilers. The MIPS compilers are derived from compilers developed at Stanford, and are widely viewed as among the best available. Stanford-derived compilers are available for C, Fortran, and Pascal. Compilers for Ada, COBOL, and PL/1 are also available, but have been licensed from other sources and customized by MIPS.

The compilers do not produce machine language, but rather "Ucode," which is a stack-based machine-independent intermediate language. Ucode modules produced by different compilers can be combined into one program, allowing intermodule (and interlanguage) optimizations to be performed. Ucode modules are first linked together by the Ucode linker. The linked Ucode then passes through several optimization stages, including function inlining, loop unrolling, and global optimization. Finally, the code generator converts the linked, optimized Ucode to machine language, which is further optimized by the pipeline scheduler.

The MIPS compilers are among the few that perform interprocedural register allocation; most compilers optimize register use for each procedure independently. Interprocedural optimization reduces the amount of register saving and restoring that is required. In the MIPS view, it is this software technology that makes register windows an unjustified hardware expense.

An assembler is provided as well, of course, but nearly all applications are expected to be written in a high-level language. Assembly-language code passes through the pipeline scheduler just like compiler-produced code, so the order of the instructions in the object code is not necessarily the same as the order of the assembly language instructions.

Several simulation and performance profiling tools are available from MIPS. Sable is a Unix-hosted simulator that simulates the full instruction set (including floating-point) and the memory management functions. It works with a symbolic debugger called sdbx, which is derived from the standard Unix dbx debugger.

For performance tuning, a program called Pixie adds information to an application's executable object files that create profiling information while the application runs. Pixie produces address traces for later analysis, plus statistics about the instruction mix, the time spent in each procedure, and the number of times each procedure is called. This information helps find the "hot spots" in a program to guide optimization efforts.

Another tool uses the address traces generated by a "pixified" program to evaluate the behavior of various cache architectures. The performance impact of changing the cache size, refill block size, memory latency, and other parameters can be measured.

MIPS also provides source code for a basic system ROM, which includes startup routines, exception handlers, and a basic debug monitor.

Source-level debugging of code running in target hardware is also supported. A special debug monitor is resident in the target hardware, and a remote symbolic debugger (called pdbx) runs on the Unix host. The host and target are connected via a serial port and/or an Ethernet link.

No in-circuit emulators are available for the MIPS processors. A traditional ICE is very expensive for processors running at these speeds, and it is unnecessary for most applications. Once the hardware is basically functional, the remote source-level debugger provides a software development tool superior to most emulators. The only places where an in-circuit emulator makes a real contribution is in getting the prototype hardware to this stage and in performing real-time tracing. For developers of real-time control systems, real-time tracing can be important; logic analyzers with disassemblers for the MIPS instruction set are expected to be available soon.

MIPS and their semiconductor partners have recognized the need to encourage software developers to port to the MIPS architecture. They have set up an independent company called Synthesis Software Solutions, Inc., which is working with third-party software developers and is also porting applications for them. The current Synthesis catalog lists 72 software packages that have been ported to RISC/os. This does not include packages sold by companies such as Silicon Graphics specifically for their MIPS-based computers; including these vendor-specific packages, the total number of packages ported to the architecture is 300 to 350. However, these are not all binary compatible, so the number of packages available for any one machine is much more limited. In time, the DECstation 3100 will presumably attract a large variety of applications.

The Byte Sex Dilemma

In the early days of microprocessor development, the byte ordering choice was split between Intel-style processors, which use little-endian ordering, and Motorola-style processors, which use big-endian ordering. (This split goes back even further, with IBM using big-endian ordering and DEC using little-endian ordering.) Several RISC processors, including MIPS, the 88000, and the 29000, support both ordering schemes. Being able to match the byte ordering of existing systems is important for retaining data compatibility, and also eases porting of software for earlier architectures.

In the case of MIPS, however, this flexibility has come back to haunt them. All existing MIPS-based systems (except DEC's) use big-endian ordering, and the MIPS Application Binary Interface (ABI) specifies big-endian ordering. Unfortunately, MIPS' highest-profile design win is DEC's DECstation 3100. It was more important for DEC to maintain data compatibility with their existing VAX machines than to conform to the existing MIPS systems. As a result, the DEC system does not conform to the MIPS ABI. This scuttles any chance for shrink-wrapped software compatibility among all MIPS-based machines. (Note that DEC still does not have full data compatibility with their VAX, since the VAX floating-point formats are different.)

(Since the "endian-ness" is selected only at power-up, the MIPS processor cannot dynamically adjust to alternative byte orderings. A more elegant solution to this problem would be to tag each memory page with an attribute bit, which would specify whether data in that page should be accessed as big-endian or little-endian.)

Recent Developments

Since this introduction to the MIPS architecture was written, the R6000 ECL implementation has become available. Although faster than the CMOS implementations that came before it, the cost of getting that extra performance—in terms of the lower integration level of the chips, their high power consumption, and the challenges of ECL system design—was difficult to justify. Production problems at the foundry (Bipolar Integrated Technology) severely limited the supply of chips, which hurt the R6000 in the marketplace.

In mid-1991, MIPS began demonstrating early silicon of the R4000. This is a superpipelined CPU running at 100 MHz internally from a 50-MHz external clock. The R4000 integrates the CPU and floating-point unit, and it includes on-chip instruction and data caches of 8 Kbytes each. Architecturally, the R4000 is a 64-bit superset of the 32-bit R2000/R3000/R6000 architecture.

References

MIPS publishes an extensive benchmark report, which lists the performance of a dozen or so systems on a wide variety of benchmarks. It is available on request from MIPS or from any of their semiconductor partners.

The central reference for the MIPS architecture is *MIPS R2000 RISC Architecture*, by Jerry Kane. This book is published by Prentice-Hall, and may also be available from MIPS or their semiconductor partners.

MIPS Computer Systems, Inc., 928 Arques Ave., Sunnyvale, CA 94086; 408/720-1700.

12

MIPS R3000 System Design

Michael Slater

In the preceding chapter we described the architecture of the MIPS micro-processor and the general features of the existing implementations. In this chapter we explore the details of the hardware design and conclude with a preview of future implementations.

Architecture versus Implementation

Each RISC processor family has some distinctive architectural strengths and some architectural weaknesses. These differences make superb topics for academic study and theoretical arguments. SPARC can be faulted for its lack of single-step integer multiply and divide instructions. SPARC proponents fault MIPS and the 88000 for their lack of register windows. And the 88000 designers claim that the lack of addressing modes is a weakness in both SPARC and MIPS.

However, real systems must be built with implementations, not with abstract architectures; and it is in the implementations that the real performance differences exist. While Sun chose initially to implement SPARC in a gate array to minimize time-to-market, the MIPS processor is a full-custom VLSI implementation. This allowed MIPS to include on-chip functions—such as cache control and memory management—that are left to external support chips in the early SPARC implementations. Motorola's 88000 includes these functions in the separate CMMU chips.

VLSI Design Strategy

At first glance, MIPS and Sun seem to have taken the same approach to silicon implementation: let existing semiconductor companies do it. In fact, however, the two companies have taken significantly different approaches. Sun provides only an architecture specification, and has left the detailed implementation up to each semiconductor company. While Sun's engineers did work with the semiconductor companies, Sun does not provide chip designs to their semiconductor licensees.

MIPS, on the other hand, designed the R2000 and R3000 using their own in-house VLSI design team.. Each of the semiconductor partners is provided with a complete chip design. This has made it much easier for small companies, such as IDT and Performance Semiconductor, to enter the microprocessor business.

Each semiconductor company is contractually required to produce the exact design provided by MIPS, guaranteeing that chips from all vendors will be 100% compatible. (While pin-compatible SPARC chips are also available from several vendors, this is a choice made by the semiconductor companies, and was not dictated by Sun.) MIPS' semiconductor partners are encouraged to produce derivative designs, as long as they also produce the standard version.

In the short run, this means that there is less diversity of MIPS implementations than of SPARC implementations. This lack of diversity is good (guaranteed compatible alternate sources) and bad (not as wide a range of price/performance points).

All of MIPS' semiconductor partners are seeking ways to differentiate their products, and are thus likely to introduce derivative versions of the processor before long. The design team at MIPS is also hard at work, and has at least two new processor designs under development. (We'll take a look at what the future may hold at the end of this chapter.

Cache Implementation

Figure 1 shows the connections between the R3000 CPU and the cache memory. Unlike SPARC and the 88000, the R3000 includes the translation look-aside buffer (TLB) and cache control logic on the processor chip. This eliminates the need for an external CMMU or complex cache control logic. (The R2000 is similar, but requires external buffers for the cache RAM control signals. It also supports data and instruction caches of 64K bytes each maximum, whereas the R3000 supports up to 256 Kbytes each.)

The R3000 is the only CPU design to use standard static RAMs for both the cache data RAM and the cache tag RAM. Motorola includes both the data RAM and the tag RAM on their 88200 CMMU chip, along with

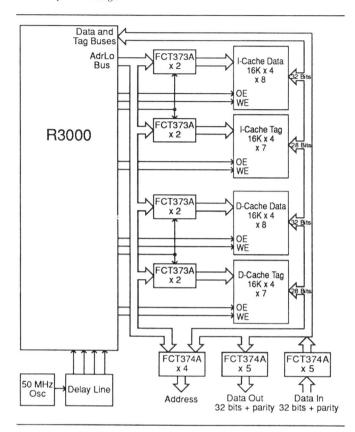

Figure 1. R3000 CPU, 64K Instruction and Data Caches, and Bus Interface

the cache control logic. Cypress' SPARC chip set includes the cache tags on their 7C604 CMU chip, and uses special SRAMs for the cache data RAM. While the MIPS approach results in a higher chip count, the design is simple, and the competitive market for standard SRAMs will keep the cache costs down. To make the design even simpler, IDT recently introduced a surface-mount module that includes all the latches and memory chips for a complete cache subsystem for use with the R3000. While the cache memory and bus interface circuitry is straightforward, it does require a lot of chips—54 in the example in Figure 1.

Another innovative feature of the R3000 is the use of a single address and data bus to interface to separate instruction and data caches. Thus, a Harvard memory architecture is used, even though separate instruction and data buses are not present.

To accomplish this, the bus is cycled twice during each clock cycle, as shown in Figure 2. One phase is used for data access, and the other for instruction access. During phase 1, a data address is output, and instruction information is read on the data bus. In phase 2, the data addressed in the previous phase is read on the data bus, and the address of the next instruction is output on the address bus.

This scheme minimizes pin count, but makes the bus timing very tight. For 25-MHz operation, 20-ns RAMs are required. To provide the critical timing control signals, the R3000 requires four clock signals, each at twice the basic clock rate, which are phase-shifted to provide edges at the right times for controlling the bus. All four signals are produced by a single delay line, whose specifications are provided by MIPS; no "tweaking" is required.

Cache Operation

There are two banks of cache RAMs, one for instructions and one for data. Each bank is a total of 60 bits wide, and thus requires 15 four-bit-wide RAM chips. The 60 bits are allocated as follows:

- Data/Instructions: 32 bits
- Data/Instruction parity: 4 bits
- Tag: 20 bits
- Tag parity: 3 bits
- Valid flag: 1 bit

The caches are direct-mapped and are physically addressed. The R3000 is unique in providing parity bits for the cache; this may be attractive for military applications, but seems unnecessary for commercial systems.

Address bits A_0 and A_1 are not used for cache accesses, since the cache is addressed as words (not bytes). For the smallest cache size allowed (4K bytes, or 1K words), address bits A_2–A_{11} select one cache word. The cache tag stores the upper 20 bits of the physical address. Larger caches use more address bits to select the cache word, and thus some of the tag bits are irrelevant.

The tag and the instruction/data information are read at the same time. If the Valid bit is set and the tag matches the high 20 bits of the physical

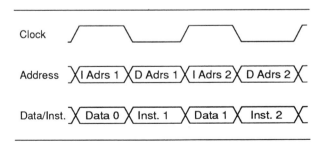

Figure 2.   R3000 multiplexed instruction/data bus operation

address, then a hit has occurred and the processor uses the instruction/ data from the cache. If not, then a miss occurs, the pipeline is stalled, and the data is retrieved from main memory. The RdBusy control signal is asserted by the memory system to keep the processor stalled until data is available.

The R3000 supports cache refill block sizes of 4, 8, 16, and 32 words. The refill block size is the number of words that are read in response to a miss; a block refill is a form of prefetching. The block size can be independently selected for the instruction and data caches. A large block size is desirable when memory latency is long, since the latency is generally incurred only for the first word in the block, after which successive words are provided relatively quickly. There is a tradeoff, however, since the larger the block size the more likely some of the data or instructions read will not be needed, and may displace other useful information in the cache. The flexibility to select the block size allows the cache design to be optimized for various applications.

The R3000 also provides a feature called *instruction streaming*. When a cache miss occurs, the processor is provided with the instruction fetched from main memory at the same time as it is read into the cache. The processor can then proceed to the next instruction while the block refill is still in progress, and it is likely to find successive instructions already in the cache.

Most other RISC cache designs, including the early SPARC implementations, the 88000, and MIPS' earlier R2000, have a fixed block size and do not provide instruction streaming. Instead, the processor is stalled until the entire block has been read into the cache.

In contrast to the direct-mapped caches used by MIPS and SPARC, the 88000 has a 4-way set-associative cache, which provides a higher hit rate for a given cache size. However, caches in a R3000 system will tend to be bigger, since an 88000 system gets quite expensive if more than the minimum 16K bytes each of instruction and data cache is used. The 88000 also has a two-clock load delay, versus one clock for the R3000.

The caches are write-through, which means that every write operation is passed through to the main memory. Byte and halfword write operations are processed as read-modify-write cycles. The processor attempts to read the word containing the addressed byte or halfword from the cache. If the word is found in the cache, then the appropriate byte or halfword is modified, and the entire word is then written to main memory and to the cache. The R2000, on the other hand, writes bytes and halfwords directly to memory, and the associated word in the cache is invalidated.

Write Buffers

In many cache controllers, writes are buffered so that the processor does not need to wait for main memory to accept the data. Such systems generally provide only a single-level buffer, however; so if another write occurs while the previous write is still in progress, then the processor must stall.

The R3000 does not include any write buffering on the CPU chip. Write buffering is provided by a separate chip, the R3020; this chip provides a byte-wide data path, so four are required. The write buffers contain four-word FIFOs, so up to four memory write cycles can be pending without requiring the processor to stall. If a fifth write is attempted, the WrBusy signal is asserted, causing the processor to stall until a pending write is completed and the buffer is able to accept another word. The write buffers also provide a "byte gathering" function. If the processor performs a series of byte writes, the write buffer will combine them into word or halfword writes if possible. This reduces the number of memory write cycles required. Because the write buffers require access to the address lines as well as the data lines, they require relatively large packages—68 pins, just for a byte-wide buffer.

Since the write buffers queue up memory writes, the main memory is not always fully up-to-date. When the processor reads a memory location shortly after data was written to that location, precautions must be taken to ensure that the data in memory is not stale. The write buffers include conflict checking logic, which can be used to stall the read cycle if the read access is to a memory location for which the write buffer has data. However, in MIPS' own system designs, they have chosen to always stall the processor on a memory read cycle until the write buffers are empty. With a main memory system that takes advantage of page mode DRAMs, this may have higher performance than allowing the read to occur in the midst of a burst of writes. Since a series of writes will often be to locations within a page, inserting a read operation is likely to cause an access out of the page, thus slowing the execution of the following write cycles.

Standard FIFOs can also be used in place of the write buffer chips, although this sacrifices the byte-gathering function. FIFOs also do not provide conflict checking, so they must be allowed to empty before a memory read can be completed. MIPS chose to use FIFOs rather than write buffers in their own high-end R3000-based system. For cost-sensitive applications, the write buffers can be replaced with single latches, but this requires a stall when a write is attempted if the previous write cycle has not yet completed.

Multiprocessor Support

For shared-memory multiprocessor systems, some method must be used to maintain cache coherency. The most common approach is to provide "snooping" logic as part of each processor's cache controller, which monitors main memory accesses by other processors. If a write to a cached memory location is detected, then the affected cache word is invalidated.

The R3000 does not provide snooping logic, but it does provide control signals to support external snooping logic. Although it is possible for snooping logic to share the main cache tags, the performance degradation due to contention for tag access makes this an undesirable design. Most multiprocessor designs use either a second-level cache or a second set of tags.

When snooping logic detects a "snooping hit," it asserts a special "multiprocessor stall" signal to the R3000. The R3000 then disables the outputs of the address latches driving the data cache. A second set of address latches, whose inputs come from the snooping logic, allows the snooping logic to address a particular cache line. The snooping logic then asserts the "invalidate" input to the R3000, and the R3000 clears the "valid" bit of the addressed cache line.

While it is thus possible to implement snooping with the R3000, it requires much more support logic than for processors that provide this function on-chip. Motorola's 88200 CMMU provides snooping logic, but since the snooping logic shares the tags with the processor, performance will suffer. Cypress' CY7C604 CMU for SPARC does not include snooping, but Cypress also has a multiprocessor CMU, the CY7C605, which will provide snooping. This CMU has two sets of tags: a virtually addressed set for use by the processor, and a physically addressed set for use by the snooping logic. This eliminates the contention for tag access between the processor and the snooping logic.

Unlike the 88200 and the 7C604, the R3000 does not support write-back cache operation, in which writes are buffered in the cache and main memory is updated only when the cache line is flushed. Most MIPS-based multiprocessor systems are expected to use a second-level cache in addition to the primary cache that is controlled by the R3000. In such systems, it is desirable for the first cache to use the write-through approach, while the second-level cache uses the write-back protocol. Existing MIPS-based multiprocessor machines, such as those from Silicon Graphics, use this approach.

Coprocessor Interface

The R3010 floating-point accelerator (FPA) watches the bus as the R3000 fetches instructions. The R3000 provides two status signals to the FPA that allow it to track the operation of the R3000's pipeline. When the FPA detects a coprocessor instruction being fetched, it initiates execution of that instruction; the R3000 does not need to feed instructions to the FPA.

MIPS calls this a "seamless" interface, since coprocessor performance is just as high as if the FPA were on the same chip as the integer unit.

This approach eliminates the instruction-passing overhead incurred by most other coprocessor designs. However, this method cannot be used with processors that have on-chip instruction caches, since not all instruction fetches are visible on such processors. Thus, future MIPS processors with on-chip instruction cache will have to use a different coprocessor interface. Such processors are also likely to include on-chip floating-point hardware, however, eliminating the primary need for the coprocessor interface.

Floating-point computation instructions take operands from, and write results to, the sixteen 64-bit floating-point registers, which are part of the FPA. Floating-point load and store operations use both the R3000 and the FPA. The R3000 provides the memory address (since only it has access to the TLB), and the FPA reads or writes the data. The R3000 also handles the cache control. Floating-point move instructions, which transfer data between the integer registers and the FP registers, are also available.

The FPA provides FP condition and FP busy signals to the R3000. The condition signal is used for the "branch on coprocessor condition" instructions. The FP busy signal causes the R3000 to stall if an attempt is made to access an FP register while an FP computation is in progress.

Applications

The R3000 was designed as a Unix engine, and the majority of its applications to date have been in Unix-based systems, either workstations or servers. It is also used in high-performance embedded control applications, such as military systems, robotics applications, and telephone switching systems.

Because the R3000 requires external cache memory, however, the minimum system chip count is relatively high. Unless very fast main memory is used, operation without an instruction cache causes a drastic performance degradation. It is more feasible to operate it without a data cache for some cost-sensitive applications, but it is questionable how effective this configuration would be.

AMD's 29000 and Intel's 80960 have an edge on MIPS for embedded control in several respects. These processors can be used without external cache while still maintaining reasonable performance, and require much less "glue logic" for the memory interface. They are also supported by in-circuit emulators and real-time kernels. Thus, in the realm of embedded control, the MIPS processor will be attractive primarily for very high-end applications.

13

IDT R3000 Derivative

Michael Slater

IDT's 79R3001 is the first derivative of the MIPS R3000 microprocessor. MIPS provides complete designs to their semiconductor partners, which must produce the standard chips. The partners then have the option to produce their own variations of the design; the R3001 is the first such device.

The R3001 maintains full software compatibility with the R3000, and no changes were made to the instruction set, pipelines, ALU, register file, or memory management unit. In most respects, the R3001 is a superset of the R3000, with additional flexibility in the cache and memory system interface. The only significant feature sacrificed was the ability to support parity on the cache tags. The R3001 will work with the same R3010 floating-point accelerator, and should also work with other R3000 interface chips, such as the R3020 write buffer, the LR3220 32-bit write buffer recently announced by LSI Logic, and ASICs that have been developed by R3000 system builders.

IDT made these changes based on feedback from their customers, which include many companies using the R3000 in embedded applications. Since this is the first time IDT has modified the R3000 design, they selected changes that did not have a major impact on the chip design, and would not have a high risk of introducing bugs or affecting software compatibility.

The R3001 is designed to lower the system cost, and thus makes it practical for a wider range of embedded applications. None of the changes hamper the ability to use the chip in workstations, however, and for many workstation applications it should be more cost effective than the R3000.

Cache Changes

The most important changes were made in the cache interface, and most involve adding flexibility that it seems, in hindsight, should have been in the original design. The R3000 provides complete cache control logic for separate, direct-mapped instruction and data caches. Standard SRAMs are used for both the instruction/data memories and the tag memories. Parity is provided for the tags, data, and instructions.

Providing parity on a static RAM cache may be appropriate for a very-high-end workstation or an embedded application in which having the utmost reliability is critical. However, the vast majority of system designs (other than those using the MIPS processors) do not implement parity on caches. The R3000 *insists* on having parity—there is no way to disable it; and since parity is checked every time a cache access is performed, there is no way to avoid implementing it.

The R3001 eliminates parity on the cache tags to save pins, and makes parity on the cache contents optional. This simple change significantly reduces the chip count and cost of a basic CPU subsystem. Not only does it eliminate the need for fast static RAMs to hold the parity bits, but it also simplifies the main memory interface and improves the memory timing. In an R3000 system, parity must be generated on all reads from the main memory, since the parity information must be written to the cache. This requires four parity generator chips. It also increases the effective access time of the memory, and to compensate for this, many R3000 system designs add another level of pipelining to the memory system, increasing both chip count and memory system latency.

The R3001 also makes the cache tag width variable. The R3000 requires 22 bits of tags on each cache line. The full tag width is really needed, however, only if the system supports the maximum 4 Gbyte main memory space and has a small cache. The R3001 allows the system designer to implement only the number of tag bits appropriate for the application. For example, a system with a 128 Mbyte main memory space and 64 Kbyte caches requires only 11 tag bits.

IDT makes special cache RAMs with on-chip address latches, which are designed to connect directly to the R3000 or R3001. Only six of these RAMs, the IDT71586, provides a complete cache subsystem for use with the R3001, with 16 Kbytes each for instructions and data. An R3000 system would require two more RAMs for the parity bits, four chips for parity generation, and one chip to buffer the parity signals, doubling the chip count of the basic CPU subsystem. (Of course, both R3000 and R3001 systems require additional chips for data bus buffers, memory controllers, and other functions.)

Other Enhancements

IDT has also made a variety of other minor changes to provide more flexibility and reduce chip count. The synchronous memory interface, intended primarily as a cache interface in the R3000, is more flexible to better support systems using only SRAM, or systems that split the instruction cache into two parts so that time-critical routines can be permanently cached. A DMA interface is also provided, and changes were made in control signals to better support a DRAM-only system.

While the changes IDT made to the R3000 are minor, they reduce system cost while sacrificing little. From a technical point of view, the R3001 appears to be a better choice than the R3000 for the great majority of applications, whether embedded or not. The only significant disadvantage is that the R3001 is (so far) sole-sourced. The R3000, on the other hand, is currently available from four vendors, with a fifth on its way.

14

MIPS Chip Set with Full ECL CPU Implementation

Michael Slater

MIPS Computer Systems' top-of-the-line RC6280 system, rated at 55 VAX MIPS, is based on their R6000 ECL chip set, and is the first system publicly demonstrated by any vendor using an ECL microprocessor.

The R6000 design is significant not just because it is one of the first ECL microprocessor-based systems, but also because it provides a preview of next-generation high-performance CMOS systems. Many of the system design aspects, such as the use of two-level caches and a high-speed block-oriented memory bus, will be equally applicable to future CMOS systems.

The R6000 is also the first unveiling of the "MIPS II" architecture, which includes load interlocks and a number of new instructions. The current R2000/R3000 architecture is now referred to as "MIPS I." To maintain a single binary standard for application programs, the new features are being pitched "for kernel use only." The application binary interface (ABI) will remain the MIPS I instruction set.

The core chip set consists of the R6000 CPU, R6010 floating-point controller (FPC), R6020 bus interface chip, and B3110 floating-point multiplier. The R6000 CPU chip incorporates about 90,000 transistors, and is packaged in a 259-pin PGA. All four chips are currently fabricated by Bipolar Integrated Technology (BIT). The first three are custom chips developed by MIPS, while the fourth is a standard BIT component.

Figure 1 shows a MIPS CPU board for the RC6230. The board-level CPU implementation in the MIPS RC6280 system design uses 76 small ECL gate arrays from Sony. These gate arrays will be available as standard devices from Sony and NEC. The gate arrays are not an integral part of the chip set, and some customers may choose to implement these functions differently. Nevertheless, their availability is important, as it makes it possible for a system vendor to produce a system without needing to design any custom chips.

Performance of the RC6280 system with a 66.7-MHz clock is rated at 55 VAX MIPS, 32 MWhetstones (double-precision), and 10.3 Linpack MFLOPS (compiled, double-precision). This places the system performance well beyond that achieved by any other uniprocessor system based on a standard microprocessor, and within range of mainframes for CPU performance.

BIT also produces the ECL SPARC chip set, but no system vendors have shown products using this chip set. It is possible that ECL SPARC systems will be in volume production at about the same time as ECL MIPS systems, but neither Sun nor other SPARC system vendors are making any promises about when they will ship ECL systems.

Figure 1. MIPS CPU board for RC6230. The large black heat sinks are on the VLSI chips; the small towers are on the gate arrays. The four blocks of chips at the left and right sides are the secondary cache RAMs. The board has 10 layers: six for signals, two for ground, and two for power.

Cache Implementation

Figure 2 shows a block diagram of the CPU board used in MIPS' RC6280 system. There are two direct-mapped first-level caches, one for data and one for instructions. The data cache is write-through. The unified second-level cache is two-way set associative, and write-back.

The CPU chip provides most of the control logic for both the first- and second-level caches. As with the R3000, standard SRAMs are used for the instruction and data caches and the tags as well.

Unlike the R3000, however, the interface logic between the CPU and the cache RAMs is more than just buffers and registers. The address and data registers for the caches are implemented in the MIPS design with ECL gate arrays. These gate arrays also include the cache tag comparators, multiplexers, and address and data registers. The R6000 CPU provides all the sequencing and control logic, and the gate arrays are simple data path chips. By including the tag comparators in the gate arrays, the need for pins for the tag bus on the CPU chip is eliminated.

There are eight different types of gate arrays, all made by Sony, each of which includes 100 to 200 gates. The instruction cache address register (ICAR) gate array, for example, provides a 6-bit "slice" of the required function. Three ICAR arrays are used for the instruction-cache address, and two for the data-cache address.

The primary address bus is shared between instructions and data, in a manner similar to that of AMD's 29000. The instruction address register is actually a counter, and the CPU provides a new instruction address only when a nonsequential fetch is performed. Instructions that create nonsequential fetches (such as branches) don't modify any data, so these instructions do not create contention for the bus. Thus, there is contention for the address bus only when crossing an 8-word instruction cache block boundary.

The primary tag array is also shared between instructions and data. The tag array is logically divided in two. Access to the instruction tags is needed only when a cache line boundary is crossed. The instruction cache has an 8-word line size, so on the average an instruction tag access is required only every eight clock cycles. The likelihood of a conflict with a data cache tag access is reduced by tag "look-ahead," which checks to see if there will be a hit on the next sequential line while the previous line is being fetched.

The data cache has a 2-word line size. According to MIPS, the data cache line size was made smaller than that of the instruction cache to simplify the implementation of the store double-word instruction. A long line size is also less likely to pay off for data than for instructions, which

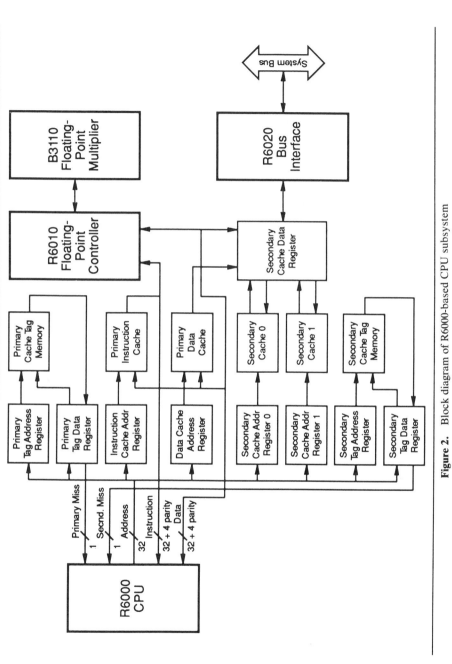

Figure 2. Block diagram of R6000-based CPU subsystem

are fetched in a more sequential pattern. (A longer line size increases the hit rate, but at the expense of a higher miss penalty.)

Both primary caches are direct-mapped and are virtually addressed. In a virtually addressed data cache, *aliasing* (having the same physical memory location cached as two different virtual memory locations, called *synonyms*) must be avoided. In the MIPS system design, this problem has been eliminated in the first-level cache by making the data cache size the same as the page size—16 Kbytes. Thus, the 14 bits used to address the data cache are the same whether the address is physical or virtual, and no aliasing can occur. Other system designs could use larger primary data caches, but software would then have to ensure that address aliasing did not occur.

The secondary cache is a unified cache (mixed instructions and data), and is two-way set associative. Accesses are interleaved by dividing the cache into two arrays, one for odd-addressed locations and one for even-addressed locations. This allows the secondary cache to provide a transfer rate of one word per clock on sequential accesses, although it has a two-clock latency. The current MIPS design uses a 512-Kbyte secondary cache, but the CPU will support up to 2 Mbytes. MIPS' literature claims "the observed cache hit rate on a wide range of programs is 99.5 percent."

The cache tags for both levels include an 8-bit address space identifier (ASID), which identifies each page of memory with a particular task. This eliminates the need to flush or invalidate the cache whenever a task switch occurs.

In the current MIPS 66.7-MHz system design, the primary cache chips are 8-ns ECL SRAMs, and the secondary cache chips are 15-ns BiCMOS SRAMs. The secondary cache line size is 32 words. In the MIPS implementation of the system bus and main memory system, each word within a block is transferred at a rate of one word per clock, but there is a 33-clock overhead associated with each block transfer. Thus, the cache miss penalty is 65 clocks, but each miss fills a 32-word section of the cache. To be able to transfer bursts at this rate, the main memory boards are eight-way interleaved.

Memory Management

The secondary cache uses an unusual design approach, with a physical cache index (which selects one cache line) but a virtual cache tag. Stored within the data portion of the cache (rather than in the tag portion) are physical tags and a translation look-aside buffer (TLB). This scheme is designed to work with the R6000's unique TLB implementation.

A typical 64-entry translation look-aside buffer (TLB) requires about 3000 bits of memory. For the R6000, MIPS needed a method that required fewer transistors to implement, and they invented the "TLB slice" approach. The CPU chip does not contain a full TLB, but only a small TLB slice, as shown in Figure 3. A full TLB is stored in the secondary cache.

(The CMOS R3000, like most other CPUs with on-chip memory management, includes a traditional, fully associative translation look-aside buffer (TLB) on the CPU chip. Each TLB entry contains a virtual page number, which is compared to the page number requested by the processor, and a physical page number, which is provided to the memory system if the virtual page numbers match.)

The TLB slice is a simple direct-mapped cache, which functions as a lookup table to convert virtual address bits 14–16 to physical address bits 14–19. The TLB slice does not include any tags to check virtual address bits 18–31, so its output is only a "guess" as to the correct physical address. Furthermore, it does not provide a full-width physical address, but only six bits.

The six-bit physical address "guess" from the TLB slice is combined with the 14-bit offset to provide a 20-bit physical index for the secondary cache. The secondary cache tags store virtual addresses, and when the

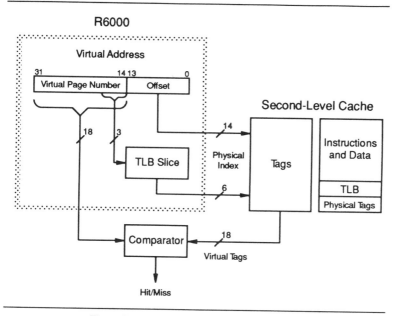

Figure 3.   TLB slice and second-level cache

desired cache line is retrieved, the virtual tag is compared with virtual address bits 14–31 from the processor, and the ASID is checked. If these match, then the TLB slice translation was correct, and the data is retrieved from the cache.

If the virtual addresses do not match, then either there was a TLB miss, the TLB slice "guess" was wrong (a TLB slice miss), or there was a cache miss. To determine which is the case, the processor reads the full TLB entry from the reserved portion of the secondary cache and checks the tag bits to see if it is valid. If not, a TLB miss trap is taken. If the TLB is valid, the processor compares physical address bits 14–19 from the full TLB entry with those provided by the TLB slice. If these do not match, then there was a TLB slice miss. If they do, there was a cache miss.

When a TLB slice miss occurs, the CPU reads the full TLB entry from the reserved area of the second-level cache, and updates the TLB slice. State machines in the R6000 chip provide all sequencing logic for handling TLB slice misses, cache misses, and address translation. The penalty for a TLB slice miss is eight clock cycles.

For each line in the second-level cache, there is a physical address tag as well as a virtual cache tag. The virtual tags are stored in the separate tag array so they can be quickly compared when checking for a cache hit. If there is a cache miss, then the physical tag is compared with the physical address from the TLB. If these match (even though there was a cache miss, which means that the virtual addresses did not match), then aliasing has occurred (two different virtual addresses are assigned to the same physical address), and what appeared to be a cache miss at first is, in fact, a cache hit. Because the R6000 can detect this situation and handle it properly in hardware, the software does not need to ensure that aliasing does not occur.

Finally, if there is a true cache miss, the cache line is refilled from main memory, using the full-width physical address from the main TLB (in the secondary cache).

This scheme greatly complicates the cache miss process, but the overall effect on performance is claimed to be very small. Whenever there is a hit in the first-level cache, the TLB slice and secondary cache are not used at all. Even when the first-level cache misses, if there is a hit on the second-level cache, then the full-size TLB and physical tags do not need to be accessed.

The TLB slice allows the secondary cache to be physically indexed without requiring a full TLB on the CPU chip. Physical indexing allows the system to automatically detect synonyms, relieving the software of this concern. It also will make it straightforward to add a second, physical set of tags for multiprocessor implementations.

MIPS II Architecture

The company "MIPS" was named after the "Microprocessor without Interlocked Pipeline Stages" architecture developed at Stanford. This approach minimizes the pipeline control logic in the CPU, but requires that the compiler track all pipeline hazards and insert no-op instructions as needed to guarantee that data is valid when it is accessed.

As the Stanford MIPS design evolved into the commercial R2000, pipeline interlocks were added for all multicycle (mostly floating-point) operations—except for load and branch instructions. The R2000 and R3000, which are now termed the "MIPS I" architecture, require a no-op between a load instruction and the instruction that uses the data loaded, unless another instruction can be scheduled into the load delay slot. Similarly, a no-op is required following branch instruction if another instruction cannot be scheduled into the branch delay slot.

Table 1 summarizes the new instructions in the "MIPS II" architecture. The R6000 is the first processor that implements the extended instruction set. One group of instructions allows the capabilities of a more powerful floating-point unit to be utilized. The other additions are in three areas: load interlocks, annulling branches, and conditional traps.

Despite its heritage, the MIPS II architecture is fully interlocked— including load instructions. Thus, no-ops can be eliminated from most programs. Since the pipeline must stall anyway if the data being loaded is needed immediately, no direct speed advantage results. The primary benefits are increased code density and reduced instruction-fetch bandwidth.

Table 1. New Instructions in the MIPS II Architecture

Mnemonic	Name	Use
	All Load Instructions	In R6000
SC rt,offset(base)	Store Conditional	Multiprocessor/multitask interlocks
LL rt,offset(base)	Load Linked	Used with Store Conditional
B(cond)L	Branch (condition) Likely	Increases code density
T(cond)	Trap conditional	Increases code density
	Floating-Point Extensions	
LDCz rt,offset(base)	Load Doubleword to Coprocessor	Use full 64-bit data path
SDCz rt,offset(base)	Store Doubleword from Coprocessor	
SQRT.fmt fd,fs	Square root	Access HW square root logic
ROUND.W.fmt fd,fs	FP round to fixed-point	Access HW rounding logic
TRUNC.W.fmt fd,fs	FP truncate to fixed-point	
CEIL.W.fmt fd,fs	FP ceiling to fixed-point	
FLOOR.W.fmt fd,fs	FP floor to fixed-point	

Another new feature of the MIPS II architecture is a new class of branch instructions (with all the conditional variants) that MIPS calls "branch likely." These instructions are the same as what are called "annulling branches" in SPARC and other architectures. When a branch likely is executed, the instruction in the delay slot is executed only if the branch is taken. If the branch is not taken, then the instruction in the delay slot is skipped.

These annulling branches eliminate the need to ever place a no-op in the delay slot following a branch. If the branch delay slot cannot be filled otherwise, the compiler can use a "branch likely" instruction and move the instruction at the branch destination to the delay slot. MIPS estimates that this produces a 4% typical performance increase.

Conditional traps combine a compare instruction and a conditional branch instruction, also increasing code density.

The floating-point additions include 64-bit load and store instructions to exploit the width of the data path, plus a square root function that matches the capabilities of the B3110 multiplier chip and rounding instructions that allow different rounding modes to be used.

The "Store Conditional" (SC) and "Load Linked" (LL) instructions are provided as primitives for implementing interprocessor interlocks. External logic must provide a status bit for use by these instructions. In the MIPS implementation, there is one such bit per memory board, in the R6020 bus interface chip.

A Store Conditional instruction completes the store operation only if no other Store Conditional instruction has accessed the linked memory location since the Load Linked instruction. The SC instruction returns a 0 or 1, indicating whether the store completed successfully or not.

Listing 1 shows the program fragment for an atomic increment. This program reads a semaphore location in memory, using an LL instruction, and then increments that value in a register. The SC instruction then stores the incremented value *only* if the semaphore location has not been modified since the LL instruction read its contents. The success or failure of the store is indicated in a register, and if the store failed, then the loop is repeated.

Listing 1. Atomic Increment Sequence Using New Multiprocessor Instructions

```
L:   LL      T1,(T0)      ;read   semphore
     ADD     T2,T1,1      ;increment  semaphore
     SC      T2,(T0)      ;store   conditional
     BEQ     T2,0,L       ;repeat  if
     NOP                  ;   not  successful
```

Attempting to execute any of the new floating-point instructions or the conditional traps on an R2000/R3000 machine produces an undefined instruction trap. The new instruction can then be emulated in software, but such emulation is too slow to be of much use. It is also possible to automatically translate MIPS II binary programs to MIPS I binary programs.

The load interlocks and annulling branches, on the other hand, cannot be emulated on earlier machines. If the critical delay-slot no-ops are removed from a program, then it will run properly only on a MIPS II machine—for now, only the R6000. The new Load Linked and Store Conditional instructions can't be emulated on MIPS I-based systems without special hardware.

So what use are the new features? MIPS is positioning them as primarily for the operating system kernel. The kernel is often specific to the machine model anyway, so having a kernel program that runs only on the R6000 is not a problem. MIPS claims that, compared to typical applications programs, the kernal has more branches with delay slots that are harder to fill. Thus, the new additions are expected to make a significant performance improvement in the kernels.

Scientific computing and other floating-point-intensive applications will be recompiled to take advantage of the new architecture as demand develops for such programs. These programs could run on MIPS I machines, as long as those machines have an operating system that provides emulation of the instruction set extensions in the trap handler. However, separately compiled versions for the MIPS I machines will have better performance than those using operating system emulation of the MIPS II instructions.

Eventually, the R3000 will be replaced by future CMOS processors that implement the MIPS II architecture. Once these new machines become dominant, software vendors will start compiling the standard version of their programs for the MIPS II architecture, and providing special versions for those "old" R2000/R3000 machines.

The R6000 also has the capability of switching between big-endian and little-endian modes (high-byte first or low-byte first) under software control. (The R3000 can also operate in either mode, but this is determined by the state of a pin at reset, and cannot be changed while the processor is running.) Because DEC operates their R2000/R3000 systems in little-endian mode while virtually all other MIPS system vendors use big-endian mode, applications programs and databases are not freely interchangeable. The ability to change the byte ordering dynamically may eventually lead to a version of the operating system that can adapt to programs and data of either byte ordering.

Conclusions

The ECL implementations of MIPS and SPARC provide an interesting comparison, since both were designed at about the same time, using the same foundry and process capabilities. Sun chose, as they did in CMOS, to implement just the basic CPU and floating-point controller, leaving memory management and cache design up to the system designer. MIPS, on the other hand, followed their own CMOS approach, and built cache and MMU functions into the chip set. While a full R6000 CPU subsystem does require a number of gate arrays, these ASICs will be available as standard products. Thus, it appears that it will be considerably easier for a system vendor to build an ECL system based on the MIPS design, as compared to the SPARC design.

The MIPS II architecture shows a surprising willingness of its architects to add features, such as annulling branches and load interlocks, that can only be exploited by new, binary-incompatible programs. It is unfortunate that programs taking advantage of the new features cannot be used on existing machines.

Embedded applications, for which software portability is much less of an issue, will be able to use the MIPS II features more readily. Until a CMOS implementation of MIPS II is available, however, it will have very few embedded applications.

MIPS' competitors will probably use these changes as a weapon against MIPS, and it is critical that MIPS promotes the changes properly. The MIPS software situation is confusing enough as it is, with two different byte orderings and several operating system flavors in use. By reserving the architectural extensions for kernel code only, their existence becomes a nonissue for application developers—at least until the installed base of MIPS II machines becomes large.

The new instructions for multiprocessor interlocks may simplify the design of new multiprocessor systems. However, the current MIPS CPU board implementation does not provide bus snooping, and it is not designed for multiprocessor systems. The multiprocessor features will presumably be exploited in future multiprocessor R6000 systems, and will become more important when highly integrated CMOS implementations of the MIPS II architecture appear.

The role that ECL will play in the future of microprocessors is not entirely clear. MIPS estimates that ECL designs currently lead CMOS designs by about 18 months in achieving a given performance level. If this lead continues, top-of-the-line servers will continue to be implemented in ECL—unless, of course, it gets squeezed from the top by gallium arsenide.

The R6000 chip set and BIT's SPARC chip set demonstrate that at least some RISC architectures are indeed scalable, in the sense of being able to take advantage of high-speed technologies. While the R6000 will never be a high-volume product like the R3000 or the rumored R4000, it provides a tremendous high-end growth path and thereby helps reinforce the MIPS architecture.

15

ECL Bus Controller

Mark Thorson

The ECL microprocessor system recently introduced by MIPS wouldn't be too useful without a bus that matches the performance of its R6000 CPU. To meet this need, MIPS has developed a new bus design and a chip to support it, the R6020 System Bus Chip. Implemented in the same ECL technology used for the CPU and floating-point arithmetic chips, the R6020 has

- 66.7-MHz clock frequency
- 266 Mbytes/s block transfer rate
- ECL 100K-compatible signals
- 259-pin package
- Two 36-entry I/O buffers (FIFOs)
- Serial scan testing

The R6020 implements an interface to the R6000 System Bus, which has

- Multiplexed address, data, and control
- 36-bit physical address space
- 32-bit data with parity
- Differential pairs for all signals except reset
- Block transfers (32 words)
- Geographic addressing
- Distributed arbitration

In the MIPS system design, every board on the R6000 System Bus, whether it's CPU, memory, or I/O, uses the R6020 to interface to the bus.

The chip handles the bus protocol, interfaces to the board ID PROM, and provides a complete set of arbitration logic, so all bus devices can track bus requests in parallel and predict which device will become the next bus master.

Two 36-entry queues in the R6020 allow any bus transaction, even 32-word block transfers, to be set up and received without slowing down the bus to the speed of master and slave devices.

Bus Signals

Figure 1 is a block diagram of an RC6280 system. All of the cards in a system share 37 differential pairs of signals, listed in Table 1. This is an unusually small number of signals for a 32-bit system bus; it is achieved by multiplexing both the address and control on the same wires used to carry the data. This both saves pins (doubly important where differential pairs are involved) and eases the ground bounce problem when signals change state simultaneously.

Also listed in Table 1 are the two clocks, which also are differential pairs, and the daisy-chained, single-ended signals used for reset and sys-

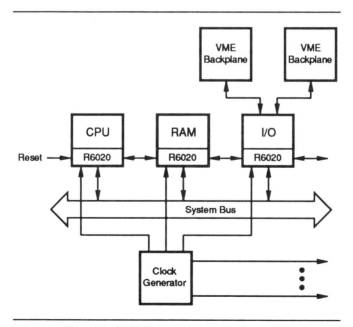

Figure 1. MIPS RC6280 system block diagram

Table 1. R6000 System Bus Signals

Name	Description
BusData<31:0> and BusData<31:0>*	Data lines, which are also used to carry address and control signals. During arbitration, BusData<31:17> are used as bus request signals.
BusType<2:0> and BusType<2:0>*	Indicates the function of signals on the data lines (see Table 2).
BusPar and BusPar*	Word parity for BusData<31:0>.
BusAck and BusAck*	Used by a bus slave to acknowledge data words received from a bus master.
TxCk and TxCk*	Clock used by bus drivers.
RxCk and RxCk*	Clock used by bus receivers.
BusLeft	Daisy-chained connection to neighbor on left.
BusRight	Daisy-chained connection to neighbor on right.

tem configuration. The clocks are distributed separately to each board by traces tuned to minimize skew. (Skew must be held within ±0.5 ns.) The transmit clock is used by the output drivers of the R6020, and the receive clock is used by its bus receivers. The receive clock is a slightly delayed form of the transmit clock.

Unlike other buses, which use card-ID pins or individual slot-select signals to implement geographic addressing, the R6000 System Bus uses the daisy-chained reset signal. Each card has separate lines for receiving a reset signal from its left neighbor and transmitting the signal to its right neighbor. Reset begins with a one-cycle pulse driven into the leftmost card slot. This pulse is propagated through the card to its neighbor, lengthened by one clock cycle. The neighbor, and every other card in the system (up to 15), propagates the pulse toward the right and lengthens it by one cycle. Each card knows which slot it's in by the length of the pulse it receives. Two cycles after its reset pulse is negated, each card echoes a one-cycle pulse back toward the left. Each card knows how many cards are in the system by adding the number of echoes to its own slot number.

Bus Arbitration

Figure 2 shows a read cycle, in which two clock periods are required for arbitration and seven for the data transfer. Before the read cycle takes place, the future bus master must arbitrate for control of the bus. During arbitration, each card "owns" one of the bits BusData<31:17>. The winner of the arbitration is the highest-priority card (i.e., the card with the

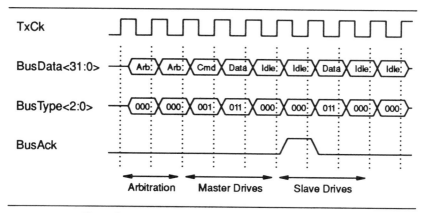

Figure 2. R6000 System Bus timing; TxCk is 66.7 MHz.

lowest slot number) that requests bus control by asserting its bit. After the first arbitration cycle in which at least one request bit is asserted, a second arbitration cycle is required so that all of the cards can recognize the winner.

When a card takes control of the bus, each R6020 chip latches the request bits asserted at the end of the second arbitration cycle. Requests that become asserted during the second cycle are too late to win immediate control of the bus. After the current bus master gives up control of the bus, the highest-priority latched request is serviced. No more arbitration cycles are performed until all latched requests have been serviced. This enforces fairness, so high-priority devices won't monopolize the bus.

Bus Protocol

After receiving control of the bus, the new bus master issues a command word, which is identified by the encoding of the BusType<2:0> signals (see Table 2). The command word specifies the direction of the data transfer, whether it is a single word or a block transfer, and the 14 least-significant bits of the physical address.

After issuing the command word, the bus master issues a data word, which specifies the remaining bits of the physical address. On a write cycle, this word also specifies the byte enables. For a read cycle, the master then hands off the bus to the slave. Two no-data (idle) cycles are required when one board stops driving the bus and another board starts. The first board drives one no-data cycle, and then the second board drives at least one no-data cycle before driving any command or data words.

Table 2. BusType<2:0> Encoding

Value	Function
000	No data (idle)
001	Command word
010	Data word
011	Data word and switch
100	Bad data (bus is undriven)
101	Reserved
110	Data word, write-disabled
111	Data word, write-disabled, and switch

Two clock periods after being presented with the data word from the master, the slave asserts BusAck. This is not a cycle termination signal like READY# on the Intel 386 or DTACK on the Motorola 68000. Because the R6020 can buffer any bus transaction, the bus protocol does not need a mechanism for extending a cycle. It is assumed that slaves can receive and transmit at the maximum speed of the bus. A slave acknowledges a data word two cycles after it is issued, but this only indicates that a slave has decoded the cycle and that it is capable of servicing it. Failure to acknowledge a data word causes the master to rearbitrate for control of the bus and rerun the cycle. There is no acknowledgment when a slave sends data to the master.

The slave inserts wait states by driving no-data cycles until it is ready to service the read request. Then, it drives a data word followed by a no-data cycle.

Two encodings of the BusType<2:0> signals specify "switch" cycles, which are used whenever the bus is about to be driven by a different board. Switch cycles occur when a master has issued command and data words and begins waiting for a slave response, and when a master gives up control of the bus. Switch cycles also occur when a slave response completes a bus cycle.

Two encodings of the BusType<2:0> signals specify write-disabled data words. These are used for performing a block write to less than 32 words. Any of the 32 words in a block write may be write-disabled.

A bus master is limited to one read cycle and one write cycle each time it gains control of the bus. These can be single-word cycles or 32-word block transfers. The longest time a master can hold the bus occurs when a block read immediately follows a block write, which happens during cache line replacement.

Semaphores are implemented by locked reads and conditional writes, both of which are specified by encodings of the command word. Conditional writes are similar to reads, in that both require a response from the slave. After performing a locked read, a slave returns a "success" word when accessed with a conditional write, if no other device has accessed the destination with a conditional write. Otherwise, the slave returns a "failure" word.

Bus Performance

Considering the amount of effort that has been put into making the bus signals fast, it seems surprising how many cycles are consumed by the bus protocol. Because it is a multiplexed bus, a command word and a data word must be issued before any data transfer can take place. Arbitration takes two cycles, as does handing off the bus from one set of drivers to another.

Although nine clock periods may seem rather long for reading a single 32-bit word (seven, if arbitration does not need to be performed), it should be kept in mind that most of the bus traffic will be block transfers between the caches and main memory. A 32-word block transfer does not require more overhead for bus protocol than a single-word cycle, so the average overhead per word is small.

The MIPS' literature quotes 266 Mbyte/s as the maximum transfer rate, but this figure is merely the bus clock frequency multiplied by the number of bytes that can be transferred over the data bus in one clock cycle. This rate is achieved only in the middle of a block transfer. If the overhead for bus protocol is included, the maximum rate drops to 237 Mbyte/s on reads and 225 Mbyte/s on writes.

Unlike other recent bus standards, such as the EISA bus and Sun's SBus, the R6000 System Bus does not support "critical word first," in which an instruction operand or the target of a branch is read in the first cycle of a block transfer to release the CPU, with the remaining cycles filling the rest of the cache line. This feature is not supported in the bus interface because it is not supported by the R6000's cache design.

Conclusion

Whether implemented in ECL, GaAs, or CMOS, the coming generation of superfast microprocessors will demand superfast buses. The R6000 System Bus is among the first of these new bus standards, and it illustrates techniques that might become commonplace in the future, such as differential pairs for all bus signals, small number of bus signals, clocks tuned for each slot to minimize skew, and multiple idle cycles when handing off the bus from one set of drivers to another.

Although MIPS is not promoting this bus as an industry standard, anyone using the R6000 chip set is likely to use the R6020 and, consequently, this bus. Documentation will be freely available to assist prospective third-party vendors developing products for this bus.

16

IDT Embedded MIPS Processors

Michael Slater

IDT has announced the first MIPS processors with on-chip cache, the R3051 and R3052. As Figure 1 shows, the chips are based on the R3000A processor core and include a 2-Kbyte data cache, a 4-Kbyte (R3051) or 8-Kbyte (R3052) instruction cache, and four-word read and write buffers. The new chips will make the MIPS architecture available to a far wider range of applications and provide strong competition for AMD's 29000 family and Intel's 960 family.

The R305x chips are the second derivative of the R3000 design. The first derivative, also from IDT, is the R3001, which is a minor modification to the R3000 to make it more suitable for embedded systems. Like the R3000, however, the R3001 requires external SRAMs and bus interface logic to achieve its performance potential. The R305x brings these functions on-chip, dramatically reducing system complexity and cost.

The R3052 chip includes about 500,000 transistors, as compared to the 115,000-transistor R3000. Because of the density of the cache RAM, however, the die size increase isn't nearly as large: the R3000A is about 75,000 square mils, while the R3052 is 105,000 square mils. The R3000A is also pad-ring-limited, so it will not benefit from further shrinks. The R3052, with less than half as many pins, is not limited in this way.

Despite its larger die size, the R3052 has one cost advantage over the R3000: a cheaper package. Bringing the caches on-chip eliminates the tag bus, and multiplexed address and data buses reduce pin count further, allowing the R305x chips to fit in an 84-pin package. IDT modified the CPU core to reduce its power consumption, making plastic packaging possible

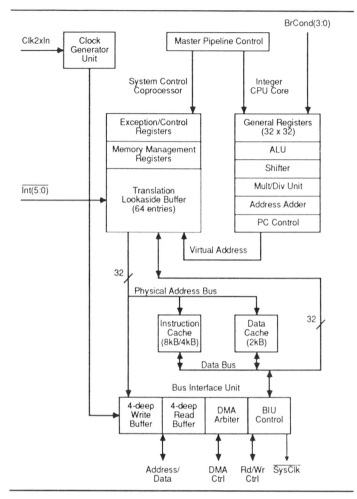

Figure 1. Block diagram of the R3052

at lower clock rates. The 20- and 25-MHz versions, and perhaps the 33-MHz version, will be available in plastic. A 40-MHz version will be available only in ceramic. Power consumption is expected to be about 2 watts at 33 MHz.

The aggressive pricing of the R305x chips is a sign of IDT's determination to make the MIPS architecture a contender for cost-sensitive embedded applications. Previously, MIPS processors have been popular in high-end embedded applications, but their appeal was limited to applications that could justify a several-hundred-dollar CPU subsystem.

On-chip caches will make it significantly easier to build systems at high clock rates. R3000 processors have recently become available at 40 MHz, but a 40-MHz R3000-based system requires very fast (8 ns) cache RAMs and careful board design. An R305x-based system needs no external cache RAMs, and its external bus does not need to operate at the CPU frequency.

IDT rates the performance of the chips for integer programs at 16 to 35 VAX MIPS, depending on clock rate. Performance is claimed to be over 64,000 Dhrystones at 40 MHz, but since Dhrystone fits in the on-chip caches, it is not a good indicator of performance for larger programs.

No on-chip floating-point hardware is provided, nor can an external floating-point accelerator be attached, so performance on floating-point-intensive applications won't be exciting. The lack of an FPU option makes the chips unsuitable for even low-end workstation applications. IDT plans future members of the family with an on-chip FPU. IDT has written a new floating-point emulation library that it claims is 20 times as fast as the MIPS-provided library, but it is still five times slower than a system using the R3010 FPA.

Four Variants

Four different versions have been announced: the R3051, R3051E, R3052, and R3052E. The difference between the '51 and '52 is the size of the instruction cache (4K versus 8K). The E versions include a full MMU, identical to that in the R3000. The non-E versions maintain the separation of user and kernel address spaces as well as cacheable and noncacheable addresses, but do not include the translation look-aside buffer (TLB).

The four versions of the chip are made from the same die, with the TLB disabled for the non-E versions and one 4K instruction cache block disabled for the '51 versions. This is a common method of addressing multiple price points with a single design, and also improves yield. A similar technique has been used by AMD to create the 29005 from the 29000, and by Intel to produce the 960KA, 960KB, and 960MC chips. The cache and TLB structures are large and dense and are most likely to be affected by defects. A fully functional device can be sold as a '52E; a chip with a defect in the TLB will be sold as a non-E version; and a chip with a defect in one of the two 4K cache blocks will be sold as a '51 or '51E. Defective blocks will be disabled through bonding options or modifications to the die, so users won't have access to the defective areas.

Most embedded applications don't need a full MMU and will use non-E versions. The E versions will be useful in high-reliability applications, in which the protection capability of the MMU is important. The MMU is also necessary for applications, such as X terminals, that depend on paged virtual memory.

On-Chip Caches

Selection of a 4K or 8K instruction cache will depend on the nature of the application program and the cost sensitivity. Applications with small, speed-critical loops may perform just as well with the smaller cache, while others may perform substantially better with the larger cache. Since the R3051 and R3052 are pin-compatible, users don't need to select the cache size until the PC board is stuffed.

R3000-based systems typically use instruction and data caches of 32K or 64K each. IDT's simulations showed that the R3052 performed at 85 to 90% of an R3000 with 32K external caches on most programs. Of course, some "cache buster" programs will degrade much more with the smaller caches, and others—such as Dhrystone—fit almost entirely in the smaller caches and achieve essentially the same performance regardless of cache size.

Both caches are direct-mapped. The instruction cache has a four-word (16-byte) line size and performs a four-word block read on a cache miss. The miss penalty is three clock cycles to the first word with the fastest external memory. Instruction words are read into the read buffer and are "streamed" to the processor as soon as they are read into the chip; the processor does not need to wait for the entire line to be read.

The data cache has a one-word line size and uses a write-through memory update policy. The four-word-deep write buffer minimizes processor stalls due to write cycles. A data cache miss causes either a one-word or a four-word refill, as selected by a configuration input pin when the processor is reset.

No snooping logic is provided for the caches, and the R305x chips are not intended for multiprocessor configurations. In systems that use DMA, software must flush the caches if a DMA transfer is performed to a cacheable address range. Because the caches are physically addressed, cache flushes are not required when a task switch occurs.

Bus Interface

The R305x uses a 32-bit multiplexed bus to minimize pin count. All bus cycles begin with an address cycle during which address latch enable (ALE) is asserted. In successive cycles, the processor provides data (for write cycles) or waits for data (for read cycles) until the acknowledge

(Ack/) signal is asserted by the system's control logic. The shortest possible bus cycle requires two clock cycles, one for address and one for data. DRAM memory systems require two or more additional cycles (wait states) for random accesses.

During read cycles caused by an instruction cache miss, the Burst/ output is asserted and a single address cycle is followed by four data cycles. Data cache misses create either single-word reads or four-word reads, depending on the option selected at reset.

Figure 2 shows the timing for a four-word read with two wait states for the first access and none for subsequent accesses. Two dedicated address pins provide address bits 2 and 3, which indicate the word number within the line. Accesses are always in the order 00, 01, 10, 11, so nibble-mode DRAMs can be used. Ack/ is asserted by the system's control logic when

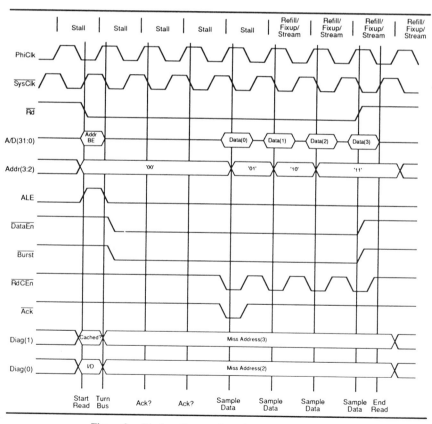

Figure 2. Timing diagram for a four-word burst read

the first word is ready, and the read buffer clock enable (RdCEn/) is asserted to clock in each word.

Write cycles are always individual accesses; bursts are not used. The Burst/ output pin is redefined during write cycles as WriteNear/, which is asserted when the previous access was a write cycle and was within the same 256-byte page. This is useful for page-mode and static-column memory systems.

Five interrupt inputs are provided. Three are internally synchronized, so they can be driven by asynchronous signals. The other two must be synchronous with the system clock but have one clock cycle less latency than the asynchronous inputs.

A bus arbiter is included on-chip and allows an external device to take control of the bus with a simple BusReq/ and BusGrn/ handshake.

Several features ease real-time tracing and debugging. When emulation mode is enabled (via an input pin), the address for all instruction cache accesses is output on the address bus whenever the bus is otherwise idle. This allows a logic analyzer (or an emulator's trace buffer) to trace most instruction fetch activity, although the instruction trace is interrupted whenever the external bus is needed for a data transfer.

Two diagnostic output bits indicate, during the address cycle, whether a bus cycle is due to a cache miss and, if so, whether it was an instruction cache or data cache miss. After the address cycle, these pins indicate the state of address bits 2 and 3 for the access that caused the miss. (This address is not otherwise apparent, since a four-word cache refill always starts at the first word in the line.)

Support Chips

The R305x chips do not include DRAM control logic, programmable chip selects, or DMA controllers. IDT decided to focus its efforts on providing functions on-chip that could not be replicated externally and are used by all applications. This kept chip size, design time, and pin count to a minimum.

To simplify system design, IDT will provide three peripheral chips designed to work with the R305x processors. Figure 3 shows a system using the three chips. The R3721 DRAM controller, packaged in an 84-pin PLCC, provides programmable timing for interleaved or noninterleaved memory systems and supports page-mode access. It can directly drive four banks of DRAMs. With two interleaved banks of 80-ns DRAMs, it can stream data to the processor at one word per clock cycle (at 33 MHz) after the initial three-clock latency.

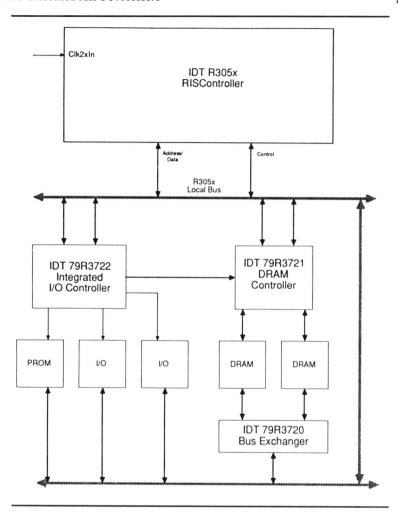

Figure 3. System using the R305x and IDT's peripheral chips

The R3720 bus exchanger is a three-port, 16-bit, bidirectional multiplexer, which connects the processor's bus to two memory banks. Two of these chips are required to create the 32-bit data path. It is packaged in a 68-pin PLCC.

The R3722 I/O interface controller is the most complex of the peripheral chips. In a 132-pin PQFP package, it provides eight programmable chip select outputs, an 8-input priority interrupt encoder, a 4-channel DMA controller, four programmable timer/counters, a dual UART, and eight parallel I/O lines. It also allows a single 8-bit-wide boot EPROM to be used by reading four bytes from the EPROM, assembling a 32-bit word, and passing this word to the processor. (R305x processors do not support dynamic bus sizing.)

Conclusions

The R305x family promises to provide serious competition for AMD's 29000, Intel's 960, VLSI Technology's ARM, and various embedded SPARC processors. No other processor provides nearly as much on-chip cache memory at the price of the R305x chips. The R305x chips benefit from the sophisticated compilers and software development tools available for the MIPS architecture. SPARC processors have this same advantage, but so far, no SPARC implementations provide on-chip cache or memory management.

The R305x chips demonstrate the value of a licensable CPU core. AMD and Intel invested large amounts of time and money in developing processor cores and software development tools. In the meantime, IDT started with a high-quality CPU core and built from that point. It is unlikely that a company such as IDT could have produced chips like the R305x family in a reasonable period of time if it had to develop the CPU architecture and core design from scratch.

Like other vendors of embedded RISCs, IDT has its eyes on the market now served by Motorola's 68020. IDT claims the R3051 has five times the performance of a 68020 at a lower price. With Motorola's new 68300 family, however, the picture is a little different. Motorola's CPU performance is still much lower than the R305x, but chips such as the 68340 match the price of the R3051 while providing on-chip peripherals. The functions of IDT's R3722 I/O controller, for example, are included in the 68340. When the price of the two IDT chips is compared to that of the 68340, the IDT solution is seen to cost twice as much.

Thus, tradeoffs among price, performance, and chip count remain. Applications that can get by with the CPU performance of the 68340 will require fewer chips and have a lower system cost than those based on R305x processors. Of course, in many applications, the raw CPU performance of the R305x chips will be a significant advantage.

The R305x family offers a strong upgrade path. Staying with the same pinout, a design can be upgraded from the R3051 to the R3052, and can also move from 20 MHz to 40 MHz. For maximum performance, the software-compatible R3000 or R3001 can be used with large external caches, and the R4000 will provide a very-high-end option.

The 68300 family parts, on the other hand, are available only in 16-MHz versions. The 68020 and 68030 are available at clock rates up to 50 MHz, but system design is difficult at these clock rates. To get significantly higher performance within the 68000 family, the only option is the expensive 68040.

So far, the R305x is a paper tiger; IDT does not yet have silicon on the chips, and their production schedule is predicated on moving into production with relatively few changes. The CPU core is essentially unchanged from the R3000A, so there is little risk (no pun intended) in this most-complex part of the chip. IDT has experience designing SRAMs and processor/cache modules. The R305x chips are, however, IDT's first attempt at an on-chip cache subsystem and bus interface logic.

It remains to be seen how quickly the chips move into production and when the full range of clock rates will be achieved. Other MIPS vendors have similar devices in the works, and IDT may have some serious competition by the time the R305x chips reach silicon.

The R305x is the first sign of RISC architectures originally designed for Unix moving aggressively into the embedded arena. Intel and AMD benefit from their focus on embedded applications, for which previous MIPS and SPARC implementations have been relatively weak. With the R305x and future embedded SPARC versions expected, competition for embedded RISC applications will grow more intense. As prices drop and system designs become simpler, the CISC processors that still dominate embedded control applications will come under increasing pressure.

17

High Integration on
MIPS-Based Processor

Michael Slater

Just weeks after IDT's announcement of their R3051/3052 embedded MIPS processors, LSI Logic announced their own embedded MIPS design—the LR33000. The IDT and LSI devices both aim to reduce chip count for embedded applications but each results from a different design approach and includes different features on-chip.

The LR33000 (Figures 1 and 2) includes an R3000A-compatible CPU, 8-Kbyte instruction cache, 1-Kbyte data cache, write buffer, DRAM controller, and three timer/counters. The bus interface provides programmable wait-state generation and supports 8-bit-wide boot ROMs. It will be available in 25-, 33-, and 40 MHz versions, with maximum power consumption of 2, 2.5, and 3 W, respectively. All three versions will be available in a 155-pin ceramic PGA, and the 25-MHz version will also be available in a 160-pin PQFP. LSI claims to have over 20 design wins, including QMS (laser printers), Tandem (disk arrays), Electronics for Imaging (color processing), and Dataco A/S (LAN products).

Unlike IDT, which based its chips on the MIPS-provided R3000A implementation, LSI Logic reimplemented the CPU as a standard-cell design. By creating a new CPU implementation, LSI gained the flexibility to add new features and eliminate unnecessary features. Unlike the original MIPS design, the LSI Logic implementation is fully static. This allows the clock to be slowed or stopped to reduce power consumption without losing register contents or other processor state information.

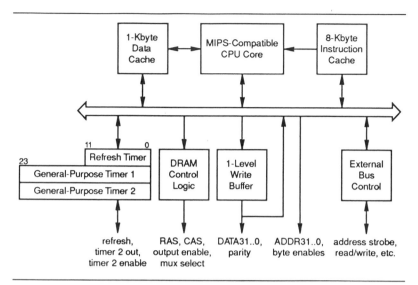

Figure 1. Block diagram of the LR33000

Table 1 shows the key differences between the LSI and IDT devices. LSI chose not to include the translation look-aside buffer (TLB). Since IDT used the standard MIPS core, they couldn't easily delete the TLB. Instead, IDT chose to provide the chip in two versions, one with a functioning TLB and one with the TLB disabled. IDT claims that the TLB is important for some applications, such as X terminals. LSI counters that the TLB is a nicety, but not a necessity, and claims to have a design win for the LR33000 in an X terminal.

LSI added several debugging features to the CPU. There are two breakpoint registers, one for a data address and one for an instruction address. This provides the hardware needed for a monitor program to implement rudimentary breakpoints. A trace capability captures the address of the last nonsequential instruction executed (i.e., the most recent branch target). In addition, the BRTAKEN output is asserted whenever a branch is taken by the processor, to aid in tracing program flow externally. An in-circuit emulator for the LR33000 is being developed by Embedded Performance.

On-Chip Caches

Both LSI Logic and IDT chose the same 8-Kbyte size for the instruction cache, while IDT provides twice as much data cache (2K versus 1K), IDT

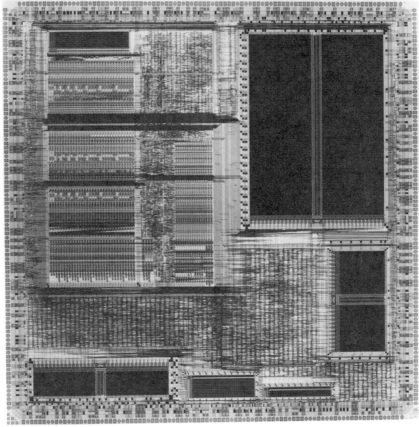

Figure 2. Die plot of the 700,000-transister, 500-mil-square LR33000

claims that their simulations showed a significant performance increase for a 2-Kbyte cache as compared to a 1-Kbyte cache. LSI on the other hand, produced simulation data showing a performance gain from 0 to a maximum of 3.6% as a result of increasing the data cache from 1K to 2K. Whether the larger cache in the IDT part is justified will depend on the nature of the application program and the speed of the external memory system.

Both caches in the LR33000 have a four-word line size. When a cache miss occurs, the refill size (number of words read from memory) can be set to 1, 2, 4, 8, or 16 words. This flexibility allows the system to be optimized for various algorithms and memory systems. It is not clear if the ability to select from this range of refill sizes will be a significant advantage over the IDT device, but it can't hurt.

Table 1. Major Differences between LSI and IDT Embedded MIPS Processors. Note that IDT will provide peripheral chips with DRAM control, DMA controller, timers, boot ROM support, and other functions.

	IDT R3051/52	LSI LR33000
Instruction Cache	8K (3052) 4K (3051)	8K
Data Cache	2K	1K
Snooping	No	Yes
I-Cache Refill Size (words)	4	1, 2, 4, 8, or 16
D-Cache Refill Size (words)	1 or 4	1, 2, 4, 8, or 16
D-Cache Line Size (words)	1	4
TLB	Yes (E versions)	No
Static Design	No	Yes
Write Buffer	4-Level	1-Level
DRAM Control	No	Yes
8-Bit ROM Support	No	Yes
Programmable Wait States	No	Yes
Breakpoint Registers	No	Yes
Timers	None	2 General-Purpose 1 Refresh
Address/Data Buses	Multiplexed	Non-Multiplexed
Clock Input	2×	1×
Price (25 MHz, 1000s, PQFP)	$81 (R3052)	$99.95

Both caches are direct-mapped, and the data cache is write-through. Unlike the IDT processor, snooping is supported for both caches; cache lines are invalidated if a DMA controller or other bus master writes to a memory location that is present in the cache. Either cache can be disabled under program control. In addition, an input signal controls whether each data memory access should be cached. This input can be used to lock cache entries by decoding the address and allowing only certain addresses to be cached.

Timers and DRAM Control

The LR33000 includes three timers, all of which are decremented by the system clock; there is no prescaler or external clock option. Two are general-purpose 24-bit counter/timers which, when enabled, produce an interrupt when they reach zero. One has an output pin to indicate when zero is reached and an input pin that can be used as a clock enable. In a

25-MHz system, the timers provide a maximum interval of about 11 minutes with a resolution of 40 ns. The third timer has only 12 bits and is intended primarily as a DRAM refresh timer.

Accesses to the lower 256 Mbytes of the address space are assumed to be to DRAM, and the DRAM controller provides the data ready signal to pace the bus interface for accesses in this range. The DRAM controller provides RAS, CAS, output enable, and multiplexer control signals. An external multiplexer is required to produce the multiplexed address required by DRAMs. In a system with eight or nine DRAMs, the control signals can drive the memory chips directly; in larger systems, buffers are required. Parity generation and checking logic is provided on-chip, and can be disabled.

DRAM timing is programmable to a limited degree. CAS is always asserted two clock cycles after RAS. The CAS active time can be programmed to be either 1.5 or 2.5 clock cycles, and the RAS precharge time can be set to either 2 or 3 clock cycles. A typical DRAM access requires four clock cycles for the initial access and two clock cycles for each subsequent access in a block refill. With two interleaved banks of DRAM and an external control PAL, successive accesses within a block can be performed on each clock cycle. The DRAM speed required is 100 ns for 25-MHz operation, 80 ns for 33-MHz, and 70 ns for 40-MHz.

When enabled, a refresh cycle is generated whenever the refresh timer reaches zero. If a bus cycle is not in process, the refresh cycle is performed immediately; otherwise, it is performed as soon as the current cycle completes. Refresh uses the CAS-before-RAS method (i.e., no refresh address is provided on the bus).

Bus Interface

The bus interface includes a single-level write buffer that stores one 32-bit word waiting to be written to memory. This allows the processor to continue executing while the memory write cycle is completed; but if another write is performed, the processor must wait for the buffer to be emptied. IDT's R305x chips, like the external write buffers commonly used in R3000-based systems, provide a 4-level write buffer. The deeper write buffer will increase performance slightly by reducing the number of processor stalls when successive writes are performed. One drawback of the deeper write buffer is that when a memory read occurs, the processor must be stalled until the write buffer empties to ensure that the read does not return stale data.

Chip-select outputs and programmable wait-state generation are provided for two fixed address ranges of 16 Mbytes each. One of these address spaces is intended for ROM, and the other for I/O. Each can be independently programmed for 0 to 15 wait states. Alternatively, the on-chip wait-state generator can be ignored for either space, with the external DRDY signal controlling the timing. If the BWIDE/ input pin is asserted during access to the ROM space, the bus interface performs four 8-bit reads to assemble a 32-bit word. This allows a single 8-bit-wide boot ROM to be used.

Two different bus arbitration request/grant pairs are provided. The BREQ/BGNT pair provide a typical bus arbitration function. When BREQ is asserted, the processor completes any transaction in process, and then puts the address, data, and control buses into the high-impedance state and asserts BGNT. While BGNT is asserted, the processor monitors bus write cycles and invalidates any cache lines containing memory locations modified by an external bus master. The snooping logic requires access to the cache tags. Instead of providing arbitration logic for the tags, LSI chose simply to halt the processor when the bus has been granted to another bus master. This makes the design far from optimal for multiprocessor systems.

The on-chip DRAM controller continues to monitor the address bus when an external bus master is in control. If it detects an access to the DRAM address range, it generates the RAS, CAS, OE, multiplexer, and write-enable signals required for DRAM access.

An alternative method for an external bus master to access DRAM is provided by the DMAR/DMAC signal pair. When DMAR/ (DMA request) is asserted, the processor completes any bus cycle in progress. It then asserts DMAC (DMA cycle) and begins a DRAM access cycle, driving RAS, CAS, OE, write enables, and the multiplexer control signal. The processor does not tri-state its address and data buses, however; the DRAM system must have two address and data ports. Since the processor cannot see the address provided to the DRAM by the external bus master, no snooping is performed. One benefit of this access method is that the processor continues executing from cache until it requires access to the external bus.

Comparing the IDT and LSI Designs

LSI Logic has aimed to provide a minimum chip-count solution for DRAM-based systems. The on-chip DRAM control, chip-select logic, and wait-state generation will allow simple systems to be built with very little glue logic.

IDT, on the other hand, chose to provide DRAM and I/O control in separate peripheral chips. A simple system design will require more chips using the IDT approach. IDT's I/O interface controller, DRAM controller, and bus exchanger chips, however, will provide many more functions in a modest number of chips. The three-chip set will provide eight chip-select outputs instead of two, and four general-purpose timers instead of two. It will also provide a dual UART, eight parallel I/O lines, a 4-channel DMA controller, an 8-input priority interrupt encoder, and support for interleaved DRAM systems. All of these functions are left to the system designer using LSI's processor.

The IDT processor should have higher performance due to the larger data cache and four-deep write buffer. On the other hand, the programmable refill sizes of the LSI processor may provide some modest benefit. LSI claims that their implementation of the processor core has the same performance as the standard R3000A design. There may be some performance differences between LSI's on-chip DRAM controller and IDT's external DRAM controller. Final evaluation of the performance differences between the two designs will have to await benchmarks run on real silicon.

Each design has some unique features that may sway a designer's choice depending on the needs of the application. IDT provides the optional MMU, which is valuable in some applications. On the other hand, the LSI design is fully static, allowing power consumption to be dramatically reduced when the system is idle.

LSI's pricing is substantially higher than IDT's. LSI's chip provides more functions. This is not entirely fair either, however, since the IDT chip set provides many more functions than LSI's processor. At higher clock rates, the price difference is more dramatic. This is due in part to the fact that the LSI part has many more pins (155 versus 84) because of its nonmultiplexed buses and DRAM control signals. LSI uses an expensive ceramic pin-grid array package for the higher clock rates, while IDT uses a ceramic chip carrier. LSI's die size is more than twice IDT's, so LSI's manufacturing costs will be substantially higher.

IDT also offers a 20-MHz version and the R3051 version with only 4K instruction cache, providing even lower price points. These low price points should make the IDT part attractive for a considerably broader range of applications. Competition between the two companies is likely to drive LSI's pricing for the higher-speed parts down toward IDT's.

At the moment, neither chip is ready for sampling. LSI is promising samples somewhat earlier, but only at the 25-MHz clock rate and only in the PGA package. LSI's design may have more schedule risk than IDT's, since it includes an entirely new CPU core implementation and more interface logic. LSI is confident that there will not be problems with the chip, having completed the design in March of 1990 and spent six months on simulation and verification.

Conclusions

RISC processors are clearly coming of age for embedded control, and the MIPS architecture appears well positioned to be a significant player. In addition to the LSI and IDT chips, NEC is rumored to be developing a MIPS implementation for embedded control. These processors will provide serious competition for AMD and Intel, who have so far been concentrating on fighting each other. MIPS-based processors will also challenge Motorola's 68300 family and National's 32000 family.

Intel and AMD have the significant advantage of having been active in the high-end embedded market for over two years, and have spent considerable sums building a base of third-party development tools. They also have field sales and application support organizations that LSI and IDT can't match.

The existing "embedded" SPARC implementations don't have on-chip caches, DRAM control, or flexible bus interface logic, and aren't likely to fare well. Fujitsu is close to announcing new embedded SPARC designs, however, and Philips-Signetics is due to introduce embedded SPARC products next year. Selecting an embedded processor is only going to get harder, but the alternatives are getting more and more appealing.

MIPS with 64-Bit R4000 Architecture

Michael Slater

MIPS Computer Systems has unveiled the long-awaited R4000, its third-generation microprocessor. As expected, the R4000 includes on-chip instruction and data caches of 8 Kbytes each, a second-level cache controller, a floating-point unit, and a superpipelined CPU that implements the same instruction set extensions as the ECL R6000. The surprise is that it also extends the architecture to 64 bits—the integer registers and ALU are 64 bits wide, and linear, 64-bit virtual addressing is available when the 64-bit mode is enabled. It is the first microprocessor to provide this capability.

MIPS stopped short of making a product announcement, and the company steadfastly refuses to discuss three key issues: price, availability, and performance. Many technical details have been released, but data sheets and users' manuals remain under nondisclosure. This strategy is reminiscent of Motorola's preannouncements of the 88000 and 68040 months before their formal announcement, but MIPS has provided far more technical detail than did Motorola. Still, MIPS won't discuss many implementation details.

It has been rumored that MIPS originally expected to have silicon in late 1990, but design changes and simulation problems delayed the project by as much as a year. The company says that it decided to make the technology announcement because of misleading rumors being spread by its competitors—presumably Sun, and perhaps Motorola—so customers would not be confused about what the R4000 really is (or, more accurately, what it will be). MIPS was no doubt also motivated by the opportunity to be the first to reveal a microprocessor design of this performance class.

MIPS won't speculate on performance and prefers to wait until measured SPEC benchmark results can be quoted, but company officials were "comfortable with" our previous estimate of 50 VAX MIPS at 50 MHz. There have been rumors that MIPS has backed off from its 50-MHz target and is planning to introduce the chip at 33 MHz, but MIPS denies this.

The premature nature of the announcement makes it difficult to claim titles such as "world's fastest CMOS microprocessor," "first true 64-bit microprocessor," or "most highly integrated microprocessor." If the chip were available today, these claims would be valid. What really counts, of course, is not when chips are disclosed but when they are shipped, and it is uncertain how many of these honors MIPS will have earned when judged by that standard.

The R4000 design uses about 1.1 million transistors, less than Intel's 486 and Motorola's 68040, yet it has twice as much cache memory as either of those chips. It also includes a much faster CPU and FPU, a second-level cache controller, and a more sophisticated bus interface. The R4000 gets much more out of the same transistor count for several reasons. To some degree, it is the advantage of RISC over CISC—the instruction decoder is simpler and no microcode ROM is needed. Another key reason is that the cache memory uses four-transistor memory cells, instead of six-transistor cells as used by Intel and Motorola, so even though the caches are twice as large they only use a third more transistors.

The R4000 is designed in 1-micron (drawn) CMOS technology, through some vendors may fabricate it using a denser process. MIPS would not disclose the die size, but one of the semiconductor vendors indicated that it is at the limit of the reticle size, which is a circle 21.2 mm in diameter. (One recent microprocessor, Intel's military-only 960MM, is so large that it is octagonal, rather than rectangular—the round reticle cuts off the corners.) A 15-mm square chip (590 × 590 mils, or 348K square mils) is the largest die that can fit within this circle. Like most microprocessors, however, the R4000 is rectangular rather than square, so the die area is probably closer to 330K square mils, roughly the same as the 68040. Intel's 486 is considerably smaller at 256K square mils, and the future three-level-metal, submicron version of the 486 is a mere 125K square mils.

As compared with the anticipated next-generation SPARC, the R4000 transistor count is quite modest. Cypress/ROSS's Pinnacle is expected to be over 1.5 million transistors, and TI's Viking is rumored to be over 3 million transistors. This should make the R4000 manufacturable somewhat earlier than these chips, and could make it less expensive as well. Some analysts are skeptical whether all the MIPS semiconductor partners are capable of manufacturing the R4000, but MIPS says that all of them expect to produce it.

Pricing for the R4000 will be set by the semiconductor partners, so there is little MIPS can say in this regard, and the partners aren't talking yet. The chip will be produced in at least two versions that differ only in their packaging. The full-function version with second-level cache support requires 447 pins. A version without the second-level cache interface requires only 179 pins, and probably will be priced several hundred dollars lower. This version will not support multiprocessor systems. A third version with the second-level cache interface but not the multiprocessor support may also be produced.

CPU Subsystem

Figure 1 shows a block diagram of an R4000 subsystem. The chip includes the following functions:

- Integer unit, which implements a superset of the R3000 instruction set.
- Floating-point unit, which implements a superset of the R3010 FP accelerator instruction set.
- System control coprocessor, which provides memory management and exception handling.
- Instruction and data caches of 8 Kbytes each, both direct mapped.
- Control for a second-level cache with its own dedicated 128-bit data bus and associated address and control lines.
- Interface to a 64-bit multiplexed address/data system bus.

The on-chip paths from the instruction and data caches are 64 bits wide, allowing a pair of instructions or a 64-bit data value to be accessed in a single clock cycle.

Many aspects of the chip's operation, such as the configuration of the second-level cache and the timing of the system bus, are programmable. The R4000 loads its configuration information when it is reset by reading a serial data stream of 256 bits from a dedicated configuration EPROM. In previous MIPS processors, programmable options have been set by using the interrupt inputs as configuration inputs when reset is asserted. For the R4000, there are too many options for this approach to be practical, but since many of these options must be set before the system can operate, they cannot be programmed via software-written control registers.

The system bus is designed for block-mode transfers, and several timing protocols are provided. The 64 system bus signals are multiplexed be-

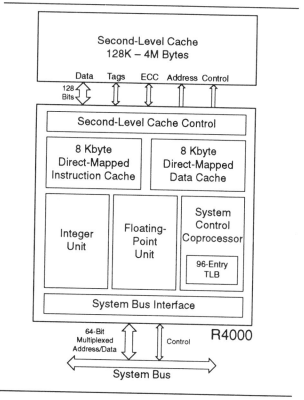

Figure 1. R4000 CPU system

tween a 36-bit physical address and a 64-bit data transfer. An address cycle may be followed by a single data transfer or as many as sixteen 64-bit words, allowing the longest possible cache line to be transferred in a single burst. The bus is synchronous, and slow I/O devices will typically be connected via interface chips that provide FIFO buffering. Either parity, ECC, or neither can be selected.

Bus timing can be varied in two ways. First, the bus clock can be the same as the system clock, or it can be divided by 2, 4, or 8. Second, nine different data patterns can be selected, in which one or more data transfer cycles are followed by one or more idle bus cycles. For example, a very fast memory system might want consecutive transfers (DDDD); a slower memory system might want one or more intervening idle cycles (DxDx or DxxDxx); and a 128-bit-wide memory system might want pairs of transfers followed by idle cycles (DDxx).

Figure 2 shows the R4000 pipeline, which has eight stages as compared to five for the R3000. The instruction and data cache accesses are both split into two stages, and an additional stage is added for the cache tag check after the data cache lookup. MIPS won't discuss how the caches are pipelined, but conceptually, a register could be added between the address decoders and the memory array, for example. Because of the deeper pipeline, there is one-half-clock stall when a taken branch is executed. In future implementations, branch prediction may allow the taken path to be prefetched, eliminating this stall cycle.

The R4000 is called superpipelined because the caches are split into two pipeline stages. The ALU, instruction decode, register file read, and write-back operations remain single stages, however. An on-chip phase-locked loop doubles the external clock to provide the 2× clock for the pipeline. Instructions are issued at a 100-MHz rate with a 50-MHz external clock, so in some sense it is a 100-MHz processor. The 100-MHz clock never leaves the chip, however, and MIPS decided not to market it as a 100-MHz device. To avoid confusion, in this article we use the term "one clock cycle" to mean one cycle of the external 50-MHz clock, and refer to the internal clock cycles as half-clock cycles.

Unlike a superscalar design, which requires issue restrictions because of data dependencies and resource conflicts, the R4000 implementation has no issue restrictions whatsoever; two successive instructions can always enter the pipeline on successive half-clock cycles. For example, the R4000 can execute two successive store instructions or two ALU operations in a single clock cycle, while a superscalar design would not be able to do so without a dual-ported data cache or dual ALUs.

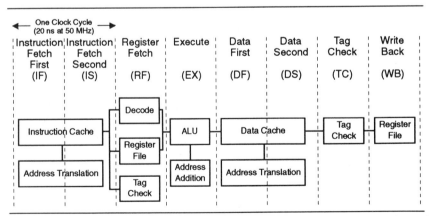

Figure 2. R4000 pipeline. Each stage uses only half a clock cycle (one cycle of the internal 2x clock), or 10 ns at 50 MHz.

Integer multiply speed has been doubled in the R4000, while division remains the same (in clock cycles). The latencies of floating-point operations are similar to those of the R3010, with a 25% improvement (in clock cycles) in multiply and a small improvement in divide. The faster clock rate will produce an additional gain. The floating-point unit is also more highly pipelined, so the maximum issue rate is increased.

Architecture Extensions

The R4000 includes the same architecture extensions as the ECL R6000. These extensions have not been given a formal name by MIPS, but are commonly called "MIPS-II." MIPS-I remains the application binary interface (ABI) for general-purpose applications, since programs using the MIPS-II extensions won't run on R2000- and R3000-based machines. Operating-system code on MIPS-II machines will take advantage of the new features, as can custom programs written by users of such machines. As the installed base of MIPS-II machines grows, some software vendors might produce two versions of their applications, one using the standard ABI and another taking advantage of the MIPS-II extensions. Embedded applications will also be able to use the MIPS-II extensions when an affordable implementation is available.

One of these extensions, the "reverse-endian" (RE) bit, has also been retrofitted to the R3000 design, creating the pin-compatible R3000A. If set, the RE bit causes the processor to switch byte ordering mode (high byte first or low byte first) when changing from kernel to user mode or vice versa. This allows an operating system running in either mode to execute applications running in either mode, and, with the proper operating-system support, will allow a single system to run both big-endian applications (as used by MIPS, SGI, and most other MIPS-based systems) and little-endian applications (as used by DEC). MIPS has not, however, made any commitment to provide the required operating system support. The RE bit does not solve the problem of the different operating-system versions used by DEC and other MIPS vendors, but it provides the fundamental capability needed to unify the MIPS software base. Whether the operating system and application software will evolve to take advantage of this capability remains to be seen.

The MIPS-II architecture also interlocks load instructions, so if an instruction attempts to use data loaded by the immediately preceding instruction, the pipeline will stall. In an R3000 system, such an attempt produces an incorrect result, and a no-op instruction must be added after a load unless a useful instruction not depending on the load can be placed there. The R4000 allows the no-ops to be eliminated, but programs that eliminate the no-ops will not run correctly on R3000-based hardware.

The MIPS-II architecture extends the floating-point instruction set with a square root instruction, FP-to-fixed conversion instructions that specify the rounding mode, and 64-bit load and store instructions. Note that MIPS-II defines 64-bit load and store instructions only for floating-point data. The as-yet-unreleased 64-bit extensions to the architecture will provide 64-bit integer load and store instructions.

Two new integer instructions, Load Linked and Store Conditional, provide the mechanism for implementing interprocessor or intertask synchronization primitives, such as test-and-set and compare-and-swap. The Load Linked instruction operates as a standard load instruction but has the side effect of setting the "link" status bit. As part of the cache coherency mechanism, the processor monitors accesses to the linked location and clears the link status bit if another processor accesses that location. Store Conditional performs a store operation only if the link bit is set, and it provides a result in the destination register indicating if the store was successful. These two instructions, combined with the hardware mechanism that controls the link status bit, allow indivisible test-and-set and other semaphore operations to be implemented without requiring bus locks. (MIPS assures us that this really works, even though conventional designs require an indivisible series of bus transfers to implement reliable semaphores.)

Finally, the MIPS-II architecture adds conditional traps and annulling branches (called "branch likely"), both of which increase code density.

MIPS has released few details of the 64-bit extensions to the architecture. The entire integer unit, including the registers and the ALU, is extended to 64 bits wide. A control bit determines whether the processor operates in 32-bit or 64-bit mode. When in 64-bit mode, 64-bit linear, virtual addresses are produced. (Now we know why John Hennessy has been so vocal in his criticism of Intel for calling the 860 a 64-bit architecture.) A 32-bit or 64-bit operating system can dispatch applications running in either mode. MIPS says that the transition from 32 to 64 bits will be smooth, and its designers cringe at the word "mode" because of the terrible associations with the modes in the 286 and 386 architectures. Compiler support for the 64-bit mode is planned for late 1991 or early in 1992.

Caches

The on-chip instruction and data caches are both direct-mapped and are 8 Kbytes each. For caches this small, a two-way set-associative design is generally believed to provide a significantly higher hit rate. MIPS did not implement set-associative caches, as in the 68040, because of the access time penalty and complexity that results and because it expects future implementations to have larger on-chip caches, for which the benefit of set-associativity is smaller.

Both caches are virtually indexed and physically tagged. This means that the untranslated virtual address selects a cache line, and the address is translated to a physical address while the cache access occurs. The cache tag is then compared to the physical address to determine if a hit has occurred. Because the caches are larger than the smallest page size, some system configurations will require software to ensure that synonyms don't occur. MIPS won't describe the details of this mechanism because of a pending patent application.

Both caches are parity protected. If a parity error occurs on an instruction cache access or an access to a clean data cache line, the information can be re-fetched from memory. Both caches have 64-bit data paths to the CPU and an access can be initiated twice each clock cycle. The current R4000 design uses only half of the available instruction cache bandwidth; it fetches a single 32-bit instruction during each half-cycle. The line size of each cache can be either four or eight words (16 or 32 bytes).

The data cache uses a write-back memory update policy. When a line must be written back to memory, it is transferred to a single-line write buffer that holds the data while the series of memory write cycles occurs, freeing the cache for CPU accesses.

The R4000 includes complete control for an external second-level cache; only standard synchronous SRAMs are needed externally to implement a cache of 128K to 4 Mbytes. A 512-Kbyte cache could be implemented with 22 RAMs, each 32K × 8. (The memory must be 176 bits wide to provide the 128-bit data path, 16 ECC bits, and 32 tag bits.) Four copies of each control signal are provided, allowing up to four banks of SRAM to be driven without external buffers. Error detection is implemented in hardware, and if an error occurs, an exception is generated that transfers control to error correction software.

For maximum-speed operation, 17-ns RAMs are needed with a 50-MHz clock. On a first-level cache miss that hits in the secondary cache, the miss penalty is two clock cycles. The cache timing is programmable, so a system designer can choose to implement a slower second-level cache. In some applications, a larger but slower secondary cache may be a better tradeoff than a smaller, faster cache.

The second-level cache is direct-mapped and uses a write-back memory update protocol. It is physically indexed and physically tagged. The line size may be programmed to be 8, 16, or 32 words. The cache can be partitioned into separate instruction and data areas if desired to prevent instruction accesses from displacing data, or vice versa.

The R4000 includes a fully associative translation look-aside buffer with 96 entries arranged in 48 pairs. Each pair must consist of adjacent pages. Each TLB entry can be locked to provide guaranteed minimum access time to critical pages. Page size is selectable from 4 Kbytes to 16 Mbytes on a per-page basis. Large pages are useful for frame buffers and large program and data structures, and they allow large amounts of memory to be mapped at one time. This will be especially important in systems using 64-bit addressing. Like the R3000, a TLB miss generates an exception, and the TLB is reloaded by software.

Multiprocessor Support

The R4000 provides a comprehensive set of functions to support multi-processor systems. The R4000 itself does not implement any specific cache coherency protocol, but it provides all the facilities necessary for external logic to do so. MIPS plans to introduce a system bus interface chip that will provide one standard implementation of such protocols.

State bits for each line in the primary data cache and secondary cache allow each line to be flagged as invalid, clean exclusive, dirty exclusive, shared, or dirty shared. Both snooping and directory-based protocols can be implemented, and various schemes can be used to identify accesses to shared and private data.

The primary cache is maintained as a subset of the secondary cache. In most cases, only the secondary cache must be "snooped" to maintain cache coherency. Multiprocessor cache coherency is not supported for systems using only the on-chip primary cache.

The TLB includes status bits to specify the cache coherency protocol on a per-page basis. Each page can be marked as noncoherent, coherent, write invalidate, or write update. (The R4000 is the first microprocessor to implement write update, which allows the on-chip cache to be updated from the bus when snooping logic detects that another copy of the cached data has been modified.) The status bits from the TLB are output on the bus with the address, allowing cache coherency logic elsewhere in the system to take the appropriate action. If a page marked "not coherent" is accessed, for example, other processors do not need to snoop on accesses to this page.

Conclusions

From the earliest days of the commercialization of RISC, MIPS Computer Systems has had a reputation for having one of the best architectures and outstanding implementations. The R4000 appears destined to continue that reputation. The biggest questions with regard to the R4000 are when it will be available, how it will perform, and at what price. (Much to the chagrin of MIPS and Motorola, technical excellence isn't everything, of course. The success of SPARC and the 80x86 are dramatic illustrations of how strong marketing and the support of a leading systems vendor can overwhelm technical issues.)

In choosing a superpipelined, rather than superscalar, implementation, MIPS has taken a different path than most, if not all, other next-generation RISC implementations. MIPS says that this design choice is a result of extensive simulations. The R4000 began as a superscalar design, but MIPS was unhappy with the simulated performance characteristics. MIPS says that the superscalar design provided a good performance boost for floating-point applications, but not for integer programs. Issue restrictions are a key weakness of superscalar designs.

One weakness of the superpipelined approach is that it is not easily extended beyond two instructions per clock cycle. According to research results quoted by MIPS, issuing four instructions per clock cycle (as some superscalar implementations may be able to do) instead of two produces a performance gain of only 6 to 18%. Furthermore, the more complex logic required by superscalar designs will limit their clock rates. The tradeoffs are complex, and it is very difficult to judge each design on paper. By the end of this year, benchmark data on the R4000 and two or three superscalar SPARC implementations should be available, and a real-world comparison will be possible.

MIPS's decision to implement a 64-bit extension to the architecture in the R4000 delayed the design by an estimated four to six months, and added 5 to 10% to the chip area. MIPS feels that the cost was well justified as an investment in the future. Few systems need 64-bit processors today, but when the need arises, MIPS will be there. It may also provide MIPS with a key competitive advantage for large-system customers. Sun is known to be developing a 64-bit version of SPARC, but it will not comment on the time frame for its introduction. The SPARC chips due out in late 1991 are not expected to implement the 64-bit architecture, however.

MIPS has designed the R4000 to provide a technology base upon which it can build for the better part of a decade. As semiconductor technology advances, simple changes such as increasing the size of the on-chip caches will boost the chip's performance. MIPS has tackled the hard issues, such as extending the architecture to 64 bits, up front, so a major redesign should not be needed for several years. The future planning in the R4000 is also evident in the secondary cache and bus interfaces, both of which are designed with programmable options to allow them to operate at a fraction of the processor's clock rate as clock frequencies rise.

IV

Motorola 88000

19

Motorola 88000 RISC Chip Set

Michael Slater

Motorola has formally introduced the first members of the 88000 RISC processor family: the 88100 processor and the 88200 cache and memory management unit (CMMU). Simultaneously with Motorola's announcement, 13 hardware vendors announced plans to use the chips and 21 software vendors announced plans to provide support software. The 88000 chip set provides the highest level of integration of any RISC processor, and claims performance near the high end of the range claimed by other RISC processors.

Motorola's announcement should silence most claims that RISC technology does not have any real performance advantages over CISC technology. If Motorola thought they could get the same level of performance from the 68000 architecture, they would not have introduced a new architecture with all of its attendant marketing and support problems. While Motorola remains committed to the evolution of the 68000 family, the message is clear—for the highest performance, you must switch architectures.

The 88100 CPU includes on-chip floating point with a claimed performance of 14 to 17 VAX MIPS and up to 7 million floating-point operations per second (MFLOPS). The processor is divided into five independent execution units: the data unit, the instruction unit, the integer unit, the floating-point adder, and the floating-point multiplier. Each is pipelined, and all can execute concurrently. All units are connected to the 32-word register file via internal operand buses. Register scoreboarding logic provides the necessary coordination to manage the concurrency and ensure

159

that no instruction can be executed before the data it requires is valid. The companion 88200 CMMU chip provides memory management logic and 16 Kbytes of fast cache RAM with sophisticated cache control logic.

The 88100 is quite a pure RISC architecture, with only 51 instructions and all instructions occupying a single 32-bit word. There is no microcode. Unlike the MIPS architecture with its roots at Stanford and the SPARC architecture with its Berkeley origin, Motorola traces the genesis of its designs to Seymour Cray. Cray has long advocated inclusion of floating point as part of the basic instruction set, and used register scoreboarding in the CDC 6600.

High Integration and High Performance

Motorola is a latecomer to the RISC processor game. There are already too many architectures for the market to support, and there will likely be only two or three big winners.

For pure performance, Motorola is in the top few. AMD claims about the same level of performance for their 29000, and MIPS claims 20 MIPS for their latest R3000. SPARC is currently a little behind, but will soon catch up. While it is not clear which architecture will be the performance leader, it is evident that they are all in the same ball park. Intel's 80960 is not yet in the same performance league, although if Intel meets their promised schedule of improvements it may catch up.

Motorola's key advantage is the level of integration that they have achieved. Neither MIPS, SPARC, nor AMD have processors with on-chip floating point announced or expected soon. SPARC does not even have an MMU chip, and requires multiple chips for floating point support. And no other vendor has a cache chip with all the RAM on-chip. AMD and SPARC do not yet provide any cache support at all; MIPS provides cache control on the processor but requires external memory chips and glue logic.

Motorola was able to build such complete cache chips because of the range of technologies available to them. Most other vendors do not have sufficient static RAM technology in-house to match Motorola's accomplishment. Motorola also has a marketing edge because there is no question that they have the resources and staying power to support this architecture in the long term.

Scoreboarding Manages Concurrency

The 88000 architecture allows multiple instructions to execute concurrently. Register scoreboarding ensures that an instruction does not use data that is not yet valid. When an instruction that will modify a given register begins execution, the scoreboard bit associated with that register is set, indicating that the contents of the register are not valid. If another instruction attempts to make use of that register's contents before the scoreboard bit is cleared, that instruction will be stalled. When the scoreboard bit is cleared by the completion of the first instruction, the stalled instruction will be continued.

Use of register scoreboarding guarantees that "stale" data will never be used. The MIPS architecture does not provide such a guarantee in hardware, but depends on the compiler to schedule the instructions to avoid data dependencies. This approach simplifies the silicon, but places great dependence on the compiler and requires that all instructions be stalled any time there is a delay in a memory access. Note that scoreboarding does not prevent the compiler from optimizing performance by rearranging instructions; indeed, it should be the goal of the compiler to keep the scoreboarding logic from ever causing a stall. When this is not possible, however, the scoreboarding logic will automatically stall only the affected instruction(s). This eliminates the need to pad the instruction stream with no-ops, and also ensures that existing code will run reliably on all future versions of the processor, even if the pipelining is modified or load-and-store times are changed.

Floating Point a First-Class Citizen

While on-chip floating point has been implemented in other processors, such as Intel's 80960, Intergraph's Clipper, and INMOS's T800, the 88100 is the highest-performance processor to do so. The SPARC processors use external floating-point coprocessors, and require a gate array to provide the interface between the coprocessor and the main processor. MIPS and AMD both provide their own floating-point coprocessor chips for their RISC processors. Having the floating-point unti on-chip eliminates the coprocessor communication overhead, provides significantly higher performance, and reduces system complexity.

The floating-point units are fully pipelined and are capable of initiating a new single-precision operation every clock cycle. Mixed-mode floating-point operations eliminate the need for size conversion instructions.

The CMMU

The 88200 CMMU combines 16 Kbytes of on-chip static RAM with 4-way set associative cache control logic and memory management logic. While the 88100 can be used without the CMMU chips, it is optimized to work with a minimum of two of them—one for data and one for instructions. Up to eight 88200s (four for data and four for instructions) can be used with a single 88100, for a total of up to 128 Kbytes of cache. No additional logic is required for paralleling of CMMUs. In addition to increasing cache size, adding CMMUs increases the size of the address translation cache; each CMMU chip provides a 56-entry page address translation cache and a 10-entry block address translation cache.

System Architecture

Figure 1 shows the basic three-chip configuration. The three internal buses allow the transfer of two source operands and a destination operand in each clock cycle. The register file has three ports to support this concurrent access. The 88000's multiple independent pipelines boost performance. Because the data and instruction units have their own pipelines, other pipelined units continue to advance even when a cache miss occurs.

The P-bus provides the interface between the CMMUs and the processor chip. A full Harvard architecture is implemented, with separate 32-bit address and data buses for data and for instructions. While this consumes a large number of pins (there are 180 altogether), it provides the highest possible performance by eliminating conflicts between instruction fetching and data transfers. Because the 88100 does not have any on-chip cache, its instruction bus must be able to provide an uninterrupted instruction stream. Since the P-bus can transfer a 32-bit word every clock cycle, its maximum transfer rate with a 20-MHz clock is 80 Mbytes per second on each of the instruction and data buses.

The M-bus links the CMMUs to the main memory system. Both the P-bus and the M-bus are synchronous. The M-bus uses multiplexed address and data to minimize the number of signals needed. Since an M-bus access occurs only if there is a cache miss, the relatively slow speed of the M-bus does not significantly reduce system performance.

The M-bus is a multimaster bus. This allows multiple 88100/88200 chip sets, or multiple 88200s connected to a single 88100, to connect directly to the same M-bus. Most system designs are expected to use a common M-bus and common main memory for instructions and data, but it is possible to keep the data and instruction M-buses separate, providing a Harvard architecture for the main memory system as well as for the CMMUs.

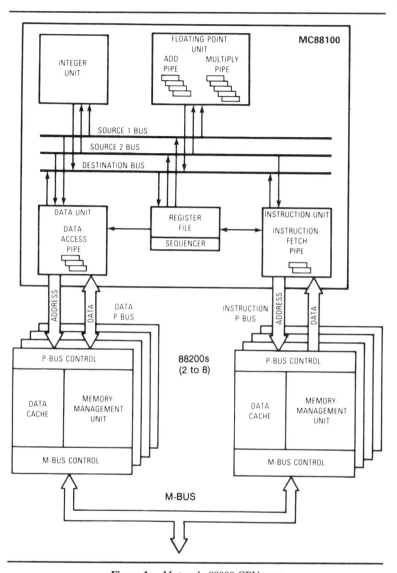

Figure 1. Motorola 88000 CPU core

Instruction Set

The 88000 has only a single set of 32 registers, which is used for integers, floating-point values, and addresses. According to Roger Ross, manager of the 88000 development team, adding more registers is not only unnecessary with a good optimizing compiler, but makes it more difficult to speed up the processor because of the increased capacitive loading on the internal buses. Ross called register windowing "an accommodation to mediocre compiler writing."

There are many control and status registers in the 88100. Only two are accessible in user mode: the floating-point status and control registers. Other registers are accessible only in supervisor mode, and are intended for operating system use only.

Table 1 shows the instruction set. All integer instructions except loads, multiply, and divide execute in a single clock cycle. Integer multiplication and division are in fact performed by the floating-point units. Because the floating-point units are fully pipelined, integer and single-precision floating-point multiplications can be initiated each cycle.

All instructions use a three-operand format. Memory addressing modes supported are register indirect with 16-bit unsigned immediate offset, register indirect with index, and register indirect with scaled index. These addressing modes eliminate the need for multiple-instruction sequences for accessing data on the stack, arrays, and other structures, as are required on processors such as the SPARC. Data types supported are shown in Table 2. In a concession to the Intel/DEC style of byte ordering, the 88000 supports both little-endian and big-endian ordering (least-significant or most-significant byte first); the order is selected by a control flag in the processor status register.

The bit-field instructions are useful for bit-mapped graphics processing, and are also designed to support efficient decoding of other processor's instruction sets for emulation. The Exchange Register with Memory instruction provides an indivisible read-write operation to support semaphores in multiprocessor systems.

Like other RISC processors, the 88000 uses delayed branches. Rather than always executing the instruction following the branch, as do most other RISC processors, the 88000 has a bit in each branch instruction that indicates whether or not the instruction following the branch should be executed before the branch is taken. The compiler can thus simply set this bit, rather than inserting a no-op, if it is unable to fill the branch delay slot with a useful instruction. This feature, when combined with register scoreboarding, completely eliminates the need for no-ops to control pipeline scheduling, and helps minimize code size.

Table 1. Instruction Set Summary for 88100

Integer Arithmetic Instructions	Logical Instructions	Flow Control Instructions
Add	AND	Unconditional Branch
Add Unsigned	OR	Unconditional Jump
Subtract	Exclusive-OR	Conditional Branch
Subtract Unsigned	Logical Mask Immediate	Branch on Bit Clear
Compare		Branch on Bit Set
Divide	**Bit-Field Instructions**	Branch to Subroutine
Divide Unsigned	Clear Bit Field	Jump to Subroutine
Multiply	Set Bit Field	Return from Exception
	Extract Signed Bit Field	Trap on Bit Clear
Floating-Point Arithmetic Instructions	Extract Unsigned Bit Field	Trap on Bit Set
Floating-Point Add	Find First Bit Clear	Trap on Bounds Check
Floating-Point Compare	Find First Bit Set	Conditional Trap
Floating-Point Divide	Make Bit Field	
Floating-Point Multiply	Rotate Register	
Floating-Point Subtract		
Convert Integer to Floating-Point	**Load/Store/Exchange Instructions**	
Round Floating-Point to Integer	Load Register from Memory	
Round Floating-Point to Nearest Integer	Store Register to Memory	
Truncate Floating-Point to Integer	Exchange Register with Memory	
Load from Floating-Point Control Register	Load Address	
Store to Floating-Point Control Register	Load from Control Register	
Exchange Floating-Point Control Register	Store to Control Register	
	Exchange Control Register	

All integer instructions except multiply, divide, and load execute in a single clock cycle. Integer multiply and divide are executed in the floating-point unit and require four and 37 clocks, respectively. Single-precision floating-point adds take five clocks, and multiplies take six clocks; because of the fully pipelined design, an add or a multiply can be initiated on every clock cycle and will complete five or six clocks later.

Table 2.   Data Types Supported by 88100

Bit Fields	Signed and Unsigned, 1–32 bits
Integer	Signed and Unsigned Bytes
	Signed and Unsigned Half-Words
	Signed and Unsigned Words (32 bits)
Floating Point	Single Precision (32 bits)
	Double Precision (64 bits)

Extensibility

The 88100 processor is designed to allow additional functional units to be added; Motorola calls these Special Function Units, or SFUs. The instruction encoding reserves 256 opcodes each for up to eight SFUs. This will make it possible for future versions to extend the instruction set while maintaining full compatibility with the existing instruction set, and without requiring escape sequences that would be antithetical to the single-cycle RISC approach.

The 88100 and 88200 were designed with the GDT silicon compilation tools from Silicon Compiler Systems Corp. This technology makes it relatively easy to modify the designs; changes such as modifying the cache size are trivial. Motorola could, for example, produce a less expensive version with smaller caches, or make a version with larger caches as they move to denser fabrication technologies.

Motorola will provide large customers with all the design tools needed for them to develop their own versions of the processor with added SFUs. One such project, which Motorola will not identify, is already underway. It is also possible to remove any of the existing function units, such as the floating point unit. Apple is rumored to be working with Motorola to develop a customized version of the 88000 with a proprietary instruction set. This would erect a major technical barrier to another vendor making a system compatible with Apple's, even if the legal barriers were surmounted.

Multiprocessor Support

The CMMUs are designed to support multiprocessor systems with no additional logic. The CMMU includes "snooping" logic to monitor all data transfers on the M-bus. This allows the CMMU to invalidate cache entries that have been modified in main memory, ensuring cache coherency.

Because the typical traffic on the M-bus is infrequent as compared to P-bus traffic, it is possible to connect a number of processors in parallel without running out of bus bandwidth. The highly integrated 3-chip set makes it possible to build multiprocessor systems with a remarkably small number of chips, and each processor is provided with its own substantial cache. Building multiprocessor systems with other processors is far more complex and requires much more board space; each processor requires a number of SRAMs for cache memory, separate cache tag RAMs, and cache control logic, plus additional logic to implement a multimaster bus interface and snooping logic. Because of the complexity involved, such multichip implementations generally do not use a 4-way set associative cache structure but instead use the simpler direct-mapped approach, which can make the cache significantly less effective.

Fault Detection

The CMMU and the processor chips can operate in a checker mode, in which they monitor all inputs but do not drive any output pins. By connecting two chip sets in parallel, with one set in checker mode, full redundancy is provided. The checker chip compares the state to which it would have driven its output pins with the state that it senses on the output pins, which are driven by the master chip. If the checker detects a mismatch between its idea of what the output signals should be and the detected signals, it asserts an error halt signal. (As a side benefit, this same logic also allows a single CPU to detect if a bus conflict is preventing it from properly driving the bus.)

Note that this scheme does not provide any way to know whether the master or the checker failed; both must be disqualified. Another chip set pair can then take over. Thus, a "duplex pair" fault-tolerant system requires four chip sets (two master-checker pairs).

HYPERmodules

In addition to individual chips, Motorola will produce modules containing one to four processors and two to eight CMMUs. Master-checker configurations will be available as well. Called "HYPERmodules," the modules use special surface-mount packages, which are smaller than the standard pin-grid arrays, on a copper-core substrate. All modules will be the same size (8.5″ × 3.4″) and use the same connectors for the M-bus interface, making it trivial to upgrade a system by switching to a module with more CMMUs and/or more processors.

Third-Party Support

Motorola went to great lengths to demonstrate that the 88000 has a wide base of support. The press information included a bundle of releases from third-party "adopters," both hardware and software vendors. Table 3 shows the language support. Rather than relying on any single compiler vendor, Motorola is encouraging multiple vendors to provide 88000 support. (This is a prudent move, considering Motorola's poor reputation for development tools.) Motorola will resell the Green Hills compilers. Uni-Soft is working with Motorola on the UNIX port. Real-time operating systems will be available from Software Components Group (pSOS) and JMI Software Consultants (JMI C Executive). Both Informix and Relational Technology plan to port their database engines to the 88000.

Both Tektronix's NuBus add-in card (Figure 2) and Motorola's Platform-88 development system are already available in limited quantity. Tadpole's VME card is also available—but does not include the currently

Table 3. Language Support Products for the 88000

Company	Languages Supported
Green Hills (818) 246-5555	C, Fortran, Pascal
Oasys (617) 890-7889	C, C + +, Fortran, Pascal
DIAB Systems (415) 571-1700	C
Tadpole Technology (415) 828-7676	C
Absoft (313) 853-0050	Fortran
Micro Focus (415) 856-4161	COBOL
Incremental Systems (412) 621-8888	Ada
aitech (408) 720-9400	Ada
Telesoft (619) 457-2700	Ada
NKR Research (408) 249-2612	BASIC compiler and interpreter
Franz Inc. (415) 548-3600	Common LISP
Applied Logic Systems (315) 471-3900	Prolog

Note that most of these products are cross-development products and are hosted in a variety of environments.

Figure 2. The Tektronix TL88K-P 88000 add-in board for the Mac II, which includes one 88100, three 88200s (one for data and two for instructions), and 8 Mbytes of dynamic RAM

scarce 88000 chips. Prices are steep but will surely drop dramatically as production ramps up and, hopefully, memory prices drop.

Motorola and a group of 88000 supporters have formed the "88open Consortium Limited" to coordinate software standards, recruit third-party applications and software, and organize joint development and marketing efforts.

Software Emulation

The 88000 instruction set was designed to provide efficient emulation of other instruction sets. Motorola claims that it will be able to emulate 386 code faster than a 386, presumably at an equal clock rate. Both Phoenix Technologies and Insignia Solutions plan to port their current DOS emulation products, now hosted on 68000-family processors, to the 88000. Motorola is working on a 68000 emulator, but has not disclosed any details. As you might imagine, they are more interested in emulating the 386 than the 68020. (Note that the only major body of 68000-specific assembly-language software is for the Macintosh. Macintosh application programs require the Mac operating system to execute, and the operating system is impossible to emulate without incurring Apple's legal wrath.)

A Bright Future

The 88000 architecture seems to have a very bright future. Faster versions of the existing chip set are sure to come, as the design is moved first to 1.2-micron and then over time to submicron processes. With submicron technology, it will be possible to combine the processor and CMMUs on a single chip.

Recent Developments

Since this introduction to the 88000 architecture was written, a pact between Apple and IBM to standardize future architectures on derivatives of IBM's RS/6000 architecture has dashed hopes that the 88000 might find sockets in Apple personal computers and workstations. Motorola was included in the pact, to work jointly with IBM to develop three different price/performance versions of an RS/6000-based architecture called the "PowerPC." Motorola and IBM will have rights to make the chips, with Motorola having the right to sell them to the merchant market.

Lack of a major customer will starve the 88000 family of the funds needed to stay competitive with general-purpose architectures like SPARC and MIPS. If the 88000 survives at all, it is likely to be used as the core for future embedded processors.

Although the IBM–Apple partnership has suddenly dimmed the prospect of future investment in the 88000 family, there is an unreleased next-generation product at an advanced stage in the design pipeline. Motorola has shown die photos of the 88110, the 1.3-million transistor successor to the 88000. It is a superscalar design with on-chip instruction and data caches of 8K each. On-chip floating-point is included, along with support for graphics operations similar to the support provided on Intel's i860. Motorola hasn't quoted pricing or availability for this part.

20

Motorola 88200

Michael Slater

In the preceding chapter we described Motorola's 88000 chip set, with emphasis on the 88100 processor. This chapter covers the second part of the 88000 chip set—the 88200 cache and memory management unit.

RISC microprocessors are very demanding of their memory systems. It's not much use being able to execute one instruction per clock cycle if the memory system can't supply one instruction per clock cycle.

One of the strengths of Motorola's 88000 design is that the 88200 CMMU chips provide a highly integrated cache memory solution. Although the 88100 can be used without the 88200, most 88000 systems will include at least two 88200s—one for instructions and one for data. Up to four 88200s can be paralleled to increase the size of the cache and address translation buffers.

The 88200s connect to the 88100 CPU via the nonmultiplexed P-bus, and to the memory system via the multiplexed M-bus. There are separate P-buses for instructions and data. Most systems use a common M-bus and common main memory, but it is possible to keep them separate.

Memory Management

The 88200 includes two address translation caches, called the block address translation cache (BATC) and the page address translation cache (PATC). (Address translation caches are often called translation look-aside buffers, or TLBs.) The PATC holds a subset of the full address translation table that is stored in main memory. This tree-structured translation table consists of a segment table containing up to 1024 segment pointers, each of which selects a 1024-entry page table. (Actually, there are two of these trees—one for supervisor accesses, and one for user accesses.) Each segment is 4-Mbytes, and each page is 4-Kbytes.

The operating system must maintain this table in main memory; the CMMU chips automatically fetch entries from memory as needed. No software intervention is required when there is a PATC miss; the CMMU hardware automatically searches the table in main memory and loads the required descriptor. Once an entry has been fetched by the CMMU once, it remains in the address translation cache until the cache is full; then, the next time another table entry is needed, the oldest entry in the translation cache is discarded.

The BATC has 10 entries, and maps blocks of 512 Kbytes. The PATC has 56 entries, each of which maps a 4-Kbyte page. Both translation caches are fully associative. The BATC is intended for use by the operating system and other programs using large contiguous areas of memory.

Without the BATC, large programs would require many PATC entries. The small page size of the PATC supports demand-paged operating systems. The BATC must be explicitly set up by the system software; unlike the PATC, the BATC entries are not automatically fetched from a table in main memory. This keeps them from being flushed due to paging activity.

In addition to specifying the physical address, each page descriptor includes protection and control information. Descriptor flags can be set on a block, segment, or page level to mark an area as cacheable or not, global (shared) or nonsharable, and write-through or copy-back. "Used" and "modified" flags are maintained for each page to support demand-paged virtual memory.

Data/Instruction Cache

The data/instruction cache is the largest available on a single chip—16 Kbytes. Figure 1 shows the block diagram of the 88200. The cache is 4-way set-associative, so most thrashing problems are eliminated. When multiple CMMU chips are used in parallel, they effectively increase the associativity of the cache; two chips in parallel act as an 8-way set-associative cache. Note that adding CMMUs increases the size of the PATC and BATC as well as the data/instruction cache.

Each cache line includes a "disable" bit that allows the self-test software to turn off any cache line that shows errors. Motorola could increase their yield by selling less-expensive versions in which not all cache lines are guaranteed to work. Since RAM cells rarely go bad once they have

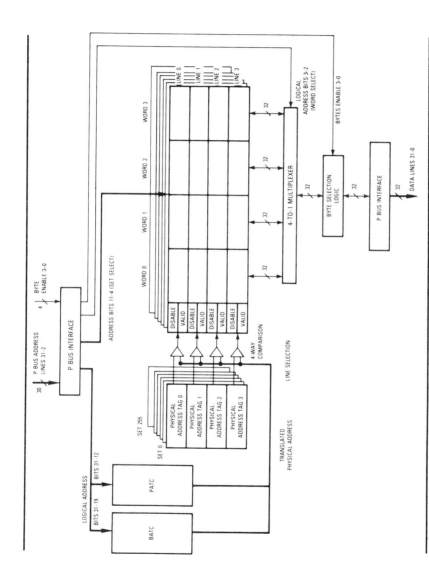

Figure 1. Motorola's 88200 cache and memory management unit provides 16 Kbytes of data or instruction cache, a 56-entry page translation cache, and a 10-entry block address translation cache.

passed manufacturing testing, it's not clear that the disable bits are otherwise of much use.

The MMU is overlapped with the cache access to provide zero-wait-state performance even though it is a physical, rather than a virtual, cache. Since the MMU's page size is 4K, the least-significant 12 bits of the address are not translated, and thus are not delayed by the MMU. Eight of these bits (A4–A11) select one of 256 cache sets at the same time that the MMU is translating the upper bits. When the MMU translation is complete, the translated address is compared with the address tags of the four lines in the set. If any of the four match, then there is a cache hit. Address bits A2 and A3 then select one of the four words in the line, and the four byte enable signals from the CPU (which eliminate the need for A0 and A1) enable the appropriate bytes.

When a read miss occurs, the entire cache line is filled. The CMMU uses a 4-word block transfer on the M-bus to get the data from main memory. The transfer itself takes a minimum of five clock cycles, one for the address cycle and four to transfer the data. Another three clock cycles are used in the CMMU, so the minimum delay on a miss is eight clock cycles. With real-world DRAMs, this delay is extended to at least 10 clock cycles. Because the access is a four-word burst, page-mode and nibble-mode access techniques can be used.

One shortcut taken in the 88200 design is that the P-bus access is not satisfied until the entire line is filled. A more sophisticated approach is to fill the needed word first, and immediately pass it along to the CPU; the cache controller can then fill the remainder of the line.

Snooping Ensures Coherency

Either a write-through or copy-back memory update approach can be used, and is selected by a control bit in the page descriptor. Copy-back provides higher performance for multiprocessor systems, but requires read snooping to guarantee cache coherency. The 88200 includes the snooping logic.

Even when copy-back is selected, the first write to a cached location is written through. This updates the main memory and invalidates any other copies of the data that may be present in other caches. Successive writes to that memory location are then not written through to memory. When the cache line (or the entire cache) is flushed, it is written back to main memory if it is "dirty"—that is, if it has been modified since it was last written to main memory.

One of the page and segment descriptor control bits indicates whether or not that page or segment is global, meaning that it can be shared among processors. This information is output on the M-bus during each access. All CMMUs monitor the M-bus, and any access to a global location causes the snooping logic to be activated. The address is compared to the cache tags to see if the addressed memory location is present in the cache and if it has been modified. If so, the cache chip asserts the M-bus reply code signals to abort the transaction.

The cache chip that made the original request must give up the bus and wait at least one clock cycle before re-requesting it. During this one-clock delay, the cache that detected the snooping hit takes control of the M-bus and updates the main memory. When it releases the M-bus, the requesting cache retries its read cycle, and gets the updated data from main memory.

Another approach is for the cache to provide the data directly to the requesting device, rather than aborting the cycle and requiring that the requestor retry the access after main memory has been updated. This has slightly higher performance but is more complex to implement, and it is not implemented in the 88200.

Because the snooping logic requires access to the cache tags whenever an M-bus access to a global location occurs, normal operation of the cache is affected. If a P-bus request occurs while the snooping logic is checking the tags, a wait state is generated. This causes some drop in performance in multiprocessor systems if there are many M-bus accesses to global memory locations. Eliminating this problem requires a duplicate set of tag bits for the snooping logic, and Motorola's designers felt that the silicon area required was not justified. The CMMU provides additional tag state outputs to allow an external set of tags to be maintained, so high-performance multiprocessor systems can implement snooping externally to the CMMU and eliminate this performance degradation.

Snooping is generally disabled on the instruction cache, since programs should not be modified while they are executing.

If the cache chip's snooping detects an M-bus write to a cached location, it invalidates that cache line. The other aspects of the cache coherency protocol guarantee that the invalidated data is merely a copy of data in main memory.

Because the 88000 provides such a complete set of functions in only three chips, it is sure to be popular for multiprocessor system designs. In the next generation, even more sophisticated protocols are likely to be implemented.

V

Intel 860

21

Intel i860 Performance

Brian Case

The i860 microprocessor, known previously to the rumor mill as the N10, is a significant technological achievement. It is the first single-chip microprocessor to integrate relatively large instruction and data caches, a TLB-based memory management unit, a pipelined RISC integer unit, high-performance, pipelined floating-point units, and a 3-D graphics unit. The "N" in "N10" presumably stands for "numerics," and there is a heavy emphasis on floating-point performance.

Despite the fact that the ISSCC paper that first revealed the architecture mentioned only a 50-MHz version, the chip initially will be available at 33.3 MHz, with a 40-MHz version due later.

The i860 is capable of impressive peak performance because of its highly parallel architecture. Under the right circumstances, the integer core and the two floating-point units can each generate a new result every cycle. Thus, at 40 MHz, the i860 can execute bursts at 40 native integer MIPS and 80 single-precision MFLOPS. in addition, the chip has a special graphics hardware unit, which has instructions that speed up hidden-surface elimination and smooth-shading algorithms for 3-D graphics.

Architecture Overview

The i860 contains two semi-independent processing units, each with its own set of thirty-two 32-bit registers. One of the units handles integer operations, and the other handles floating-point and graphics instructions.

The two units work together in a number of modes, some of which are quite unusual.

In the most conventional mode, a program consists of a series of integer, floating-point, and graphics instructions, each 32 bits wide, intermixed as necessary. Each instruction is fetched and decoded in sequence, and executed by the corresponding section of the chip. Integer instructions operate as in a conventional RISC design, with a four-stage pipeline.

Floating-point (FP) operations are less straightforward. Most come in what Intel calls *scalar* and *pipelined* flavors. The so-called scalar instructions are the traditional instructions as present in all microprocessors. The pipelined instructions are designed for vector calculations and are more complex to use.

There are separate execution pipelines for FP addition/subtraction, FP multiplication, and graphics operations. Scalar instructions must operate in sequence; i.e., within each pipeline, the previous scalar instruction must complete before the next may begin. Each takes from two to four clocks, after which its result is stored in the designated result register.

When a pipelined instruction is fetched, the designated operation and operands are dispatched to the start of the appropriate pipeline, previous pipelined operations are advanced one stage, and the result in the final stage is written to the result register designated by the current (not the original) instruction. Thus, in the three-stage adder pipeline, for example, three successive FP adds must be issued before the result of the first can be saved, and each must designate where to store the result of one of its predecessors.

There is also a collection of dual-operation pipelined instructions, in which a single 32-bit instruction code issues operations simultaneously to both the addition and multiplication pipelines. Finally, there is a special dual-instruction mode in which a 64-bit instruction pair (one integer instruction and one pipelined FP instruction) are fetched from the instruction cache, decoded, and executed in parallel. The FP half can designate one of the pipelined multiply/accumulate combinations, in which case the chip achieves its peak performance figure of one integer plus two FP operations per clock.

System Facilities

The i860 has a rich set of on-chip system facilities including caches, a memory management unit, and a complex bus control unit. Figure 1 shows an overall block diagram of the chip, and Figure 2 shows a die of the i860. The pipelined 64-bit instruction/data bus allows up to three outstanding transactions. There is a 4-Kbyte on-chip instruction cache and an 8-Kbyte

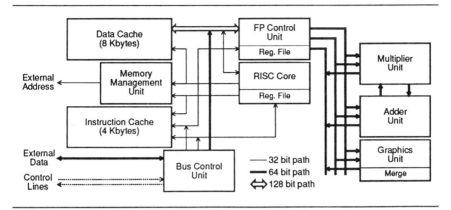

Figure 1. i860 block diagram

on-chip data cache. Both caches use 32-byte blocks. The data cache can transfer up to 128 bits in a single cycle to or from the floating-point register file. Both caches are two-way set-associative, and the data cache uses a write-back memory update approach.

The memory management unit is based on a 64-entry, four-way set-associative translation look-aside buffer (TLB). Unlike the 286 and 386, access protection is based only on user and supervisor modes. Page size is fixed at 4 Kbytes. TLB reloading is implemented in hardware, so the two-level page-table layout is fixed. The MMU implements virtual memory that is completely compatible with the 386, except that segments are not supported. The 386 compatibility allows the i860 to directly access shared memory, while using the same address translations and access protection as the 386. Intel justifies the lack of support for segments by pointing out that the i860 is designed primarily for Unix, which does not use the segmentation capability of the 386.

The on-chip caches are virtually-addressed. This takes the delay of the MMU out of the cache-access critical path. However, it means that the caches must be flushed when a process context switch occurs. Instruction cache flushing is tied to TLB flushing; both are performed when a certain bit is set in the on-chip page-table base register. Data cache flushing is performed by a software loop, which flushes one 32-byte line per iteration. This potentially time-consuming operation could significantly increase context-switching time. In addition, no traps or interrupts are allowed during data cache flushing. When there are many dirty lines, interrupt latency will be very long.

The external buses consist of a 29-bit address bus, a 64-bit data/instruction bus, 8 byte-enable control lines, and miscellaneous control

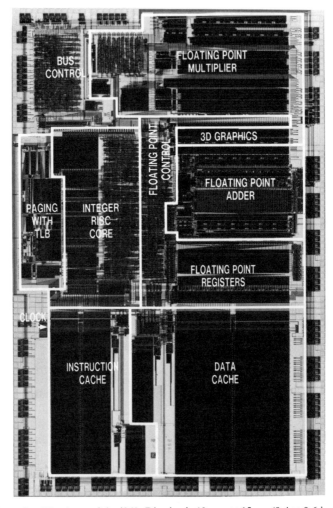

Figure 2. Die photo of the i860. Die size is 10 mm × 15mm (0.4 × 0.6 inch).

signals. (Note that byte addresses are a full 32 bits, but since the external bus is 8 bytes wide, the three least-significant bits are not needed.) Up to three outstanding transactions can be in progress at one time.

The "next near" (NENE) control line allows the i860 to take advantage of static-column and page-mode DRAMs. Based on the "DRAM page size" field in a control register, the i860 compares the current transaction address with the previous transaction address. If the current address is within the same DRAM page as the previous address, the NENE pin is asserted. In this case, a much faster DRAM memory access is possible. This signal eliminates the need for external page comparators, and may provide more time for memory access by eliminating the comparator delay.

When the microprocessor is reset, the state of the interrupt input pin is sampled. If it is high, the chip emerges from reset in "eight-bit code-size mode." In this mode, instruction cache misses are processed as a series of byte reads instead of 64-bit reads. (Three of the byte enable lines act as regular, encoded address lines in this mode.) Thus, bootstrapping from a single byte-wide EPROM is possible. Even in this mode, data transactions are still processed as 64-bit reads and writes. This mode is exited by clearing a bit in a control register.

The i860 has limited support for multiprocessing applications. Data caching can be disabled by a TLB bit on a page-by-page basis, and the external memory system can disable data caching on an access-by-access basis. There is a "lock" output signal, which tells the external memory system that it must guarantee the i860 exclusive access to memory. The lock and unlock instructions are used to bracket critical sections of code. There is no snooping or write-through option, so shared data cannot be cached.

To support software debuggers, a data breakpoint register allows a breakpoint to be produced on a read or a write to a selected address.

Integer Core Instruction Set

The "RISC Core," as Intel refers to the basic integer and system-control instruction set, is extremely simple; in fact, at least a few things found in most other RISC instruciton sets are not present in the i860.

Table 1 shows the i860 instruction set, which consists of core instructions and FP instructions. In the RISC tradition, arithmetic and logical operations use a three-address form, allowing two operands and a destination to be specified.

Like the MIPS R2000/R3000 and the Motorola 88000, the i860 has a flat, 32-word register file, with R0 as a fixed constant "zero." There are no "move" instructions; a register-to-register move is performed by using, for example, an "OR" with R0, with the result directed to the desired destination. Only load and store instructions access memory. A single addressing mode permits four useful variants: *offset+register, register+register, register,* and *offset.* This addressing mode is essentially the same as that offered by most RISC machines, and is considerably simpler than that of Intel's other "RISC" machine, the 80960. In a real departure for Intel, the i860 has an "endian" mode bit, like the 29000 and

Table 1. i860 Instruction Set

Core Unit	
Load and Store Instructions	
ld.x	Load integer
st.x	Store integer
fld.y	F-P load
pfld.z	Pipelined F-P load
fst.y	F-P store
pst.d	Pixel store
Register to Register Moves	
ixfr	Transfer integer to F-P reg
fxfr	Transfer F-P to integer reg
Integer Arithmetic Instructions	
addu	Add unsigned
adds	Add signed
subu	Subtract unsigned
subs	Subtract signed
Shift Instructions	
shl	Shift left
shr	Shift right
shra	Shift right arithmetic
shrd	Shift right double
Logical Instructions	
and	Logical AND
andh	Logical AND high
andnot	Logical AND NOT
andnoth	Logical AND NOT high
or	Logical OR
orh	Logical OR high
xor	Logical XOR
xorh	Logical XOR high
Control-Transfer Instructions	
trap	Software trap
intovr	Software trap on integer overflow
br	Branch direct
bri	Branch indirect
bc	Branch on CC
bc.t	Branch on CC taken
bnc	Branch on not CC
bnc.t	Branch on not CC taken
bte	Branch if equal
btne	Branch if not equal
bla	Branch on LCC and add
call	Subroutine call
calli	Indirect subroutine call
System Control Instructions	
flush	Cache flush
ld.c	Load from control register
st.c	Store to control register
lock	Begin interlocked sequence
unlock	End interlocked sequence

Floating-Point Unit	
F-P Multiplier Instructions	
fmul.p	F-P multiply
pfmul.p	Pipelined F-P multiply
pfmul3.dd	3-Stage pipelined F-P multiply
fmlow.p	F-P multiply low
frcp.p	F-P reciprocal
frsqr.p	F-P reciprocal square root
F-P Adder Instructions	
fadd.p	F-P add
pfadd.p	Pipelined F-P add
fsub.p	F-P subtract
pfsub.p	Pipelined F-P subtract
pfgt.p	Pipelined F-P greater-than compare
pfeq.p	Pipelined F-P equal compare
fix.p	F-P to integer convert
pfix.p	Pipelined F-P to integer convert
ftrunc.p	F-P to integer truncate
pftrunc.p	Pipelined F-P to integer truncate
Dual-Operation Instructions	
pfam.p	Pipelined F-P add and multiply
pfsm.p	Pipelined F-P subtract and multiply
pfmam	Pipelined F-P multiply with add
pfmsm	Pipelined F-P multiply with subtract
Long Integer Instructions	
fisub.z	Long-integer subtract
pfisub.z	Pipelined long-integer subtract
fiadd.z	Long-integer add
pfiadd.z	Pipelined long-integer add
Graphics Instructions	
fzchks	16-bit Z-buffer check
pfzchks	pipelined 16-bit z-buffer check
fzchkl	32-bit Z-buffer check
pfzchkl	Pipelined 32-bit Z-buffer check
faddp	Add with pixel merge
pfaddp	Pipelined add with pixel merge
faddz	Add with Z merge
pfaddz	Pipelined add with Z merge
form	OR with MERGE register
pform	Pipelined OR with MERGE register

Assembler Pseudo-Operations	
mov	Integer reg-reg move
fmov.q	F-P reg-reg move
pfmov.q	Pipelined F-P reg-reg move
nop	Core no-operation
fnop	F-P no-operation
pfle.p	Pipelined F-P less-than or equal

The w, x, y, and z suffixes specify integer word size; each suffix represents a different range of options. The p suffix specifies precision for the source and result and can be ss (both single), sd (single source, double result), or dd (both double).

the R2000/R3000, which determines the ordering of bytes within larger memory words. This is Intel's first big-endian-capable processor.

The load and store instructions for the floating-point unit can specify auto-increment to facilitate efficient vector-like operations. FP loads and stores can transfer 32, 64, or 128 bits at a time between memory and the FP register file. A special pipelined FP load instruction allows FP loads to be performed while other FP operations are in progress.

The core instruction set is complete by the standards set by other RISC architectures with three exceptions: there are no add or subtract with carry instructions, no integer multiply or divide, and no compare instructions. The omission of add and subtract with carry is partially mitigated by the long-integer add and subtract instructions in the FP set, and such instructions are rarely needed by high-level languages in any case. Integer multiply is performed by the FP unit, and integer divide requires an iterative process using the FP reciprocal function.

Like traditional machines, the i860 uses condition codes for storing information about relative values. Unlike other processors, however, it has just one condition code bit. This single condition code is set only by the integer arithmetic and logical instructions and the two FP compares, pfgt.p and pfeq.p. The logical instructions set the CC bit if their result is zero and clear it otherwise.

Compare operations are performed using add and subtract instructions, with the result directed to R0. With the appropriate arithmetic instruction followed by a branch-on-CC instruction, all the usual compare-and-branch idioms can be synthesized. However, some analysis is required. This process is best automated by either a compiler or an intelligent assembler, since the way each instruction sets the CC bit is not entirely intuitive.

Sun's SPARC architecture also uses condition codes, but with the traditional four flags (zero, negative, overflow, and carry). The encodings of the arithmetic and logical instructions in the SPARC architecture have a bit that determines whether or not the condition flags will be modified by the results of the instruction. In contrast, the i860 arithmetic and logical instructions *always* modify the single CC bit. While this simplifies instruction encoding, it will cause problems for multiple-integer-instruction-per-cycle implementations of the i860 architecture.

There are several varieties of branch instructions. The simplest (bc, bnc, bte, and btne) are traditional, nondelayed branches; that is, the flow of control is changed immediately if the branch is taken. The next simplest (bla, br, bri, call, and calli) are the familiar RISC, unconditionally delayed branches in which the immediately subsequent instruction is executed whether or not the branch is taken. The "taken" branch instructions (bc.t and bnc.t) are similar to SPARC's annulled branches; these instructions execute the immediately subsequent instruction if the branch is taken and skip it otherwise. The bri instruction performs some special functions on interrupt return.

The bla instruction is a loop primitive, which performs a decrement, test, and branch in a single instruction. Its operation is based on a special condition code, which only it can set, called the LCC bit.

Like the R2000/R3000 architecture, the i860 instruction set includes compare-and-branch instructions for branch-if-equal and branch-if-not-equal. These comparisons can be performed quickly, and thus can be done as part of the branch instruction without slowing down the pipeline; less-than and greater-than comparisons cannot.

Floating-Point

Figure 3 shows the data flow around the independent FP adder and multiplier units. (There is also a separate pipeline for FP loads in the bus control unit.) Each unit has a three-stage pipeline. Adder and multiplier instructions usually execute in three clocks, but take four clocks with some data combinations. The data types, instructions, and exception handling of the FP unit support the IEEE floating-point standard. The register file can be viewed as 32 single-precision registers, 16 double-precision registers, or eight 128-bit registers.

FP division is not performed directly. Instead, the i860 contains a small ROM that approximates the reciprocal of an operand, accurate to seven bits. A software routine is then required to increase the accuracy of the mantissa to full single or double precision. Newton's algorithm doubles the number of correct bits on each iteration but is not guaranteed to be accurate in the least-significant couple of bits. A slower algorithm is required to meet IEEE specifications. FP square root is handled similarly.

Programming the FP units can be done in either scalar mode or pipelined mode. In scalar mode, an operation is started and allowed to complete before another FP operation can begin. A scalar FP instruction specifies the two source operands, its precision, and the destination for its result.

In contrast to the intuitive scalar instructions, pipelined-mode FP instructions are unusual. In pipelined mode, each instruction (which must be one of the pipeline-mode instructions, beginning with the letter ''p'') still specifies an operation, a precision, and the source operands for that operation. However, the destination specified by the instruction is the location for the result that will emerge from the pipeline when the operation specified by the instruction is started. (The precision of a result is always that of the instruction that initiated the operation.)

Thus, a pipelined FP add instruction pushes a result out of the last stage of the adder pipeline, and this result is stored in the register specified by the destination field of the FP add instruction. Similarly, a pipelined FP multi-

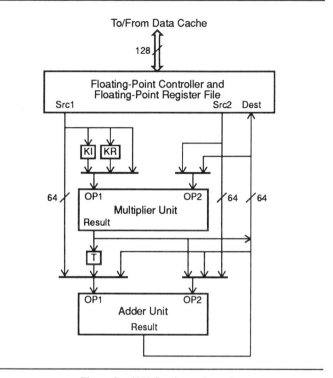

Figure 3. i860 floating-point unit

ply instruction forces a result from the last stage of the multiplier pipeline, and this result is stored in the register specified by the destination field of the FP multiply instruction.

This means that the instruction at location $i + 3$ must encode the proper destination for the result of the operation started by the instruction at location i, assuming that the pipeline latency is 3 and the instructions at $i + 1$, $i + 2$, and $i + 3$ are all pipelined FP instructions for the same unit (adder or multiplier). Pipelined add and multiply instructions can, of course, be interleaved.

The floating-point unit pipelines do not advance unless a new operation is started in that pipeline. Thus, unlike scalar FP instructions, pipelined FP instructions do not complete by themselves. This is because the pipeline does not know where to store the results that would be generated. Dummy pipelined operations (not no-ops) *must* be inserted to flush the pipes at the end of a string of pipelined operations and before a scalar operation can be performed. When adder and multiplier instructions are interleaved, one unit will be idle while an instruction is initiated in the other unit.

The i860 is the first microprocessor to expose the pipelines to this degree. Although this complicates programming, it makes possible more effective use of the register file. With the usual method of specifying the destination at the time the operation is started in the pipeline and hiding the pipeline delay from the programmer, the destination register must be reserved while the instruction is propagating through the pipeline. Using the i860's approach, a register can hold a temporary value while an instruction that will place its result in that register is proceeding through the pipeline, effectively time-sharing the register.

For single-precision operations in pipelined mode, the adder can generate a new result every clock and the multiplier can generate a new result every clock. For double-precision operations, the multiplier can generate a new result at most every other cycle.

Because the pipelines must be advanced explicitly when in pipelined mode and because scalar operations must complete before a new operation can begin, the two FP units can operate simultaneously only when the dual-operation instructions are used. Since these instructions consume more operands than the FP register file can supply, the staging registers KI, KR, and T supply some operands. KI and KR are intended to supply a constant multiplicand for a series of multiplies, and the T register is used to transfer the result from the multiplier to the adder.

The pfam.p, pfsm.p, pfmam, and pfmsm mnemonics actually stand for classes of instructions; each combination of register-file and staging-register operands has a distinct mnemonic. These dual-operation instructions facilitate common operations such as dot products, FFT computations, and graphics tranformations.

By itself, the pipelined-mode equivalent of a scalar-mode instruction requires many more instructions. Thus, pipelined mode is mainly useful for long sequences of similar floating-point operations. Short sequences are inefficient because of the overhead of getting into and out of pipelined mode.

Dual-Instruction Mode

In contrast to the implementations of most other RISC machines with floating point, in which concurrency between the floating-point and integer units is transparent and interlocked by hardware, taking full advantage of the i860 requires that concurrency be explicitly specified by the instruction stream.

In single-instruction mode, one 32-bit instruction is fetched at a time, and the instruction can be either an integer core instruction or an FP instruction. When an FP instruction with its dual-instruction mode bit set is fetched, the processor enters dual-instruction mode two instruction fetches later (not necessarily two cycles later). In dual-instruction mode (not to be confused with dual-operation instructions), instruction fetches consist of 64-bit instruction pairs. The low 32 bits are the FP instruction and the high 32 bits are the integer instruction. The integer and FP instructions are dispatched to their respective units simultaneously. Instruction pairs are fetched and dispatched in this way until an instruction pair is fetched whose FP instruction's dual-instruction mode bit is cleared. When this happens, the processor will enter single-instruction mode on the second subsequent instruction fetch. Thus, the effects of setting and clearing the dual-instruction mode bit are, roughly speaking, delayed by two instruction or instruction-pair fetches.

In light of the programming constraints of pipelined mode and dual-instruction mode, programming the i860 for maximum performance in assembly language is not for the faint of heart. However, for a compiler, exploiting dual-instruction mode should be roughly the same as exploiting delayed branches. That is, the problem is generally one of discovering independent instructions, rearranging them, and then setting the dual-instruction mode bits in the FP instructions appropriately

Note that the minimum number of adjacent FP instructions required to take advantage of dual-instruction mode is three. One FP instruction is required to turn dual mode on, one is required to turn it off, and at least one is required while dual mode is active. Thus, a sequence of three FP instructions can have, at most, one integer instruction overlapped with them. Longer sequences of FP instructions can exhibit more overlap.

Conclusion

The level of integration and performance of the i860 represents the next trend in general-purpose microprocessors. However, few microprocessors will leave the raw pipelines as exposed as they are in the i860. Fully exposing the pipelines simplifies hardware considerably but places an unusual burden on compilers and programmers. This shifting of complexity from hardware to software is, of course, one of the points of RISC. However, mainstream software may not yet be ready for such complexity. If the i860 is to realize its market potential in general-purpose applications, instead of only as an attached processor for speeding up graphics kernels or improving the floating-point performance of a host processor, Intel must provide very sophisticated program development tools.

Even so, using only the integer core instructions and the scalar FP instructions, an application will be able to realize competitive performance. Performance can then be improved by tuning the "hot spots" in an application to use pipelined-mode FP instructions and dual-instruction mode.

22

Intel i860 Graphics Unit Evaluation

Brian Case

For engineering and scientific applications, such as mechanical CAD and molecular modeling, data must be presented so that the user's innate ability to process visual information is tapped. This means generating a realistic, 3-D image rather than columns of floating-point numbers. To facilitate data visualization, the i860 microprocessor instruction set includes graphics primitives aimed at increasing the throughput of 3-D graphics rendering.

The computations needed to implement computer graphics can be partitioned into independent stages, creating a conceptual "graphics pipeline." (In high-end graphics workstations, the stages are realized by a hardware pipeline so that the stages execute concurrently.) First, the scene to be produced must be modeled and converted into a numerical representation, typically as collections of polygons. Second, the model must be transformed to the viewer's frame of reference, which involves floating-point-intensive computations, such as polygon transformation (scaling, rotation, and translation) and clipping. In this stage, the i860 graphics unit is not used, but its high-performance floating-point is valuable. Finally the mathematical description must be converted into pixel values. It is in this phase that the i860's graphics instructions come into play.

i860 Graphics Basics

The i860 graphics unit addresses two 3-D operations: hidden surface elimination and shading using intensity interpolation. The interpolation operations assume that the surfaces of solid objects are modeled as collections of polygons (typically triangles or rectangles).

The graphics instructions are implemented by the graphics unit, which is attached to the floating-point register file. This means that graphics instructions have 64-bit source and destination operands and can take full advantage of the 128-bit load and store instructions. Even though the graphics unit is attached to the FP register file, it performs only integer arithmetic.

The interpolation instructions, FADDP (pixel add) and FADDZ (z-buffer add), consider their source and destination operands as four 16-bit or two 32-bit fixed-point values. These fixed-point values correspond to pixels of different sizes:

- For 8-bit pixels, each of four values has an 8-bit integer and an 8-bit fraction.
- For 16-bit pixels, each of four values has a 6-bit integer and a 10-bit fraction.
- For 32-bit pixels, each of two values has an 8-bit integer and a 24-bit fraction.

The interpolation instructions perform the following sequence:

- Add source operands.
- Truncate each of the four 16-bit, or two 32-bit, fixed-point values to form integer values.
- Store the truncated values in the MERGE register. (The nontruncated values are stored in the destination register.)

The MERGE register is shifted right by the size of the integer value before accepting the values (see Figure 1). Since the integer values are stored in the most significant position of MERGE, it accumulates interpolated results for the three color components of multiple pixels.

The graphics instructions use the two fields in the Processor Status Register (PSR) shown in Figure 2. The Pixel Mask (PM) field is set by the z-buffer check instructions and used by the pixel values. For the pixel-add instructions, the Pixel Size (PS) field determines the partitioning of the values in source and destination operands (as four 16-bit or two 32-bit values) and the position of the binary point within those values.

z-Buffer Implementation

One aspect of image rendering in a 3-D environment is hidden-surface elimination, that is, placing pixel values in the frame buffer for only those surfaces that would be visible to the viewer if the scene being modeled

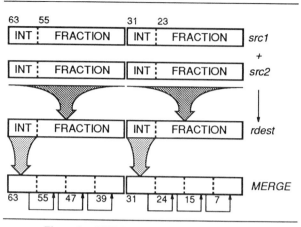

Figure 1. FADDP operation for 32-bit pixels

were physically realized. Hidden-surface elimination is essentially a sorting operation based on the z-coordinate values of objects. When multiple surfaces cover the pixel at (x,y), only the surface closest to the viewer (i.e., the surface whose z-value is smallest at that point) determines the value of the pixel in the frame buffer (x,y).

One way of rapidly eliminating hidden surfaces is with a z buffer. Like a frame buffer, which is a two-dimensional array of pixel values whose x and y dimensions match the x and y dimensions of the display device, a z buffer is simply a matrix of values (see Figure 3). The z buffer essentially shadows the frame buffer, but the value in the z buffer at (x,y) is the z coordinate value of the pixel that is currently in the frame buffer at (x,y). Thus, when a surface is to be rendered into the display's frame buffer, each pixel's z value is compared to the value currently in the z buffer. If the pixel's z value is less than the value in the z buffer, then the pixel value and z value are written into the frame and z buffer, respectively. This has the effect of sorting the image by z value.

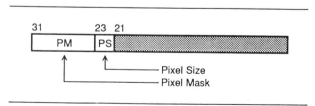

Figure 2. Graphics fields in the PSR

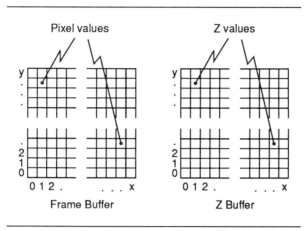

Figure 3. A Z-buffer is a shadow of the frame buffer

Implementing a z buffer requires no special hardware since it is just an array of values in main memory. (This is in contrast to the frame buffer, which is usually implemented with VRAM since the pixel values must be available on demand to refresh the display. Values in the z buffer do not affect the displayability of the pixels already in the frame buffer.) However, the z-buffer algorithm is simple and repetitive, and is therefore a candidate for hardware speed-up.

Conceptually, a pixel's z coordinate is a floating-point value since there are no constraints on the complexity of the scene being modeled. However, to permit the fastest possible z-buffer algorithm, the stored values are typically integers. To ensure reasonable dynamic range, 32-bit z-buffer values are often used; but the i860 can support 16-bit z buffers as well. An i860 graphics system could decide which to use based on scene characteristics.

Two basic introductions in the i860 permit a fast z-buffer implementation: z-buffer check and pixel store. The z-buffer check instructions perform the comparison step of the algorithm. The z-buffer checks are available for both 16-bit and 32-bit z-buffer values, and, since they are part of the floating-point unit, are available in both scalar and pipelined varieties.

For each z-buffer check instruction, two pairs of 64-bits of z values are compared at once. (The 64-bits of z may be either four 16-bit z values or two 32-bit z values.) The results of the comparisons, either two or four Boolean values (bits), are stored in the pixel-mask (PM) field of the processor status register, and the smaller of the two source operands is stored in the destination register. Before the bits are stored, the PM is shifted right by two or four bits; the stored bits go into the most significant portion of the PM. Since the PM is eight bits wide, it can buffer the results of two 16-bit or four 32-bit z-buffer check instructions.

The pixel-store instruction uses bits from the PM to determine which parts of its 64-bit source operand, in a floating-point register, to store in a 64-bit memory location. Thus, this instruction eliminates the overhead of branching around store instructions, if the pixel is not to be updated, and processes four 16-bit or two 32-bit pixels per instruction.

An i860 z-buffer algorithm consists of the following conceptual steps:

- load a z-buffer value,
- load a z value,
- compare the two values using the z-buffer check instruction,
- load a pixel value,
- store in the z buffer, and
- use the pixel-store instruction to conditionally store the pixel value in the frame buffer.

Note, however, that the z-buffer check instructions insert bits into the PM at the most-significant end, while the pixel-store instructions use bits from the least-significant end. Thus, there is some latency between the first z-buffer check instruction and the first pixel-store instruction, so the set-up code and inner loop must be written accordingly.

Of course, the i860's dual-instruction mode and pipelining can be used to achieve overlap between the integer, graphics, and cache/bus control units. According to Intel, the i860 can process two 32-bit z values every three clocks, assuming that there are no delays caused by memory. Since all the operations involved are integer in nature, it is worth comparing this performance with a generic RISC processor. A generic RISC processor would have to

- load three values,
- make a comparison,
- execute a branch,
- conditionally execute two stores,
- increment three array indices,
- compare to see if the loop is finished,
- and branch.

Thus, it could process one 32-bit pixel every 12 clocks, again assuming no memory delays. The i860 appears to be eight times faster for the inner loop of this algorithm, assuming hand-coded implementation, 32-bit z values, and no system delays. For 16-bit z values, the inner loop is an impressive 24 times faster. However, z buffering is actually a part of other algorithms, such as Gouraud shading. An eight or 24 times faster z-buffer algorithm does not necessarily translate into eight or 24 times faster pixel drawing.

Surface Shading

Rendering the image of a 3-D model, which consists of polygonal patches, on a display devise can be done at one of five basic levels:

- Wireframe: The edges of the polygons are shown.
- Constant shading: All the pixels covered by a surface have the same intensity and color.
- Gouraud shading: Assumes the surface patches are flat; the shading across a surface is determined by a linear interpolation of the intensity at the two opposite edges.
- Phong shading: Provides accurate shading for curved surface patches; the shading is computed as a function of the surface normal (vector perpendicular to the surface). The normal, instead of the shading, is interpolated across the surface.
- Ray tracing: The intensity value for each pixel is computed uniquely by following rays of "light" from the viewer back to the light source(s), through all possible reflections and refractions.

Assuming the requirement is for real-time graphics response, the computational demands of the five methods range from minimal, for wireframe, to overwhelming, for ray tracing. Real-time ray tracing of images of even modest complexity is at least several years away.

i860 Gouraud Shading

The Gouraud shading algorithm uses linear interpolation and is straightforward to implement with integer, fixed-point arithmetic. For this reason, most graphics systems use Gouraud shading. In recognition of this fact, the i860 pixel-add (FADDP) instructions support only Gouraud shading.

The operation of FADDP with PS set for 32-bit pixels is shown in Figure 1. Each execution of an FADDP performs a step of interpolation for one of the three 8-bit color components of two pixels. The side-effects (integer parts) of successive FADDPs are accumulated into MERGE, which is shifted right by eight bits before the INT portion is accumulated.

The algorithm for Gouraud shading a polygon into a raster frame buffer is much like the algorithm for drawing a line into a frame buffer. A line from $(x1,y1)$ to $(x2,y2)$ can be drawn by computing the slope of the line (i.e.,

$y2 - y1$ divided by $x2 - x1$), and then for each increment of x (one in the case of a raster display), adding the slope (one times the slope) to y. The same algorithm can be applied to each of the three color components of a pixel value: The three "slopes" are the differences between the shades of the ending and starting components divided by the number of pixels spanned in the x direction. For each increment of x, the shade of the pixel changes (but not the y-coordinate). (Monochrome shading falls out as a special case.)

Thus, a polygon is shaded in horizontal strips. A simplified C-language algorithm is shown in Figure 4. (The bias of 0.5 for R, G, and B makes the FADDP's truncation act like rounding.) For each increment of one in the x direction, three FADDP instructions are used to compute the RGB components of two pixel values. After the three FADDP instructions compute the RGB components, the accumulated pixel values are taken from the MERGE register (one in the high half and one in the low half), using the OR-with-merge-register (FORM) instruction, and placed in the frame buffer (after z-buffer checking, of course.) Thus, three FADDP instructions perform the work of the first four statements of the inner loop in the C program, but they operate on two 32-bit pixel values at once.

Not shown is the work that must be done to interpolate the z-buffer values and perform the z-buffer check. This is done in essentially the same way, but the FADDZ instruction, which has larger integer and fraction fields, is used.

The setup for the loop, as it is shown in Figure 4, includes division operations. Fortunately, the three denominators are the same. Since the i860 implements division via reciprocal-multiplication, the algorithm need compute the reciprocal only once and then perform three multiples. In addition, for small strips of pixels, the most frequent case, the precision of the division need not be great because the error cannot propagate from the fraction into the integer part (only a few FADDPs will be executed). Since only the integer part affects the pixel value, the error will not affect the display.

Analysis

The i860 graphics instructions implement the functions needed to speed up the inner loops of some parts of the final stage of a graphics pipeline. To understand their effect on the throughput of a graphic system, it is important to consider all the implications of the functions that must be performed.

The z-buffer implementation assumed by the i860 is a good match to the way existing graphics systems implement z buffering, when they do. Inte-

```
deltax = x2 - x1;
deltaR = (RED2 - RED1) / deltax;
deltaG = (GREEN2 - GREEN1) / deltax;
deltaB = (BLUE2 - BLUE1) / deltax;

R = RED1 + 0.5;
G = GREEN1 + 0.5;
B = BLUE1 + 0.5;
x = x1;
while (x <= x2) {
    R = R + deltaR;
    G = G + deltaG;
    B = B + deltaB;
    pixel = (trunc (R) << 16) +
            (trucn (G) << 8) +
            trunc (B);
    plot (x, y, pixel);
    x = x + 1;
}
```

Figure 4. Simplified Gouraud algorithm in C

ger z buffers of 16 and 32 bits, the sizes that the i860 directly supports, are widely used.

The Gouraud shading operations might be less useful for two reasons. First, they speed up only the inner loop of the algorithm. Improving inner-loop performance is clearly important, but because Gourand shading uses flat polygonal patches, scenes with curved surfaces must be modeled with many relatively small polygonal patches. When the patches are small, the horizontal strips will be short, a few to perhaps a couple tens of pixels long. This means that the inner loops will iterate a small number of times.

For a small number of iterations, the set-up code for the inner loop can dominate the execution time of the algorithm. For the i860, the inner loop must be written to process two 32-bit pixels at a time, since the graphics instructions operate on 64-bits at a time. (The C program does not reflect this fact.) Thus, the boundary conditions require some set-up on loop entry and checking on exit. Also, some checking must be done to decide what precision is required for the reciprocal.

Second, there is another technique for implementing Gouraud shading, based on Bresenham's line-drawing algorithm, that is computationally simpler. By maintaining an error term, or decision variable, this algorithm uses strictly integer operations, not even fixed-point, and the loop set-up requires no divisions. This is the algorithm of choice in high-end graphics systems because it is simple to implement in special hardware. Even for some low-end systems, using special hardware can be cheaper than the i860 alone.

In comparing the i860 to high-end graphics workstations, the i860 is appropriate for use as a transformation engine, i.e., in the part of the graphics pipeline that is most floating-point intensive, because of its floating-point performance. Silicon Graphics workstations, for example, have the line drawing, shading, and z buffering implemented in special hardware (the Geometry Engine). This allows their workstations to perform transformation and pixel manipulation in parallel. The Geometry Engine is fully pipelined so that even the set-up code for shading operations is overlapped.

To achieve the same kind of parallelism, two or more i860s would be needed. While this is certainly possible, it is not clear how much improvement would be realized, and is probably more costly than the special hardware.

Conclusion

The graphics functions of the i860 can greatly speed up the inner loops of some parts of 3-D rendering, but they do not bring to single-chip microprocessors the same kind of performance found in high-end graphics workstations. According to Intel, the intent of the i860 was to bring 3-D graphics to the mainstream of workstations without requiring the end user to purchase an extra-cost graphics option.

Without a doubt, the powerful floating-point capabilities of the i860 will provide a level of performance previously unattainable in a single-chip microprocessor for the transformation stage of a graphics pipeline. Also, the 64-bit bus can ease hardware implementation, depending on system design philosophy.

However, the graphics instructions do not necessarily speed up pixel drawing significantly. Thus, it seems that the i860 is appropriate for graphics applications more because it is a fast integer and floating-point processor than because of the functions implemented by the graphics unit. The decision about whether to use the i860 or another RISC processor in a graphics system will be based primarily on cost. For system vendors who cannot afford to design and implement special line-drawing and shading hardware, the i860 might prove to be the best choice.

One caveat about graphics benchmarks: Programs that generate and display the familiar Mandelbrot set are not "graphics" programs. The Mandelbrot set is an array of numbers that, when used as pixel values, just happens to generate pleasing images. Thus, while it is very impressive and a good demonstration of the i860's floating-point capabilities, the high performance of the i860 in displaying the Mandelbrot set is not done to the graphics unit.

Acknowledgments

Sincere thanks go to Les Kohn of Intel, Forest Baskett of Silicon Graphics, Randy Geottsch of Wyse Technology, and Tony Masterson of Apple Computer for help in understanding graphics in general and the operation and implications of the i860 graphics unit. However, any conclusions made or positions taken with respect to the i860 are those of the author.

23

Intel i860 Parallel Processing Support

Michael Slater

Intel and Alliant Computer Systems Corp. (Littleton, Massachusetts) have announced plans for a set of extensions to the i860 hardware and software to support parallel processing. The standard, called PAX (Parallel Architecture eXtension), covers several levels of the system design, including the application program interface (API), application binary interface (ABI), operating-system calls, and low-level hardware mechanisms. The companies claim that the PAX standard will make it possible for a single "shrink-wrapped" binary program to operate, without modification, on both uniprocessor and multiprocessor machines.

Alliant makes a line of minisupercomputers, and last year entered the graphics hardware business by buying Raster Technologies. Alliant claims an installed base of over 400 machines—tiny by PC or workstation standards, but respectable by supercomputer standards.

Intel has promised to provide hardware support for the PAX standard in the next-generation i860 processors. No details were provided, and Intel said that some of the support hardware may be in peripheral chips designed to be used with the i860. While it will be possible to build PAX-compliant systems with the current version of the i860, Intel and Alliant expect most system designers to wait for future i860 versions with hardware support for the PAX mechanisms. Intel will use the PAX architecture in their "Touchstone" project, a 2000-processor i860 system Intel is developing under a DARPA contract.

Intel also gains the rights to distribute Alliant's C and FORTRAN compilers, which Alliant has recently ported to the i860. Alliant claims that their compilers effectively utilize the i860's unique features, including pipelined floating-point, dual-operation instructions, and dual-instruction mode. Compilers now available for the i860, such as those from Metaware and Green Hills, do not support these features.

Intel benefits from this agreement in several ways. The PAX standard establishes an ABI that allows the same version of a program to be used on machines ranging from single-processor workstations to multiprocessor supercomputers. Intel hopes to differentiate the i860 from the RISC masses with this parallel processing support, something Intel says will take at least a year to be developed for other architectures.

The Alliant compilers will presumably improve the performance of the i860 and provide a level of software technology that is hard to find in the microprocessor world. The i860, which Intel has hyped as their "supercomputing" solution, also gains credibility from the endorsement by a genuine (if struggling) minisupercomputer vendor.

The i860 will also gain application software, something it desperately needs. As part of the Alliant/Intel announcement, 20 software vendors provided press releases endorsing the PAX standard, although most stopped short of explicitly promising to port their software to the i860.

What does Alliant get out of this? First, they got some cash—Intel purchased $3 million in stock, representing about 4% of the company. Most important, Alliant gets silicon support for their next-generation systems, without having to design it themselves. Alliant's previous systems are based on a proprietary CPU that implements a superset of the 68020 instruction set with proprietary vector-processing extensions. The minisupercomputer business has been a difficult one for all vendors, and the Intel accord should reduce Alliant's R&D cost by letting them build upon work done by Intel. Alliant will also receive income from Intel's distribution of the Alliant compilers, and will gain from Intel's high public profile.

Alliant should also have an easier time convincing software vendors to port to their system—if, as Intel and Alliant hope, other companies introduce PAX-compatible workstations. Alliant is engaged in a fierce market battle with Convex Computer, and building the software base is a key element of this struggle.

Levels of Parallelism

To understand the PAX approach, it's helpful to first see where it fits in with other schemes for exploiting parallelism. Parallelism can be implemented within a single processor using techniques such as pipelining, independent functional units, and superscalar execution, which exploit instruction-level parallelism—they allow instructions to overlap. This is called *fine-grain* parallelism.

The simplest type of multiprocessor parallelism is to distribute entire tasks among processors, with each processor responsible for one task. This is, of course, useless in a single-tasking system, but a system that is executing *n* tasks can very effectively make use of *n* processors with this scheme. This is sometimes called *coarse-grain* parallelism.

The PAX scheme is at an intermediate level—loop-level, or *medium-grain* parallelism. All processors in a system can cooperate on a single task. When a repetitive loop is encountered, it is parceled out to as many processors as are available—up to the number of loop iterations required. Each processor handles one iteration of the loop. In theory, this would allow a 100-processor system to execute a loop with 100 iterations in very nearly the same time that a uniprocessor system could execute a single iteration of the loop, assuming that there are no data dependencies and that the memory system can keep up. Alliant plans to build i860-based systems with "dozens" of processors.

This type of parallelism is a natural fit to many scientific applications, which tend to use loops with many repetitions. Typically, different data points are handled in each iteration, so there are no data dependencies between iterations. The one common dependency is the loop counter, which is eliminated by the PAX scheme—it is implemented directly in hardware.

Note that these approaches are not mutually exclusive. A single computer system could use all three at the same time. Fine-grain parallelism simply speeds up instruction execution. Medium-grain parallelism uses multiple processors to speed up repetitive loops within a single task. Finally, coarse-grain parallelism allocates different tasks to different processors.

PAX Implementation

The PAX parallelism scheme involves additional instructions for concurrency control, which are inserted by the compiler, and special hardware associated with each CPU that interprets these instructions and provides control among the CPUs. Alliant calls the hardware scheme the Concurrency Control Architecture (CCA), and the company treats details of the CCA operation as a trade secret. (The logic that implements the CCA is called the Concurrency Control Unit, or CCU, in Alliant's existing machines.) Even after Intel incorporates these functions in the next-generation i860 processor and support chips, it is not clear how much of the detailed operation will be disclosed.

Intel and Alliant have not yet revealed what instructions will be added to the i860 to implement the CCA. They will, however, presumably be similar to the concurrency control instructions used in Alliant's current products, which are shown in Table 1.

The cstart and cquit instructions replace the normal loop control primitives. The cstart instruction includes among its parameters the number of iterations required. One of the CPUs acts as the "main" CPU, and when concurrent loops are not being executed, all other CPUs are idle. When a cstart instruction is encountered, the concurrency control hardware broadcasts a command to all the CPUs, providing them with an iteration count and an initial program counter value. (Alliant claims as part of their proprietary edge the low-overhead technique they have developed for this communication. Additionally, once the setup is complete, there is no operating-system overhead involved in coordinating the processors.)

Each of the CPUs then fetches the loop, and each executes a different iteration. If there are as many CPUs as there are loop iterations, then all iterations are executed in parallel. Otherwise, the loop is executed n iterations at a time (where n is the number of CPUs available) until all iterations are complete. The cawait and cadvance instructions provide a mechanism for synchronization among iterations, if needed.

Table 1. Concurrency Control Instructions Used in Alliant's Existing FX/Series Systems

Instruction	Operation
cadvance	Advance synchronization register
cawait	Await synchronization register advance
cidle	Place CE in idle state
cnest	Store current loop status
cquit	Exit concurrent loop
cstart	Start concurrent loop
cstartst	Start concurrent loop and serialize traps
cunnest	Load concurrent loop status
cvector	Start vector concurrent loop
cvectorst	Start vector concurrent loop and serialize traps
cmove	Load/store CCU status register
crepeat	Branch if more iterations
crestore	Restore CCU state
csave	Save CCU state

CCU = concurrency control unit; CE = computation element (CPU)

The demands on the memory system are considerable. Alliant's systems use a switch-based shared memory architecture; i860 systems will be able to use a variety of architectures to achieve various price/performance goals. As long as the loop fits in the on-chip cache, instruction fetch bandwidth will not be an issue after the first iteration in each CPU is complete. The memory system must, however, be designed to handle the data bandwidth requirements of multiple processors executing simultaneously. Since each CPU is generally working on a different part of the memory, multiple-bank interleaving techniques are effective.

Conclusions

Intel appears to have jumped ahead of their RISC competitors in providing a standard mechanism for implementing loop-level parallelism. Since the announcement is only one of intent, however, it is possible that other vendors will have similar schemes ready by the time Intel is shipping chips that support PAX. Developing the necessary compilers is a considerable barrier, however.

It remains to be seen how wide a range of applications will benefit from the PAX standard, what form the silicon support will take, and how many vendors will produce systems and software to support it.

On the other hand, the PAX standard may give the i860 the boost it needs to become a significant player in technical computing. Other RISC vendors are attempting to broaden their base beyond technical computing. Intel, however, has the 486 for the broad-based market, so it can afford to focus the i860 evolution on high-end technical applications. If—and this is a big if—the PAX standard is widely supported by hardware and software vendors, it could push the i860 ahead of its competitors for these application areas.

24

MASS860

Brian Case
Michael Slater

Intel defines MASS860 as "a cooperative association committed to the promotion of hardware standards and software development for a variety of systems based on the 64-bit 860 microprocessor architecture." The founding members are Alliant Computer Systems, IBM, Intel, Oki Electric Industry Company, Olivetti Systems and Networks, and Samsung Electronics.

The goals of MASS860 appear similar to those of 88open and SPARC International. As such, MASS860 provides developers with various kinds of technical and marketing support, including porting assistance (a hot line is planned for those late-night debugging sessions), ABI (application binary interface) verification, and compatibility testing. MASS860 has little to do with hardware standards, except in the case of multiprocessor implementations.

MASS860 is intended to prevent software incompatibilities among 860-based systems. By making sure that all 860-based systems can run all 860 ABI applications, software developers are given greater incentive to port applications to 860 hardware platforms. With more applications, more platforms will be sold, and Intel will sell more chips.

The Show

The MASS860 demo room had 14 hardware stations set up. Of these, six were CP486 PCs from Olivetti, three were Okistation 7300 workstations from Oki Electric Industry, three were PCs with IBM Wizard cards, one was an Alliant FX/2800, and one was simply a show of support from Samsung (hardware not available). The Okistation is the same product that Intel has shown as the Intel "Imagestation."

Among the software shown was FrameMaker, Pixar RenderMan, and Cadence CAD software. These are some of the premier programs in their respective classes. FrameMaker is a good technical publishing package. It is popular on Sun workstations and has recently become available for the Macintosh. Curiously, its performance on the 860-based machines seemed no better than on a fast Macintosh. Perhaps performance tuning has not yet been done—or this application isn't a good match for the 860's capabilities.

BDS Systems showed its Xcalibur image processing system based on IBM's Wizard card. BDS also had a nonfunctional prototype of a two-board, four-processor 860-based Wizard card from IBM. BDS says that this card will attain 95 MFlops (using the next-generation 860) on image convolution. The multiprocessing improvements incorporated into the next version of the 860 were said to account for about 30% of the performance gain. BDS seemed to have the best marketing strategy of all the participants: develop specific software that needs the 860 and bundle it with existing hardware (the IBM Wizard card).

What wasn't at the MASS860 show may be more significant than what was there. Olivetti did not show their 860-based workstation, the MR8600. An Olivetti marketing manager said the company is "reevaluating" the timing of the product introduction. The system is rumored to be ready to go into production, but Olivetti is probably concerned about there being enough demand to justify the expense of introducing it.

Neither the Oki nor Samsung product was formally announced. It seems that developers of 860-based workstations are hesitant to introduce products until there is a more significant base of applications. But without any workstations on the market, there is little incentive for application developers to target the 860.

Intel is reselling the Oki workstation as the "Imagestation." Intel has not formally announced this product, and does not plan to sell it except as an OEM development platform.

The Software Standards

On closer inspection, the 860 ABI is revealed to be not one, but three different standards:

- APX, a subset of UNIX V.4 system calls
- Unix System V.4

- PAX, an extension to Unix V.4 that includes multiprocessing and parallel processing primitives.

The APX environment is used on PC add-in cards, such as IBM's Wizard, and in systems such as Olivetti's CP486 that include a 486 and an 860 on the system board. This software environment provides virtual-memory support, trap handlers, and a scheduler, and transfers I/O requests to the host processor. The application interface is a subset of the Unix system calls. APX eliminates the need to provide a full Unix implementation when the 860 is operating as an auxiliary processor. It allows the same binary applications to run on different hardware configurations, including those with the 860 on the system board and those with the 860 on an add-in card.

The current APX implementation includes only character-based I/O. A new version will be Posix-compatible and provide X "sockets" for communication with an X-windows server running on the host 386 or 486 processor.

The Unix V.4 implementation for the 860 is now in certification at AT&T. The initial version will include support for the Okistation 7300 workstation, a system board that includes a 486 and an 860 from Hauppauge Computer Works, and an X.11 R4 server.

The name PAX, originally used to refer to the loop-level parallelism scheme licensed from Alliant last year, is now being applied to more conventional multiprocessor support as well.

The PAX loop-level parallelism scheme requires modifications to both hardware and software. The hardware must provide a concurrency control unit (CCU) that coordinates parallel operations, while the software must include special instructions for the CCU. At the start of a loop, for example, a special instruction tells the CCU how many loop iterations are required. Instead of implementing the loop counter with the usual decrement, test, and conditional branch instructions at the end of the program segment, the CCU provides the loop control in hardware. If multiple processors are present, all processors fetch the loop, and each processor's CCU tells that processor what iteration of the loop it is to perform.

The current 860 does not provide PAX support. The next-generation N11 includes a minimal CCU on-chip so a single-processor system will be able to run PAX code. For multiprocessor systems, an external CCU chip will be required for each processor.

These three software standards don't provide an entirely cohesive compatibility standard. The only way to write applications that can run on all 860-based systems is to limit the system calls to those provided in APX. This means that only character-based I/O can be used. The APX environment provides a mechanism for applications to make calls to OS/2 Presentation Manager running on the host processor, but applications that take advantage of this capability won't be compatible with native 860 Unix systems. The next version of APX will remedy this by providing an X-windows interface, but for now, software developers using the APX environment must choose between having graphics capability and being compatible with other 860 platforms.

The PAX loop-level parallelism scheme further fragments the software environment. A single version of a program can't take advantage of the PAX capabilities and remain compatible with systems built with the first-generation 860. Developers will therefore have to provide two versions of their software if they want to exploit the PAX capabilities of the N11 and remain compatible with the 860.

The Compiler Problem

Compilers remain a critical problem for the 860. One of the real contributions of the RISC phenomenon is the value of coupling compiler design with the architecture definition. The 860 appears to be the only recent architecture designed without this collaboration.

To achieve its potential floating-point performance, software must be carefully hand-coded. This is acceptable for a graphics accelerator running a dedicated set of routines, but not for general-purpose systems that need to run a wide range of application programs. When Alliant announced their joint venture with Intel on 860 technology late last year, they expressed confidence that their compilers could fully exploit the 860. Judging from the schedule slips, it seems they are finding it's not so easy.

In addition to the Alliant compiler, Intel has worked with AT&T and The Portland Group to enhance the PCC compiler included with the V.4 release. Added features include a global optimizer and software pipelining. Intel claims this compiler uses all the 860's features, including dual-instruction mode and pipelined floating-point. How effectively it uses them remains to be seen. Intel has also funded 860 compiler work at MetaWare, and the same features that are included in the PCC compiler are being added to MetaWare's compiler.

The 860's Prospects

Intel has successful microprocessors in every market except one: technical workstations. It seems that Intel believes its best chance to succeed in this market is by pitching the 860's floating-point capabilities as a differentiating feature. Intel is also promoting the ability to run the same applications on a wide range of platforms, from PC plug-in cards to multiprocessor minisupercomputers. MASS860 is intended to provide the standards and compliance testing necessary to ensure that a wide range of 860-based systems will be software compatible, thereby attracting application developers.

There is essentially no installed base of 860-based workstations and no major companies are yet marketing such systems. Thus, the only real hope for building an 860 application base is if systems such as Olivetti's CP486, which combine an 860 and a 486, or PCs with an 860 add-in card, provide enough of a hardware base to encourage software developers. Unfortunately, the APX software environment provided by these systems is currently too weak to support competitive workstation applications. By the time the next-generation version of APX and the N11 begin shipping, other RISC processors will have an even bigger lead in the race for applications. Even the 88000 has a significant lead over the 860 in developing an application software base, and this will be very difficult for Intel to overcome.

The MASS860 consortium lacks any major computer companies that are committed to the 860 as a central processor. IBM's motives for promoting the Wizard card are tied to their need to find a justification for the Micro Channel; IBM certainly isn't going to promote the 860 as a Unix CPU, since it would compete directly with the RS/6000. Olivetti is selling the CP486 product, but their level of commitment to the 860-based workstation is questionable. Samsung and Oki aren't exactly major players in the workstation business.

If Intel and its 860 partners are going to crack the workstation market, they must differentiate themselves somehow. It is unlikely that they will be able to differentiate on price. It is also unlikely that they will be able to differentiate on integer performance, which shows up mainly in programs such as word processors, the user interface, and the operating system. The 860's integer performance looks good today only because boards using 40-MHz processors are available. As next-generation implementations of SPARC, MIPS, and the 88000 appear with on-chip caches, however, this edge will disappear.

Differentiating based on the range of systems is also going to be difficult. PC add-in boards based on SPARC, MIPS, and 88000 processors are (or soon will be) available. Supercomputer-class systems based on each RISC architecture are also in development.

The best way for Intel to differentiate the 860 is exactly the way they have chosen: emphasizing floating-point performance. Unfortunately, their market window is closing and the market itself may also be small. Within a short period of time, the major workstation processor architectures will be available in versions with on-chip floating-point performance comparable to that of the 860. The IBM RS/6000 is already there. Of course, Intel isn't standing still, and the N11 provides higher floating-point performance than the 860.

Even if the MASS860 participants are able to win every seat in the floating-point-intensive market, it is unlikely that enough units will be sold to convince many software vendors to port their applications. The 860 proponents must hope for an explosion in the number of floating-point-hungry workstation users.

When asked about the 860's unit volume, an Intel representative answered that the volume is expected to match Sun's SPARC volume, or about 30,000 chips per quarter. Clearly, the vast majority of this volume has come, and will come, from the embedded market (primarily graphics accelerators). This may make the 860 a success from Intel's point of view. From a software developer's perspective, however, the number of systems with an 860 CPU is tiny.

Intel's plans for the 860 were, for some time prior to its introduction, to pitch it as an accelerator and not as a general-purpose processor. The fact that it was designated the N10, while all of Intel's general-purpose processors had "Pxx" product names, is one indication of its intent.

Apparently out of fear of losing the Unix market to SPARC, MIPS, and the 88000, Intel decided to push the 860 in the Unix market. This was probably a mistake. Intel is expending a tremendous amount of effort trying to push the 860 into a market that doesn't want it. One indication of how ill-suited the 860 is for its new target market is the fact that, almost from the day of its introduction, Intel began talking about how the next-generation part would fix the 860's problems. There have already been at least two conference presentations on system architectures that depend on the next-generation part, but won't work with today's 860.

Intel's efforts to sell the 860 into the Unix workstation market are misdirecting its attention. The next-generation 860, the N11, has many features that make it more attractive as a general-purpose processor, including larger caches and hardware cache coherency. If Intel had remained focused on the accelerator market, it probably would have chosen a different set of features, resulting in a better solution for the application area in which the 860 has a real chance for success. In the meantime, many other vendors—including AMD with their 29050, Motorola with their 96002 and 88110, and TI with their next-generation 340-family processor—are making a push into the high-end 3-D graphics market where Intel has had so much early success.

If Intel wants to penetrate the Unix market, a 486 variant with a faster floating-point unit and larger caches would be a better bet than a next-generation 860. To make the 860 a success, Intel should focus its efforts on 3-D graphics engines and accelerators for floating-point-intensive applications.

VI

Intel 960

Intel Register Scoreboarding

John H. Wharton

In a paper delivered at an International Solid State Circuits Conference in San Francisco, Intel "announced" a new register scoreboarding mechanism to improve the performance of microprocessor systems. Motorola had two days earlier announced that scoreboarding would also be implemented in the 88000. Register scoreboarding is not a new concept—it has been used in mainframe computers since Control Data's CDC 6600 in the early 1960s. What's significant is that scoreboarding techniques are now starting to penetrate the microprocessor world.

Basically, register scoreboarding is a control mechanism by which a heavily pipelined processor keeps track of what resources are busy at any given instant. It is useful when relatively slow operations in a instruction stream are followed by instructions that use different processor resources and don't require the preceding instructions' results. In such cases, the later instructions may be safely initiated even though the prior ones are not yet done.

This enhances performance by allowing some degree of parallel program execution. The CDC 6600 contained multiple dedicated processor execution units—several adders, some multipliers, a couple branch-processing blocks, a floating-point section, and so on. Under optimum conditions, scoreboarding let the instruction decoder dispatch each instruction to a separate, idle execution unit, achieving a level of instruction pipelining not otherwise attainable.

What Was Said

The paper, presented by Glenn Hinton of Intel's Hillsboro, Oregon operation, showed how micros can use scoreboarding logic to avoid waiting for slow external memory systems. Part of an example program cited by the paper appears in Figure 1.

The first instruction loads an external memory-based variable into register R5. To execute this instruction, the processor simply sends the destination register code and the requested variable memory address to the Bus Interface Unit (BIU), and marks the register as "busy" (i.e., not yet valid) by writing its code to one of the three "checking registers" shown in Figure 2. At this point, execution proceeds immediately to the next instruction, which loads a second register. Again, a destination register code and memory address are sent to the BIU and the destination register R3 is marked busy. The BIU can queue up to three such memory requests.

The third instruction then begins. Scoreboading logic determines that this instruction does not reference either of the two busy registers, and can therefore also begin executing immediately. Its destination, R0, is likewise marked busy. All three checking registers are now in use.

The fourth instruction has R0 as its source operand. If R0 has not yet received the results of the previously initiated addition, the comparators detect a collision on the source operand field and assert the "Instruction Stall" control output. The instruction is therefore prevented from completing; instead, it is decoded, compared, and aborted repeatedly ("stalled") on each succeeding instruction cycle.

Figure 3 shows the scoreboard logic at this point. After some (presumably short) processing time, instruction 3 completes. R0 is written with the computed sum, and its checking register cleared to show that R0 is now valid. On the next cycle the instruction decoder will be free to dispatch instruction 4 safely. A request to store R0 to memory is sent to the BIU.

Seq	Inst	Src1, Src2, Dest
1	Load	0x40,R5
2	Load	0x100,R3
3	Add	R4,R6,R0
4	Store	R0,(R7)
5	Add	R5,R3,R0
6	Load	(R0),R6
7	Add	R6,30,R7

Figure 1.   Example program instruction sequence

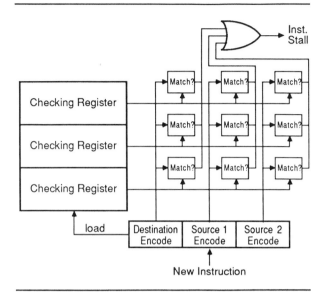

Figure 2. Scoreboard logic block diagram

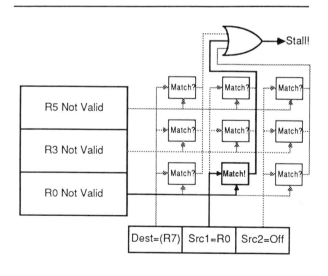

Figure 3. Register collision detection

Instruction 5 now stalls, since it references both R5 and R3, and neither is assumed to have been returned from memory yet.

In time, the two memory fetches will be performed. As each completes, the BIU writes the returned data to its destination register and clears the register code from the checking logic. Instruction 5 becomes unblocked, so it may finally proceed. Figure 4 shows the overall execution sequence thus far. The example in the paper goes on to show that instructions that change a particular register will likewise get stalled if outstanding memory references will need the register's original contents to address an external variable.

Complicating matters somewhat is the fact that multiple-precision instructions can alter or make use of two or more adjacent registers. A pending instruction to load registers 4 and 5, for example, should collide with an ensuing instruction that references either of the two, and vice versa. Depending on instruction precision, the instruction decoder translates each bit of a register number into a two-bit code, indicating whether that bit position should be tested for one, zero, or don't-care. Comparator logic checks accordingly (see Figure 5).

Intel's paper illustrated the logic functions performed by the entire scoreboard block at the device level, with individual transistors and internal clock phases shown. Hinton mentioned that pains were taken to minimize the number of gate delays within the block, and alluded to the use of domino logic and to the device-sizing and charge-sharing concerns that had been addressed to maximize its speed. When the first fabricated chips were tested, he said, the scoreboarding mechanism did indeed meet the

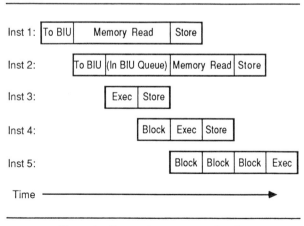

Figure 4. Instruction sequence time line

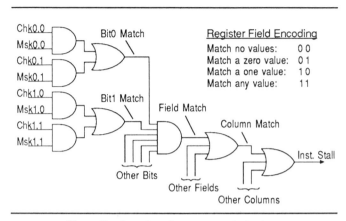

Figure 5. Scoreboard comparator logic detail

target design speed and proved not to be the clock-frequency limiting resource.

An annotated die photograph was projected and included in the proceedings to illustrate that the scoreboarding logic added less than 1% to device size and fabrication cost. Intel's computer analyses indicate that object code produced by their current C compiler runs about 10% faster than it would without scoreboarding.

Note that the degree of performance increase provided by the scoreboarding mechanism depends on the nature of the dynamic instruction stream. A memory read followed immediately by an instruction that uses the returned value would show no improvement. For best results, memory accesses should be initiated some time before their return values are needed.

Thus, performance is partly dependent on how clever the compiler is at staggering address and data calculations. The prospect of further enhancements as the compiler evolves appears promising: hand-tweaked inner program loops show improvements of from 20% to 50%.

What Was Left Unsaid

At least as intriguing as the formal paper were the questions asked afterward and at an informal discussion session with Hinton and fellow engineer Randy Steck. Paraphrasing a bit:

Q: Is this technique applicable to any architecture Intel now supports?

[The 8086/286/386 architecture is oriented toward an instruction set that implicitly ties each memory access to the instruction that needs the data. Scoreboarding works best when memory references precede usage. Thus 286 offshoots would not benefit much from the scoreboarding technique described.]

A: "The purpose of this paper is to present a register scoreboarding mechanism, not to discuss a processor architecture. However, the technique could be equally useful in a variety of architectures, whether the memory accesses were initiated at the macroinstruction level or by microcode instructions."

Q: One of your slides indicated that the collision detection logic compares six-bit register fields. What Intel processor has 64 registers?

A: "Did it really? Oh . . . well, I guess all you could really conclude was that the mechanism supports no more than 64 registers." [At the physical device level, microcode must be able to access temporary registers and other internal resources, in addition to those visible to the programmer. Thus, internal register-select buses are often wider than the corresponding macroinstruction register fields. This may explain the somewhat stilted answer.]

Q: What chip was that in the die photograph?

A: "The purpose of this paper is to present a register scoreboarding mechanism, not to announce any new products."

Q: What's the other 99% of the device used for? Test circuits?

A: "No comment."

Q: How fast does the chip run? What was the target design speed you felt so inspired to meet?

A: "No comment."

Q: Intel has two microprocessor product operations. The embedded controller [8051, 8096] operation does all its design work in Chandler, AZ. The personal computer products [80x86] people do all of their design work in Santa Clara. Where do you folks live?

A: "Hillsboro."

It's clear that Intel has something very secret and very significant up its sleeve. Intel would not analyze architectural tradeoffs, design complex chips, fabricate silicon, characterize performance, and develop and refine compilers for the sake of a three-quarter page paper.

Steck insisted that Intel was most definitely not trying to exploit ISSCC for publicity, and had not been responsible for the press leaks that occurred when this late paper was added to the program. On the contrary, Steck said, Intel had been studiously trying to keep a low profile. The device designers, though, felt that the work they had done was technically significant enough that it needed to be presented.

Still, it must have been clear to management that such a paper could not help but fuel speculation that new product design efforts were well underway. The formal announcement of a major new product line architecture must be imminent. What can we infer about the ISSCC Mystery Chip?

First, it will be fast. Processor speed depends equally on process technology and logic implementation. The Mystery Chip is fabricated using Intel's 1.5-micron double-layer-metal HCMOS process, the same as that used by the 80386. What may be more significant is the attention given to reducing the number of gate delays within the scoreboard block. This suggests that the amount of logic between reclocking points has been held to a minimum throughout the chip design, with a resultant frequency at least as high as as the 386.

[In addition to the scoreboarding mechanism described, the Intel paper may be hinting at another whole area of optimization allowed by concurrent execution of parallel instructions.]

RISC, CISC, or Something In Between?

There has been much industry speculation about a possible upcoming Intel RISC machine, and indeed this device has many RISC-like characteristics. The register load/store-oriented instruction set suggested by the example program is certainly reduced versus that of the 80286. Support for a large number of working registers smacks of several recent RISC machines. Motorola's 88000 has 32 total; the Berkeley SPUR designs and Sun Microsystems' SPARC make 32 visible at a time.

Also, the concept of evaluating architectural features in conjunction with compiler development and of giving the compiler the burden of rearranging the code generation sequence to more fully exploit hardware facilities is fundamental to the philosophy of RISC design. It has been suggested that RISC really stands for "Relegate the Impossible Stuff to Compilers."

On the other hand, the authors of this paper all hail from Hillsboro, former home of Intel's ill-fated iAPX432 "micromainframe." The Intel paper lists Konrad Lei as one of its coauthors; Lei wrote the microcode for the 432. Glenford Myers is given an acknowledgement. When Intel hired Myers away from IBM seven years ago, he was one of the industry's best-known champions of what might be called Extremely Complex Instruction Set Computing architectures.

Myers' books tout the importance of "lowering the semantic gap" between high-level constructs and machine instructions, to the point of computing array element addresses in hardware and tagging memory data objects with size and type attributes. This philosophy is the antithesis of RISC-style design, and in some ways spurred the research at IBM, Berkeley, and Stanford that led to the current RISC philosophy.

Perhaps the upcoming Intel product line may include provisions for hardware-implemented complex data objects and 432-style high-level constructs for automatic multitasking or operating system interface functions. The 432 failed, some feel, because it carried the complexity of its instruction set throughout. If the Mystery Chip also includes a full repertoire of simple, fast instructions, it could avoid the 432 pitfall and represent the best of both worlds.

Presumably the design work is being done in Oregon to take advantage of the architectural and design engineering talent amassed there for the 432. Whether the resulting product(s) are marketed by Santa Clara, Chandler, or a whole new business unit remains to be seen.

Whatever the machine is, it will herald the first all-new Intel architecture in years. For all its speed and architectural sophistication, the 386 can be considered just the latest step in a progression of processors dating all the way back to the 8008, each of which was constrained to be object-code compatible with or a functional superset of its predecessors. The 8008 was constrained to be compatible with a Datapoint CRT controller.

26

Intel 960 Architecture

John H. Wharton

Intel's 80960 family of RISC-inspired top-of-the-line embedded controllers includes a radically new architecture, three processors, hardware and software development tools, and run-time operating system support. On scanning the initial documentation, one is reminded of a radio ad for Prego spaghetti sauce that's getting a lot of air time these days. You want fresh, wholesome ingredients? "It's in there," says the store clerk. You want plump tomatoes, onions, green peppers? "It's in there." Oregano, garlic, herbs, and spices? "It's all in there."

The 960 family is the Prego of Embedded Control. You want a RISC-style processor with a load/store architecture and large register set? It's in there. You want complex multipart addressing modes? It's in there. On-chip floating point? Demand-driven 32-level real-time task scheduling in microcode? It's in there.

Power-on self tests? On-chip debug, trace, and breakpoint circuitry? Generic control instructions with run-time context-sensitive operation semantics? Maskable fault-detection facilities? Hardware and software hooks for simple shared-memory multiprocessing? Interprocessor communications mechanisms? Multiple instructions executing in one clock? It's all in there.

This is the first all-new Intel microprocessor architecture since the iAPX-432, the first chance since microprocessors came of age for Intel to go all-out for ultimate performance, unencumbered by compatibility constraints. The result is a machine that is faster, cheaper, more highly integrated, and has greater long-term growth opportunities than the 386.

221

Intel claims the devices typically sustain an average instruction execution rate of 7.5 VAX MIPS, with bursts up to 20 MIPS. The Dhrystone rating is about 15,000, according to Intel, and the Whetstone rating about 4 million.

Potential applications suggested by Intel include high-speed laser printers, robotics, military avionics, CAD, data terminal concentrators, and telephone switching systems. The machine is being called a high-end embedded controller, and does have the speed and facilities vital to that market. But it also has a level of arithmetic performance and instruction set complexity that embedded control designers never knew they needed. One suspects the product placement was partly influenced by pragmatic business concerns. As long as the 386 continues to dominate the PC world, Intel's not likely to attempt to displace it.

Product Overview

This is a system with something for everyone. If you like traditional assembly language applications programming, just limit yourself to a small core instruction subset, pretend it's a RISC machine, and you'll be thrilled with the performance. If you write debug monitors and operating system kernels, there's considerable hardware support on-chip to assist you. If you build compilers and enjoy squeezing out the last 5% of run-time execution efficiency, the instruction set has optimization opportunities to keep you challenged for months.

There are just a few things the product is not: it's not compatible with any previous Intel processor—upward, downward, or sideways. It's not a single-chip microcontroller. It has no EPROM or ROM program memory on-chip, nor is any planned. And while the documentation alludes to future unnamed "Special Function Registers," the only peripheral device currently on-chip is an interrupt controller integral to efficient program execution. There are no timers, counters, or serial ports.

The simplest of the three processors announced is the 80960KA, which implements the basic 960 core architecture for cost-sensitive markets. The 80960KB includes all the functions of the 960KA, plus a full IEEE 754 floating-point unit on-chip. This is the Mystery Chip discussed in Chapter 25. Intel has had working silicon for this 280,000 transistor device for over a year, and the part is already on distributor shelves, both in component form and in board-level evaluation systems. It's rated at 16, 20, and 25 MHz. The 80960MC is a militarized version of the 960KB that also supports memory management schemes and fault-tolerant multiprocessing.

Programming Model

The 960 has a basic word length of 32 bits. It has a standard Von Neumann memory architecture, with a single, flat, 32-bit (4 gigabyte) linear address space. External 32-bits memory words contain byte-addressable subfields that can be read or modified separately. Naturally, bit and byte ordering is little-endian throughout. The programming model of the CPU (Figure 1) includes 16 general purpose "global" registers plus 16 additional "local" registers, all 32 bits wide.

Four local register windows are cached on-chip, but only one is visible at a time. The execution context represented by the local register window is saved and restored automatically during each subroutine call.

There are also assorted CPU configuration, status, and math unit control registers. The 960KB and 960MC versions add four 80-bit extended precision floating-point temporary registers. Floating-point variables up to 64 bits of precision can be loaded, processed, or stored using the special floating-point registers or any global or local register-pair.

Instructions are all one 32-bit word wide, with an optional second word containing constants or addresses for certain instructions. Register instructions support one, two, or three-operand formats, with any global or local register allowed in each operand field.

A sophisticated 256-vector, 32-level priority-driven interrupt system is integrated into the CPU. A configuration register maintains the CPU's

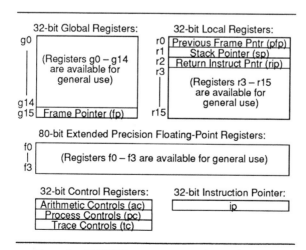

Figure 1. 80960KB program execution environment

current execution priority. Higher-priority interrupts are serviced immediately, as in traditional microprocessors. When lower priority interrupts are detected, however, the request is acknowledged, relative priority levels are compared, and flags in a latent-interrupt-pending table in memory are updated—all in microcode—but the CPU continues with the original instruction stream. Should the execution priority change, either under program control, as the result of returning from an interrupt routine, or in response to interprocessor communications messages in a multiprocessing system, the table of pending flags is retrieved, scanned, updated, and the appropriate service process dispatched automatically—again, all under microcode control.

Extended RISC?

Is the machine a RISC or a CISC? The lines are beginning to blur, and Intel seems uncertain how to position it. The cover of the 960 sales brochure announces "RISC technology goes to work in the practical world of embedded computing." Intel Senior Vice President David House seemed to avoid using the R-word, calling other RISC architectures "the last hope of the have-nots." Family architect Glenford Myers was more diplomatic. His wanted the device to take advantage of both philosophies: "RISC techniques were used for high performance, CISC techniques for ease of use."

If you look at the classical characteristics of RISC design, the machine does comply with most. Special Load/Store instructions perform all data accesses, while all other operations involve only the on-chip registers. Most instructions currently complete in 1 to 3 clock cycles. Control for most operations is hard wired.

But is the instruction set "reduced"? Not by a long shot. The Instruction Set Reference section of the 960KB Programmer's Manual is 133 pages long and lists 184 separate instruction mnemonics, not counting operand addressing mode variants. There are at least a dozen primitive data types, from single-bit fields to extended precision floating-point variables. The Load and Store instructions support seven addressing modes with up to three parts (base register plus scaled index plus constant displacement), and can transfer 1, 2, 4, 8, 12, or 16 bytes at a time. Compare this to the Sun Microsystems SPARC, probably the best-established commercial RISC processor: the SPARC CPU, minus off-chip coprocessors, supports just 6 data types, 99 instructions, and 2 addressing modes.

Design Philosophy

With the 386 and most previous microprocessors, the device architecture and the device itself are virtually synonymous. The 960 family architecture is not so much a device as an abstract design philosophy that Intel plans to exploit for years to come. It tries to reconcile two conflicting goals: to define an architecture that can support the greatest possible long-term system performance by imposing the fewest possible architectural constraints on future device designers, and to do so (at least in initial incarnations) while remaining cost-effective at a system level.

The key to such an open-ended performance upgrade path is the ability to decouple individual operations from the program instruction stream and let them execute in whatever sequence is most efficient for a given processor. This allows a level of fine-grained parallelism not previously supported in the microprocessor world. The long-term goal is to construct versions of the 960 architecture in which multiple instructions can be executed during any given clock cycle. Intel projects performance ratings up to 50 MIPS by the early 1990s.

In Chapter 25 we speculated that the Mystery Chip separated its Bus Interface Unit from its Integer Unit so it could process two separate instructions (a memory reference instruction and a traditional arithmetic operation) at once. We were off. It handles four.

First there's the Integer Unit, which executes most arithmetic and logic instructions. Next, the Bus Interface Unit can simultaneously perform external memory accesses. Meanwhile, the instruction decoder itself can process branch instructions internally, while the IU and BIU keep busy. And last, relatively slow floating-point operations (5 μs for an 80-bit square root) can plod merrily along while the other operations complete.

A single instruction decoder must classify and dispatch each instruction. This bottleneck restricts execution to at best one IPC. Even so, the ability to handle four-track parallelism lets the CPU divide multiclock instructions among the various Execution Units more effectively, so it's easier to sustain IPC rates close to unity.

This is where register scoreboarding comes in. Instructions are dispatched by the instruction decoder in the order in which they occur in the original instruction stream. In general, however, that may not need to be the order in which they should complete. Figure 2 shows a sequence of four instructions, one per EU type. When each instruction uses or modifies the same register (Figure 2a), they must each be performed in the sequence shown. When the instructions involve independent variables (Figure 2b), though, they can be performed in parallel. In this case they complete in the exact opposite order from which they were dispatched. Scoreboarding

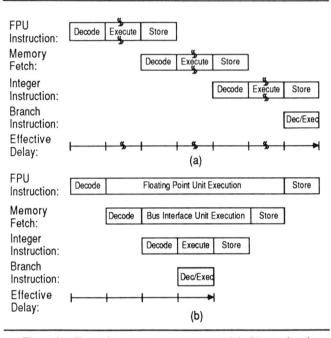

Figure 2.   Execution sequences: (a) sequential, (b) unordered

keeps track of what CPU resources are busy at each instant, and lets each new instruction be dispatched only when it is safe to do so.

Memory Interface Requirements

One notable distinction between the 960 family and prior RISC designs is the burden each places on external memory systems to attain its rated performance. Earlier RISCs generally require their external memory systems to accept or return data in a single clock cycle. If they fail, the entire internal pipeline shuts down during any wait states. Meeting this requirement demands expensive high-speed static RAM, complicated external caching systems, or both. The Motorola 88000 processor needs two dedicated external cache and memory management units to meet this constraint, one for caching programs and a second for data.

The 960 family is being pitched at embedded applications that are cost-conscious, if not cost-critical. The memory system in such a design should not cost several times more than the CPU. To reduce pin count and lower external bus interface costs, it has a single 32-bit multiplexed address/data bus. External latches, transceivers, and memory control logic reconstruct the buses and control signals needed for a standard memory and I/O interface (Figure 3).

Normally a multiplexed bus can move data on no more than 50% of its clock cycles, since the same pins hold address and data on alternate cycles and may need to allow some amount of turn-around time. A special memory burst mode on the 960 can read or write a block of up to four consecutive data or instruction words at a time. With zero wait-state memories, this hikes the ratio of cycles available for data transfers to 67% (see Figure 4). Burst-mode transfers are guaranteed never to cross four-word memory boundaries, so a simple four-bank memory system design needn't worry about address bits A31–A04 changing in mid-burst.

Exploiting Affordable Memories

To make best use of the single multiplexed bus and to avoid the need for high-speed memory subsystems, the 960 decouples internal program execution from the external memory system for both random data accesses and sequential program memory fetches. The data access decoupling mechanism is as described in the scoreboarding article in Chapter 25: to reference a memory-based operand, the instruction decoder posts a mem-

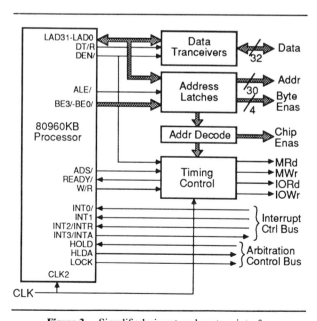

Figure 3. Simplified pinout and system interface

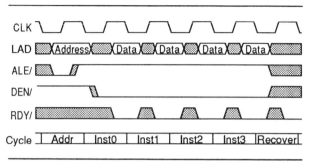

Figure 4. Four-word burst-mode read timing

ory request to the BIU before the data is needed. With sufficient warning, the BIU can retrieve the data by the start of the instruction that needs it.

Program memory decoupling is accomplished via a 512-byte (128-instruction) on-chip program cache. An instruction prefetcher predicts what execution path will be followed, to keep the cache filled with instructions that may be needed. On an instruction cache miss there will be a short delay as the new address is put out and a burst-mode fetch started. Thereafter, though, the successors to the target instruction should arrive on back-to-back clock cycles. The number of memory access wait states required for the initial fetch is thus effectively divided by four, since the delay is defrayed over all the instructions fetched.

No matter how fast external caches may be, even a fully dedicated 32-bit bus can retrieve no more than one instruction word per clock. On-chip program caching may be mandatory in order to break the IPC barrier in future microprocessor designs. CPUs attempting to decode and dispatch four instructions in parallel, for example, would need a separate, dedicated 128-pin cache interface bus just to keep pace.

Internal program caching eliminates this problem. Once the required instructions have been fetched into the on-chip cache, they tend to get executed repeatedly. Inner program loops can then continue to cycle out of cache without consuming any external bus bandwidth. Putting the cache on-chip would let it feed the four instruction decoders directly with relatively little impact on die cost and no increase in pin count or external memory system complexity.

Instruction Set Overview

The 960 instruction set is extensive and eclectic. Simple data transfer operations (Table 1) include memory loads and stores of ordinal (unsigned)

Table 1. 80960KB Instruction Set Summary

Data Transfer	Arithmetic	Logical	Floating-Point	Program Control
Load Byte	Add	And	Move Real	Unconditional Branch
Load Short (Two Bytes)	Add with Carry	Or	Add	Conditional Branch
Load Word (Four Bytes)	Atomic Add	Exclusive-Or	Subtract	Compare and Branch
Load Long (Two Words)	Subtract	Exclusive-Nor	Multiply	Branch and Link
Load Triple (Three Words)	Subtract with Carry	Complement	Divide	Call and Save Locals
Load Quad (Four Words)	Multiply	Not (A And B)	Remainder	Call System Routine
Store Byte	Extended Multiply	Not (A Or B)	Scale	Return and Restore Locals
Store Short	Divide	(Not A) And B	Round	Branch if Bit Set
Store Word	Extended Divide	A And (Not B)	Square Root	Branch if Bit Clear
Store Long	Remainder	(Not A) Or B	Sine	Conditional Fault
Store Triple	Modulo	A Or (Not B)	Cosine	Mark
Store Quad	Shift Left	Set Bit	Tangent	Force Mark
Move Word	Shift Right	Clear Bit	Arctangent	
Move Long	Rotate	Complement Bit	Log	
Move Triple	Decimal Add w/ Carry	Copy Bit to Flag	Log Binary	
Move Quad	Decimal Subtract w/Carry	Copy Flag to Bit	Log Natural	
Decimal Move and Test	Compare	Scan for Bit Set	Exponent	
Load Address	Conditional Compare	Scan over Bit Set	Classify	
Synchronous Load	Compare and Increment	Extract Bit Field	Compare	
Synchronous Move	Compare and Decrement	Modify Bit Field	Copy Real Extended	
Flush Register Cache	Scan Bytes for Equal	Atomic Modify	Convert Integer to Real	
			Convert Real to Integer	

				Machine Control
				Modify Trace Controls
				Modify Arithmetic Controls
				Modify Process Controls
				Test Condition Codes
				Synchronize Faults

and integer (signed) 8, 16, and 32-bit values, and burst-mode loads and stores of "long" (two 32-bit words), "triple" (three-word), or "quad" (four-word) blocks. Triple word blocks are best at manipulating 80-bit extended real variables. Data can be moved between local and global registers in single, long, triple, or quad word blocks.

Multiword transfers all impose the natural alignment restrictions. Long operations must start at even register and memory word numbers; triple and quad word operations must start at register and memory word numbers that are multiples of four.

Arithmetic instructions perform the operations you might expect on full-word registers: add and subtract, ordinal or integer, with or without carry. In contrast to the simplest RISC machines, the CPU also performs integer, ordinal, and extended (double-precision) multiplication and division, plus remainder, modulo, and arithmetic shift operations. There's even a set of decimal move, add, and subtract instructions that operate on individual ASCII-encoded BCD nibbles. COBOL and PL/I programmers take note.

Logic designers will appreciate the repertoire of logical operations supported. Every possible bitwise logical operation on two variables is supported: AND, OR, Exclusive-Or, and NOT, of course, but also NAND, NOR, A And Not B, Not A Or B, and so on. Bit and bit field operations allow individual register bits to be set, cleared, or complemented, or copied to or written from a status flag. Scan and span instructions find the highest-order one or zero bit in a register, respectively, while the extract and modify instructions allow an arbitrary bit field to be shifted to a separate register or spliced into an existing bit pattern.

As a rule, arithmetic and logic instructions do not modify PSW status flags. This is a pronounced break from conventional processor architectures. Maintaining flag settings would preclude the primary goal of the 960 architecture, which is to allow out-of-order and concurrent program execution. The PSW resource on conventional machines is essentially shared among all instructions that alter it. In the 960, the register scoreboarding mechanism would therefore have to block all such instructions until their predecessors completed.

Instead, only a set of explicit Compare instructions affect the result status flags checked by the conditional branch instructions. For efficiency, separate Compare-and-Branch instructions perform both steps at once.

Control Flow Instructions

Other control flow instructions in the 960 family fall into three categories. Unconditional branches simply reload the instruction pointer. Branch-

and-Link instructions first preserve the old Instruction Pointer so you can continue later from wherever you left off, but do not otherwise affect the execution context. Call instructions also save the old local register window and allocate a new one. If all on-chip windows are already in use, microcode automatically flushes the oldest to the stack and reallocates it to the new routine. Each of the three control functions can reference local (22-bit offset) or extended (32-bit absolute) addresses.

There is also a Call System instruction to let programs access operating systems and other software utility libraries despite entry addresses that shift with each new software version. This instruction uses the specified ordinal value as an index into a microcode-maintained table of system entry points, retrieves a 32-bit vector from the table, and transfers control accordingly. This function resembles the software interrupt instructions in many other CPUs.

Some conventional processors have several forms of the call instruction, as well as an interrupt system that forces implicit calls. The 8086/286/386 family, for example, has short calls, far calls, and both software and hardware interrupt calls. Each leaves a somewhat different context on the stack. To return control to the original execution thread, the 386 must execute a short return, far return, or interrupt return, respectively. This presents a logistic problem for programmers: at the end of a subroutine, function, or service routine, the programmer or compiler must ascertain how control flow got there in the first place.

The 960 has an abundance of similar implicit system call functions. Interrupts, hardware faults, software faults, debug traps, inter-agent communications messages, and so forth all resemble the call instruction. To avoid the nightmare of reconstructing how each function was entered, each call mechanism stores a special status code in the stack frame to indicate what was left on the stack and how it got there. The Return instruction can thus be generic. Subroutines, service routines, fault handlers, and the like all end with the same simple Return instruction; microcode determines how to interpret the stack data and transparently restores the original execution state.

27

Intel 80960 Features

John H. Wharton

Drawbacks of Classical RISC CPUs

In many respects, the 80960 architecture resembles some of the classical RISC architectures. The CPU contains a large array of 32-bit working registers: 16 "global" registers are always present, while 16 "local" registers are swapped out and restored with each subroutine call and return. Most instructions reference just the working registers; only various forms of the load and store instructions can move data from or to memory. There is extensive internal instruction decode and execution pipelining; most simple instructions consume just one or two clock cycles at any stage of the pipe.

However, the 960 hardware includes some decidedly non-RISC characteristics that help it overcome some of the shortcomings of traditional pure RISC designs. Having to contend with highly reduced instruction sets can greatly complicate the software development process. More of a burden is placed on the compiler due to several factors:

- Conventional RISC architectures support only very simple arithmetic operations. Longer code sequences are therefore needed to perform a given task.
- RISC architectures allow only register-based variables for most operations, though large and complex data structures must reside in external memory. Typically, up to 40% of all instructions are loads and stores. With only simple memory addressing modes supported, load and store

address calculations can require several conventional arithmetic instructions to determine the target address.

- Intricate instruction pipeline timing interdependencies in some RISC machines require that code sequences be rearranged or padded with strategically placed no-ops to make the resultant programs work or to fully exploit the optimization possibilities allowed by the architecture.

All this demands more advanced and complicated compiler technology to take full advantage of the processor architecture. Not all third-party software developers (much less all semiconductor vendors) have access to the most advanced compiler technology. To make the 960 family more attractive to systems software developers and assembly-language programmers familiar with conventional processor architectures, the 960 architecture defines a number of hardware features that lessen the software development burden.

Complex Instruction Support

In addition to its relatively simple instruction types (integer add, program branch-and-link, and floating-point multiply), the 960KB includes a number of more complex instructions (integer remainder, compare-and-branch, and floating-point arctangent, for example). While the simplest instructions (i.e., those common to standard RISC designs) execute in a single clock cycle, the more complex can take considerably longer (see Table 1). Data types range from subword bit fields to multiword burst transfers and 80-bit floating-point variables.

Multi-Part Addressing Modes

To reduce the number of instructions required to compute memory operand addresses, the 960 load and store instructions support five memory addressing modes. In the simplest version, the contents of any working register contains a simple 32-bit memory pointer. In the most flexible version, the base address in one register is added with the contents of a second register multiplied by an index scale factor (1, 2, 4, 8, or 16), and their sum added with a 32-bit signed displacement constant.

Pipeline Timing Independence

One of the fundamental 960 design philosophies is that programs targeted to any machine should execute correctly (though perhaps suboptimally) on any other 960-class machine. Run-time register scoreboarding logic ensures that no-op padding and instruction reordering are never needed for proper functionality.

Table 1.   Representative 80960KB Instruction Timings

Instruction	Minimum Clocks	Maximum Clocks
Integer Add, Subtract, Compare	1 *	2
And, Or Not, Shift, etc.	1 *	2
Bit Set, Alter, Check	2 *	3
Compare and Increment	2 *	3
Unconditional Jump	0	2
Conditional Branch	0	2
Branch and Link	2	8
Call & Save Register Set	9 **	33
Return & Restore Reg Set	7 **	31
Integer Multiply	9	21
64-bit Integer Divide	40 typ.	
Floating-Point Add	9	17
F.P. Multiply	11	22
F.P. Long Square Root	104 typ.	
F.P. Arctangent	267 typ.	
F.P. Long Remainder	67	75,878

* Lesser value when register file bypassed (see text)
** Lesser value when new register set in cache

(Certain techniques may improve performance, however. Load instructions should generally precede the point of data usage by as many instructions as practical, to give the external memory system time to respond. Also, K-series processors fetch but one operand at a time from the register file, so register operations sometimes take an extra clock cycle to fetch the second operand. However, the register access mechanism is bypassed and the extra cycle saved if either operand is a constant or the result of the immediately preceding instruction. Instructions referencing two registers complete most quickly if arranged such that each modifies the preceding computed value. This tends to be the most natural ordering in most sequential computations, so this optimization should be straightforward.)

Complex Instruction Set Rationale

RISC purists argue that any function complex enough to require more than one clock cycle should be omitted entirely from RISC architectures. Computing a square root unavoidably requires multiple steps and multiple clock cycles in a chip with any reasonable number of transistors; when considering just the overall execution time it would seem to make relatively little difference whether the multiple cycles consisted of multiple individual macrocode instructions or internal microcode sequences. For example, the 88000 floating-point unit is restricted to basic instructions such as add, subtract, and multiply. Even so, Motorola claims it can build a sine function in software that executes in fewer clock cycles than the 960KB's built-in sine instruction—at least to within single-precision accuracy.

Intel sees several advantages in supporting complex instructions, data types, and addressing modes, however. It's easier, naturally, for a compiler to emit a single instruction word for a complex operation than the equivalent sequence of more primitive instructions. Combining complex addressing modes with load and store instructions lets separate hardware perform the computation in parallel. And future 960 designs could execute complex instructions in fewer cycles, while the time taken to execute a set sequence of single-cycle primitive instructions would be fixed.

In addition, including more complex instructions and addressing modes has advantages unrelated to execution speed, in that each tends to reduce program size. In contrast to reprogrammable (disk-based) computer applications that "recycle" a common DRAM memory among multiple programs, embedded control programs are more often EPROM-based. Memory size and cost therefore increase in proportion to the number of instructions it takes to perform a complex task.

Perhaps more important, shortening the length of instruction sequences makes better use of the K-series' relatively small (512-byte) on-chip program cache. Fetching a single instruction word also causes far less instruction bus traffic than looping through the equivalent burst of single-cycle primitives. Slower and more affordable memory devices can be used with less impact on overall performance. In multiprocessing systems, reduced instruction traffic leaves more bus bandwidth available to other CPUs.

Interruptible Instructions

One down side of implementing extremely complex operations in microcode is that more time-consuming instructions might tend to slow down interrupt-response latency time. Alas, interrupt responsiveness is vital to embedded control applications. The 960 design goal was a worst-case interrupt latency on the order of 5 μs. Unfortunately, the floating-point remainder instruction, for example, takes up to 75,878 clock cycles to complete (honest!). Even at 20 MHz, that's nearly 4 ms.

To resolve this dilemma, the 960 can terminate instructions in progress in different ways, depending on what stage of completion the instruction is in when an asynchronous interrupt request arrives. If the instruction is simple, or is nearly finished, it completes normally. If a more complex instruction has just begun and has not yet altered the CPU state, the instruction is aborted before dispatching the interrupt, and restarted following service routine completion.

In addition, all instructions that take more than a few dozen cycles to complete are interruptible. When an interrupt arrives, the CPU suspends instruction execution and pushes a special instruction resumption record onto the stack. Resumption records hold the state of all microcode counters, internal status flags, and temporary registers referenced by the instruction.

When the service routine has completed or when the interrupted task resumes, the resumption record is popped off the stack and the slow instruction continues from where it left off. It's intriguing to consider that in a heavily loaded system, potentially many interrupts may be serviced during the 4 ms of main-line execution time it may take the remainder instruction to finish.

Trace Control and Debug Facilities

Another shortcoming of prior RISC architectures is that their programs are harder to debug. The triple-whammy that RISC programs contain a larger number of instructions, that the instructions may be arranged in a counterintuitive order, and that parallel execution units let instructions complete in still another order all make it more difficult to locate and fix bugs. More of a burden is placed on programmers, operating systems, and debuggers to determine how and why errant programs fail. To simplify program testing and debugging, the 960 has built-in facilities that allow instruction trace, detect breakpoints in hardware, and restrict execution concurrency.

The 960 Trace Control (TC) register contains seven trace-enable control flags and seven trace-event status flags (see Figure 1). Setting an enable flag invokes a trap when an instruction of the corresponding class occurs. For example, if bit 1 of the TC is set, execution will break following the execution of any instruction. An operating system or debugging utility program can use this facility to trace program execution or to allow software single-stepping.

Other TC control flags let a particular class of instructions cause a break. The debugger can be set to trap on any form of the call, branch-and-link, or return instructions, for example, or only on calls and returns that enter or return from particular operating system routines. Especially noteworthy is the prereturn trace, which traps before the return executes, while the return instruction pointer, stack frame variables, and local register set are still intact.

Trace facilities are individually enabled or disabled within system routines to race through known-good routines and to prevent the debugger from single-stepping through itself. Trace event flags keep track of what

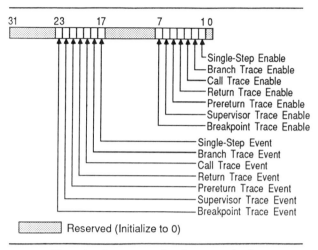

Figure 1. Trace control register organization

traceable events have been detected so the CPU can service interrupts and other, more pressing fault types without forgetting that lower-priority trace events are pending.

Software breakpoints are supported via the Mark instruction, which invokes a software interrupt. Mark instructions can be inserted throughout a program at locations that might be useful as breakpoints later. They can later be enabled or disabled under program control, so an EPROM-based system can switch back and forth between a debugging or performance measurement test mode and an uninstrumented, nearly-full-speed operation mode, without replacing EPROMs. A separate force-mark instruction forces a nonmaskable trap. It can be inserted into the instruction stream at desired breakpoints in RAM-based test and development environments.

Inserting software breakpoints in EPROM or ROM-based systems is more difficult. Instructions fetched into the on-chip instruction cache are executed later, potentially much later, if at all. External hardware cannot tell when a given instruction is executing internally. For further flexibility the 960 has two hardware breakpoint registers. Either can be set to any program memory address; execution of the corresponding instruction invokes a breakpoint trap.

Finally, out-of-order instruction execution presents a special problem, in that a debugger may not know which of several instructions in progress caused a software fault. A special "no-imprecise-faults" mode disables concurrent execution sufficiently that the cause of each possible fault can be exactly determined during debugging.

Hardware Self-Test

The 960 microcode performs an automatic memory test sequence on power-up to verify proper operation of at least the initial portions of the external memory system. The first 32 memory bytes are read and a checksum calculation performed to ensure data integrity. System designers must define the initial memory image to contain a valid data pattern. The CPU also performs an extensive self-test of its own major internal logic blocks. The sequence takes about 47,000 clock cycles, and allegedly provides an internal fault coverage of approximately 50%. If any part of the self-test should fail, the CPU asserts the FAILURE output pin and halts before attempting to execute any user code.

Inter-Agent Communications

Several system-level communications and debug facilities are supported via something called the Inter-Agent Communications (IAC) mechanism. IAC functions can involve messages sent from a CPU to itself for defining breakpoint registers or searching the interrupt-pending flag table, or to another CPU for reset initialization and task dispatching. To use this facility, the initiating CPU uses a quad-word synchronous (locked) move instruction to copy a 16-byte IAC message from its internal registers to a shared memory location allocated to the recipient processor.

The high-order 4 Mbytes of system memory are reserved for such IAC messages, with an assignment scheme that supports up to 1024 CPUs. External logic is expected to detect and decode memory writes to the IAC memory address block and alert the destination processor. The 960KB Programmer's Reference Manual describes eight IAC message types, with eight-bit type codes 40H, 41H, 80H, 89H, 8FH, 91H, 92H, and 93H. The sparse and seemingly-random code value assignments make one wonder what additional undocumented IAC message types may exist.

Dual-CPU Multiprocessing

Many of the more intriguing provisions of the 960 K-series processors come together in a facility for minimal-cost dual-CPU multiprocessing. The 960 has two configuration input pins that determine how it behaves following reset. Two identical 960 K-series processors can share a system memory and I/O interface. One is strapped as the Primary Bus Master (PBM) processor, the other as a Secondary Bus Master (SBM). Other than the configuration pins and two cross-coupled contention protocol signals, essentially all control and data signals use three-state or open drain outputs so that the CPUs may be connected in parallel as shown in Figure 2.

On reset, the PBM initializes the shared-memory system data structures and then sends an IAC to tell the SBM to begin executing its own instruction stream. Thereafter the two CPUs interleave program and data memory requests as needed, automatically resolving access contention. The SBM can perform a fully-independent set of tasks, or the two CPUs can cooperate on a single problem.

Both CPUs can share a single interrupt status table. When either finishes servicing an interrupt or otherwise changes its execution priority, it automatically scans and updates the shared list of interrupt-pending flags. The highest-priority service request currently pending will thus be dispatched, whichever CPU received the original interrupt. In multitasking applications, either CPU can resume a suspended task previously running on the other. A relatively lengthy interruptible instruction can even be passed back and forth between processors, executing short snippets on each before it finally finishes!

Presumably the combined throughput of both processors would be greater than that of a single-CPU configuration, though memory contention would reduce the performance to somewhat less than that of two fully independent subsystems. Whatever the incremental performance, the added cost is quite literally just that of the second CPU. Even with no performance enhancement, dual CPU multiprocessing constitutes a remarkably clean scheme for interrupt load sharing and reduced interrupt latency. It may also explain why the Intel project that resulted in the 960 was given the code name Gemini.

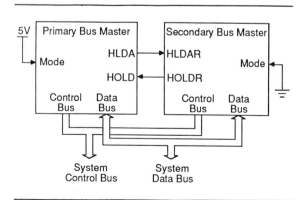

Figure 2. Dual-CPU multiprocessing interconnections

Transparent, automatic, multiple-processor task dispatching was one of the more noble and esoteric goals of the iAPX-432 family architecture; it's good to see that the concept did not die with the 432. The facility is documented in detail in the 960KB Hardware Reference Manual, but received surprisingly little attention (i.e., none) in the introductory press conference or full-day technical seminars. In fact, the Local Processor Number (LPN) and STARTUP configuration input pins described in the 960KB Programmer's Reference Manual are not even listed in the Data Sheet pinout tables. Curious.

Software Development Support

Initial software development support for the 960 family includes a macro assembler and C compiler "designed specifically for the 80960." Each can run under DOS on IBM PC/AT-compatible systems or under VAX/VMS or MicroVAX/VMS on DEC workstations. The latter supports standard ANSI extensions to C, plus enhancements useful for embedded control such as memory-mapped I/O, in-line assembly-language code, and a retargetable STDIO library. Floating-point libraries support CPU versions with or without on-chip floating-point hardware.

A PC/AT add-in board called the EVA-960KB is available for program evaluation, debug, and performance measurement. The board contains a 20-MHz 80960KB CPU, 1 Mbyte of DRAM program memory, three execution timers, and a system interface and debug monitor. A set of DOS access libraries lets the CPU access the host AT's display screen, keyboard, and disk file system.

28

Intel 80960CA Superscalar Microprocessor

John H. Wharton

After a year of suggestive ads, controlled leaks, and restrained conference presentations, Intel has taken the wraps off the 80960CA microprocessor. As expected, the key architectural feature of the device is its "superscalar" core—by dispatching multiple instructions during each clock cycle, a 33-MHz part can deliver up to 66 native MIPS, for the highest raw integer performance of any CMOS microprocessor yet announced. Performance on a range of Unix programs is claimed to be 25 to 32 VAX MIPS. On programs dominated by short loops, such as the Stanford integer suite, performance is claimed to be 40 to 50 VAX MIPS.

What Intel had not previously revealed, however, were the peripheral functions surrounding the core. Supporting the CPU are a 1-Kbyte instruction cache, 1.5 Kbytes of data RAM and register cache, a remarkably flexible bus interface controller, a four-channel DMA processing unit, and an interrupt controller (see Figure 1). Not included are any floating-point or memory-management facilities.

The device is intended for use in embedded applications demanding extremely high computational power. These include industrial robotics, laser printers and image processing equipment, and LAN and FDDI communications controllers. The latter areas will use the chip's DMA facilities and are affectionately known by the designers as "data shovels."

The 960CA contains nearly 600,000 transistors, about half that of the i860 and 486 processors. The lower count is due primarily to the difference

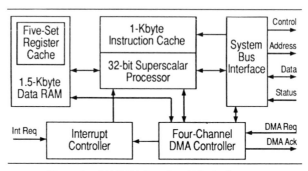

Figure 1.   80960CA functional block diagram

in cache sizes. Factoring out the respective memory arrays, the 960CA appears to contain about 500,000 transistors versus about 800,000 for the 486 and 400,000 for the i860. Chip size is 385 × 575 mils.

Superscalar Core Design

"Superscalar execution" refers to a processor's ability to execute multiple instructions per clock cycle from a conventional, linear instruction stream. This ability demands several new facilities.

For starters, the CPU must contain multiple execution units (EUs) to absorb instructions as they are dispatched. A more significant problem is that of keeping the execution units fed: the processor must include circuitry to fetch, decode, and dispatch multiple instructions at once. Finally, there must be logic to keep track of the state of the various execution units and to avoid conflicts over the use of shared resources. The 960CA provides these facilities via the microarchitecture shown in Figure 2.

The left side of the figure shows the so-called "REG" processing section, which handles register-to-register operations. This side contains two execution units. The integer execution unit (IEU) performs simple arithmetic and logic instructions, data moves, and so forth, each in a single clock cycle. The separate multiply/divide unit (MDU) performs more complex arithmetic instructions, which take from 4 to 39 clocks to complete. The units are independent, so IEU operations can continue while an MDU operation is in progress.

On the right ("MEM") side of the figure are functional blocks for addressing and transferring memory-based data. The address generation unit (AGU), which computes multipart operand addresses needed by load, store, and control transfer instructions, and the internal data RAM, DMA logic, and system bus controller all reside on the MEM processor side.

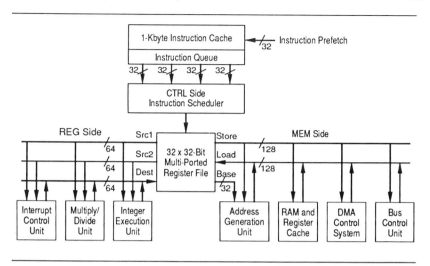

Figure 2. 80960CA processor microarchitecture

At the top ("CTRL") side of the figure are the instruction cache and logic to decode, classify, schedule, and dispatch instructions to the other two sides. The CTRL block itself performs control transfer instructions, including jumps, branches, calls, returns, and a suite of compare-and-branch combinations.

The REG, MEM, and CTRL units communicate via a register file containing 32 general-purpose registers, each 32 bits wide. The register file has six access ports of various widths, and allows a total of up to nine 32-bit words to be retrieved from and six words to be written to the file on each clock cycle. Scoreboard flags for the registers and other shared resources prevent instructions from beginning until source operands are valid.

Buses between the register file and the internal data RAM are 128 bits wide, so quad-word loads and stores can transfer all four words during each clock cycle. The 960 architecture automatically saves and restores 16 "local" working registers across each subroutine call; with the wide internal buses, all 16 can be copied in four clocks total.

Portions of two instruction cache lines can be retrieved at once, in order to supply four successive 32-bit instructions to the decoder. The CTRL block can simultaneously dispatch one REG-side and one MEM-side instruction and process a third instruction directly, for an instantaneous dispatch rate of three instructions per clock (IPC).

Intel claims only that the CA will sustain two instructions per clock within optimized program loops; in fact, this is the maximum the part can achieve. If three instructions are dispatched at once, one of the three must be a branch. On the following cycle, only the fourth instruction of the original four-word group is eligible for decoding. Intel's 960 marketing group is to be applauded for resisting the urge to claim the 33-MHz part delivers 99 MIPS, even though it can do so for an entire clock cycle.

The sustained execution claim of two instructions per clock within optimized loops does seem justified, however, since the instruction-flow resources provide wider paths at earlier stages of the execution pipeline and "funnel down" to the execution units: four instruction words are retrieved and decoded, in an effort to find three nonconflicting instruction types, for which only two of the required execution units must be available. The performance of compiled code remains to be seen.

(In contrast, Intel also claims the i860 can sustain two instructions per clock. However, this rate can be reached only when the compiler or assembly-language programmer can pair floating-point and integer instructions, when alignment restrictions are met, and when dual-instruction mode has been selected by a previous instruction. Specifically, a floating-point instruction at an even address must be paired with an integer instruction at an odd address, and a floating-point instruction, occurring two fetch cycles previously, must flag the fact that a dual-instruction mode operation is imminent. Of course, a single i860 floating-point instruction can replace dozens of 960 integer instructions, so the i860 will be substantially faster for programs using floating-point math.)

Several factors can prevent multiple-IPC operation, of course. Sequential programs fetched from external (uncached) memory cannot exceed one instruction per clock. Back-to-back multiplies can begin, at best, every four clocks. Certain instruction ordering conventions must also be met to ensure best performance. If four successive instructions all perform memory references, for example, or if all four are branches, no more than one can be dispatched at a time. Fortunately, such instruction combinations are rare.

The possibility that a series of instructions will all involve register operations is more likely, but even this hazard can often be avoided. One of the MEM-class instructions (LDA) loads a register with the effective address of a memory operand. The address calculation performed by the address generation unit can involve registers and constants in various combinations. The LDA instruction can be subverted to perform simple integer math, including register initialization, transfers, shifts, and simple arithmetic. If an optimizing compiler or diligent human programmer encounters four successive operations that would otherwise involve the REG unit, one or more can often be converted to a MEM-unit equivalent.

The 960CA raw performance statistic that is most awesome (though of questionable relevance) is its "gross aggregate internal bandwidth": the 10 internal instruction and data buses shown in Figure 2 have a combined total of 608 signal lines. If all 10 were in use at once, the effective internal data bandwidth at 33 MHz would exceed 2.5 gigabytes per second. Achieving the same level of performance with external instruction and data caches would require a CPU package with an unprecedented pin count and a complex and expensive external memory system.

Architectural Extensions

The 960 was announced last year amidst much fanfare that the core architecture was defined independent of any particular implementation. The 960CA chip designers found it necessary to extend the core architecture slightly to fit the new device's needs.

Three new special-function registers (SFRs) have been defined by the 960CA to control and monitor the built-in peripheral functions. SFRs can serve as source or destination operands for a subset of general register instructions. New system control and DMA setup instructions were invented to support the on-chip peripherals, and a new applications-level instruction (unsigned 64-bit right shift) was thrown in to enhance Bit-BLT operations.

The first 192 bytes of general-purpose system address space are now allocated to chip-specific functions, and the "inter-agent communications" mechanism, which had originally reserved the top 16 Mbytes of system address space for future enhancements, has been discarded entirely. Conditional branch prediction, which had been discussed in conjunction with the K-series devices but not actually implemented, now is.

Instruction Cache

The instruction cache has a capacity of 1 Kbyte, and is organized as two-way set-associative with an eight-word line size. It seems curious that the cache is only two-way set-associative, especially in light of its relatively small (256 instruction) size. Four-way associative caches are generally believed to have significantly higher hit rates when the cache size is small.

Instructions can be prefetched from external memory in bursts of two or four words, and are copied to the cache in pairs to improve prefetch efficiency. Prefetched instructions are not cached until the instruction executes, so speculative prefetches on behalf of an untaken branch will not corrupt previous instructions. Cache-line replacement follows a simple least recently used (LRU) algorithm.

The cache can be split into two 512-byte segments at system initialization time. Either or both halves may be preloaded with time-critical code via the new SYSCTL instruction and then "locked" to prevent later replacement. This ensures that time-critical interrupt handlers will always be present, and can begin executing without going to main memory. When half of the cache is locked, the other half continues operating as a conventional 512-byte, two-way set-associative cache.

On-Chip Data RAM

The on-chip RAM totals 1.5 Kbytes, but only the first kilobyte is program-visible. The RAM maps onto the system address space starting at address 0, and contains a number of words optionally dedicated to on-chip peripheral functions (see Figure 3). Certain interrupt vectors can be cached in the RAM, for example, and the DMA controller reads channel parameters from reserved RAM locations. The first 256 bytes of RAM can be written only in supervisor mode, to prevent corruption by application-level software; the remaining bytes are selectably write-protectable under software control.

ADDRESS	
0000 0000	NMI Interrupt Vector
0000 0004	Internal Data RAM (Optional Interrupt Vectors)
0000 0040	Internal Data RAM (Optional DMA Registers)
0000 00C0	Internal Data RAM (User Write-Protected)
0000 0100	Internal Data RAM (Optional User Write-Protected)
0000 0400	External Main Memory Region 0
1000 0000	Main Memory Region 1
2000 0000	Main Memory Regions 2 – D
E000 0000	Main Memory Region E
F000 0000	Main Memory Region F
FFFF FF00	Initialization Boot Record
FFFF FFFC	

Figure 3.   80960CA system memory map

The other 512 bytes of RAM are dedicated to internal system functions and are not software accessible. A local register cache (LRC) that saves working registers during subroutine calls uses part of this space, and temporary values for the on-chip peripherals apparently consume the rest. By default, the LRC allows up to five register sets, but can be expanded under software control to hold 15 sets total by encroaching into the visible RAM space.

System Bus Interface

The 960CA uses a 168-pin ceramic PGA package. The system bus interface has separate, nonmultiplexed 32-bit buses for address and data (see Figure 4). As with Intel's previous 32-bit processors, the low-order two address bits are predecoded to produce individual byte-enable signals. Simple, one-word transfers can take place in two clock cycles, but simple transfers (according to an early Intel technical background report) "can be embellished in astonishingly many ways."

When external memory devices allow, burst-mode transfers can move up to four data words on successive clock cycles. Individual or burst-mode transfers can optionally include address pipelining, in which case the next address is emitted one clock early, and which theoretically allows the bus to move data on every clock cycle. Operands within different memory regions can be little-endian, in the traditional Intel style, or big-endian, for compatibility with attached processors from alternate vendors.

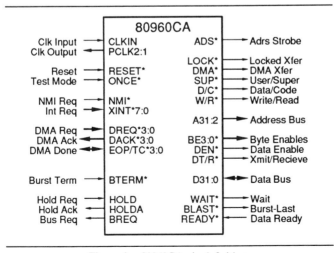

Figure 4. 80960CA pin definitions

Memory devices can be 8, 16, or 32 bits wide; full-word transfers are transformed into a series of partial-word transfers as needed. Transfers can be asynchronous, in which case an external "ready" signal paces transfer completion, or wait states can automatically be inserted, or both. When enabled, the internal wait-state generator adds up to 31 delay cycles, separately programmable for each phase of a burst transfer, and for read versus write operations.

The bus interface controller divides the system address space into sixteen regions, each 256 Mbytes long, according to the four high-order address bits. The physical characteristics of each region—burstability, pipelinability, endian-ness, bus width, pacing mode, and various wait-state counts—are defined separately for each of the 16 regions under software control (see Figure 5).

The on-chip logic can provide an indirect reduction in system cost. Providing the same level of flexibility off-chip would likely introduce buffer or decoder delays within the critical memory-access timing path. To compensate for such delays and still deliver a given level of performance might then require faster and more expensive memory devices. Many of

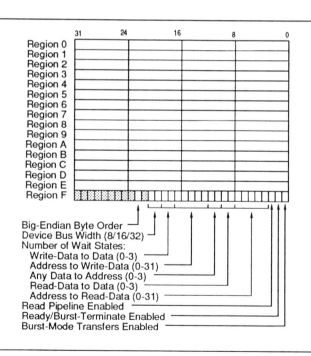

Figure 5. 80960CA memory region configuration table

the application areas that Intel is targeting require large main memory systems, so the cost savings could be significant.

At first, it seems almost absurd to include this level of flexibility within the bus control unit, while at the same time fixing memory partitions according to high-order address bits rather than software-controlled address registers. Connecting the 960CA to a slow UART, for example, might consume a quarter gigabyte of address space!

The bus interface does, however, reflect the needs and mindset of embedded system designers. The on-chip logic eliminates a host of external latches, transceivers, decoders, programmed-logic elements, and so forth, and provides flexibility for a variety of end-product price/ performance points that differ only in the size, speed, and structure of their main memory systems. Embedded system designers are generally willing to cope with the software adjustments needed to coordinate a fractured memory space, if doing so can reduce hardware size, price, and complexity.

Interrupt Control System

The 960CA interrupt system is not especially innovative, but does provide far more flexibility than most high-end processors. There are eight interrupt input pins. In the simplest mode, each is dedicated to a separate request level. In the most versatile mode, the pins accept an eight-bit interrupt-request index encoded by off-chip logic.

There is also a mixed mode in which three of the pins are dedicated to separate requests, and the other five encode additional request levels. Requests can be level-activated or edge-sensitive, and each can be debounced internally. A ninth pin requests nonmaskable interrupts at the highest priority.

External interrupts are combined with four requests generated internally by the DMA controller. The priority of each dedicated request and each DMA channel is software adjustable. The 960 architecture supports up to 248 interrupt vectors, eight each at 31 priority levels, so a fully expanded system must overload certain vectors. Interrupt vectors can be cached within the internal RAM, retrieved from external system memory, or both.

Perhaps the most intriguing facility of the 960CA design (excluding the superscalar core) is that it allows simple interrupts to be serviced entirely within the chip. Upon sensing an external event, the local registers can be saved within the LRC, the rest of the processor state can be pushed onto an on-chip stack, the requesting vector can be retrieved from on-chip

RAM, and the service routine can be executed from within a locked section of the instruction cache.

The intent is that extremely time-critical routines can begin executing in minimum time, with the guaranteed worst-case latency determined in advance, no matter what the external memory speed or how busy the bus may be when the interrupt is invoked. While the worst-case latency is predictable, it is not lightning-fast. The overhead to enter a service routine, including a register-set context switch, is typically 25 to 35 clock cycles. Under pathological worst-case conditions, including LRC spills and external instruction fetches, a nested service routine may incur up to several dozen additional clocks of latency.

I/O Channel Processor

The "I/O channel processor" is Intel's name for the complex, semiautonomous, four-channel on-chip DMA controller. The DMA system accesses memory through the same bus interface as the main CPU, so it supports the same options for memory device width, speeds, and so forth.

The DMA system operates in several modes. In block mode, large blocks can be copied continuously between memory regions or between memory and I/O until the intended number of bytes has been moved. In demand mode, external requests initiate each I/O read or write operation. Channel priority can be fixed or rotating.

Data is normally transferred in two steps: the controller first reads a word from the source device into a temporary CPU register, and then writes the word to the destination device. If the two devices have dissimilar bus widths, or if the transfer addresses have mismatched alignment, the controller automatically handles data packing, alignment, and unpacking.

Data can also be transferred in single-cycle fly-by mode, in which memory data is copied onto the bus while the corresponding DMA-acknowledge pin writes the data directly to the destination I/O device (or vice versa).

Growth Paths

Intel has a number of options concerning what next to do with the technology developed for the 960CA core. Basic superscalar concepts will no doubt appear in the 586 and future-generation i860 follow-ons, as well as product offerings from a number of Intel competitors.

In the meantime, the CA core will appear in other 960-based products. While the 960CA has impressive integer performance, the lack of floating-point hardware (either on-chip or in a coprocessor) will be a major drawback for some customers. The 960CB, now in the final stages of design, will add on-chip floating-point hardware. Another future version, internally called the P12, is rumored to provide double the performance of the CA.

Future versions will presumably include memory management and protection facilities like those of the 960MC, but perhaps better suited for embedded system requirements instead of general-purpose computers or transaction-processing systems.

The on-chip cache and RAM sizes are miserly by today's standards; apparently they were kept small to hold manufacturing cost down. Intel could presumably enlarge each array or widen cache set-associativity without too much difficulty. An additional 8 Kbytes of cache and/or RAM would add only about 400,000 transistors, and the resulting total would still fall below the 1,000,000-plus transistors used by the i860 and 486.

29

Conflict Avoidance

John H. Wharton

The Intel 80960CA introduced a new implementation technique called "superscalar program execution" to the microprocessor world. This article examines the basic concepts of superscalar execution and shows how they are implemented within the 960CA.

Superscalar designs are one way to overcome the single instruction per clock (IPC) execution barrier. An idealized superscalar processor contains a pool of execution units, each able to interpret a general-purpose instruction set, and each with unrestricted access to a common register file, bus interface, and so forth. Such a processor potentially can execute many instructions each clock cycle, and throughput would rise.

Instruction Scheduling Objectives

The control logic in such a machine must supervise a number of processor functions. During each clock cycle the processor must retrieve a series of unexecuted instructions beginning with the current instruction pointer, examine each to determine which registers or flags it uses or modifies, select a combination of nonconflicting instructions to dispatch during the next clock cycle, and assign each to an idle execution unit. The logic that decodes instructions, finds nonconflicting groups, and issues them to their respective execution units is called the instruction scheduler.

The decisions made by the scheduler concerning which instructions to dispatch are conceptually straightforward, and can be defined in terms of the conflicts that prevent a particular instruction from being issued on a given clock. In general, no instruction may begin if any of its source variables (input registers or control flags) are modified by an earlier, not yet completed instruction. Similarly, no instruction may be issued if it modifies a variable used as either a source or destination of a preceding, not-yet-issued instruction. Finally, instructions that follow conditional branch operations may be issued but must not be allowed to modify the machine state until it is known which direction program control flow will take.

In an idealized superscalar machine there is theoretically no limit to the number of instructions dispatched on a single clock. Applying these rules to the example in Listing 1, for example, it should be possible to issue the MOVE, MULT, and STORE instructions on one cycle and the ADD and SUB instructions on the next. If the MULT takes multiple cycles to complete, however, the ADD must wait, but the SUB may proceed.

Real-World Design Problems

In practice, several factors complicate the scheduler logic. Potentially, many instructions must be decoded to determine which resources each uses or modifies. The number of pair-wise comparisons of source and destination operand fields needed to detect resource collisions increases exponentially with the number of eligible instructions and operand fields. Whether or not a conflict matters may depend on when each instruction is issued. Such conflicts are easiest to resolve serially, yet the critical comparisons and decisions must be made in parallel in order to dispatch multiple instructions.

Listing 1. Sequential instruction stream

Inst	Src, Src, Dst
move	r0, r1
mult	r0, r2, r0
add	r0, r3, r3
sub	r1, r4, r4
store	r5, (r6)

Moreover, the scheduling logic must also monitor the state of each execution unit, bus, and other shared resource to determine which are available during a particular cycle. Scoreboard logic must keep track of the state of each register and status flag to determine which are awaiting the results of previously issued instructions. Finally, the scheduler should be able to anticipate when previously issued instructions will complete to avoid unneeded "dead" cycles between instructions.

Compounding these problems is the fact that a completely general superscalar processor would contain considerable redundant logic. If each execution unit can interpret any instruction, it must replicate the same arithmetic, logic, and multiplier arrays, the same address generation units, and the same connections to shared register files, system interface, and so forth.

Simplifying Assumptions

To make the control logic manageable and to eliminate the redundant execution units, real-world superscalar processors must make compromises regarding how many instructions are fetched and examined during each clock, the number and nature of the execution units, and the sorts of instruction combinations that can be simultaneously dispatched. Each of these tradeoffs affects the potential performance of the system, but software adjustments can often reduce the effects.

For example, neither the 960CA nor the IBM RS/6000 look more than four instructions ahead of the instruction pointer to locate candidates for parallel dispatch. Neither design provides multiple general-purpose execution units (EUs). Instead, the instruction set is split into several nonoverlapping groups, with a single, specialized EU dedicated to each group. Each instruction can be performed only by the corresponding EU, so instruction parallelism is possible only to the extent that different instruction types are intermixed.

The 960CA, for example, divides the instruction set three ways. Register ("REG") instructions include all register-to-register arithmetic and logic operations. Memory ("MEM") instructions include loads, stores, and other instructions that perform address calculations. Control ("CTRL") instructions include jumps, calls, and conditional branches. Instructions of each type are executed by separate portions of the chip, respectively called the REG-, MEM-, and CTRL-side processors.

The IBM America chip set design differentiates instructions in a similar manner, but with four classes instead of three. Fixed-point instructions include all register operations, loads, and stores. Floating-point operations form a second group, and branch operations a third. All instructions that affect processor status flags reportedly fall into a fourth, relatively minor, classification.

960CA Superscalar Details

The microarchitecture of 960CA subdivides the REG-side processor into two parallel execution units. The integer execution unit (IEU) performs most register operations, including simple arithmetic, moves, shifts, and so forth, each in a single cycle. The multiply/divide unit (MDU) performs multiple-cycle multiplication and division. Both units respond to the same control signals from the scheduler, and share the same source and destination data buses to the register file, so the IEU and MDU may not both initiate an instruction during the same cycle. The units operate independently, though, so IEU instructions may continue executing while a slower MDU operation is underway.

The MEM-side processor contains an address generation unit (AGU) that performs address calculations by combining shifted and sign-extended index registers and offset constants as needed. An on-chip data RAM is also part of the MEM-side processor, and automatically services data transfer requests within the low-order 1 Kbyte of system address space.

The instruction cache, decoder, and scheduling logic are all integrated within the CTRL-side processor unit to reduce conditional and unconditional branch overhead. Additional special-purpose EUs are dedicated to interrupt processing, DMA control, and external bus transfers, but will not be discussed here.

Partitioning a full, general-purpose instruction set into functional subgroups mitigates the need for multiple general-purpose EUs. It also reduces the complexity of the instruction decoder logic considerably, since the scheduler must consider only gross instruction classes, not individual opcodes. Operand fields within each class have consistent formats, which reduces the number of comparators needed to detect conflicts. Intel claims that the 960 instruction set encoding was designed from the start to simplify this sort of multilevel decoding.

Parallel Scheduling Algorithms

On each clock cycle the 960CA prefetch logic retrieves either three or four instruction words from the on-chip cache, depending on whether the current instruction pointer (IP) is odd or even. These are the only instructions eligible for dispatch, and are referred to as a "rolling quad-word" instruction group. Instructions are issued to the various processing units through the set of discrete control paths shown in Figure 1. REG instructions, for example, may be issued only from the left-most position of a quad-word group, while CTRL instructions may be issued from any of the four slots.

Instead of considering all possible instruction sequences, the decoder logic detects only certain combinations of instruction types. Table 1 shows all of the instruction combinations that can be issued on a single clock cycle. The letters R, M, and C represent the three instruction classes; x's represent "don't-care" fields, either instructions that do not match any of the preceding patterns, or 32-bit constants used for address calculations. As each instruction group is issued, the IP is adjusted to point to the next unexecuted instruction.

The fact that the instruction decode logic can only match certain instruction patterns at first seems overly restrictive. A sequence of four otherwise-independent instructions of the form M-R-M-x will have only the initial MEM instruction issued on the first cycle, with the REG instruction delayed until cycle 2. While the respective EUs would be able to complete a sequence of the form M-M-R-R in two clock cycles total, the scheduler needs four cycles to detect and dispatch all four.

These restrictions may not be as significant as they seem. There are 3^4 (81) possible ways to assign three instruction types to a quad-word group, but only 31 of the combinations are useful since a branch anywhere in the group disrupts execution of ensuing instructions. Of these, about half match the templates of Table 1 in ways that allow more than one instruction to be dispatched at a time.

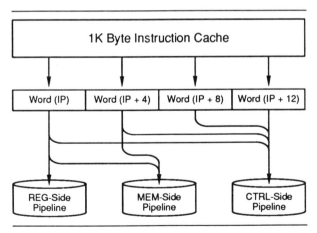

Figure 1. Instruction dispatch paths

Table 1. Instruction Dispatch Templates

IP	IP+4	IP+8	IP+12
R	M	C	x
R	M	x	C
R	M	x	x
R	C	x	x
R	x	C	x
R	x	x	C
R	x	x	x
M	C	x	x
M	x	C	x
M	x	x	C
M	x	x	x
C	x	x	x

Looking back at the instruction pattern mismatch examples presented above, the M-R-M-x sequence will fix itself by the start of clock cycle two, at which time the decoder will see a well-aligned R-M-x-x sequence. Many mismatch conditions can be avoided by an optimizing compiler or assembly-language post processor that rearranges instructions to take into account the 960CA scheduling algorithms.

The 960CA uses a number of other tricks to improve execution efficiency and keep the complexity of the scheduling logic manageable. All possible bypass paths between source and destination buses on either side of the register file are implemented. The scheduler does not try to take into account the state of all of the execution resources throughout the chip each time an instruction is issued. Instead, it only tries to find "static" instruction conflicts within the current quad-word group. Instructions that are inherently incompatible will not be issued together, but otherwise-compatible instructions will be issued regardless of the EU status and register scoreboard bits.

Each EU further decodes the instructions issued to it, verifies whether the resources it needs are available and known to be valid, and sends an acknowledgment back to the scheduler. If, for example, a REG-side operation requires a register value not yet loaded from memory, the IEU does not acknowledge the instruction and aborts its operation. The scheduler in turn aborts any instructions positioned later in the instruction stream that had already been issued, and the IP is adjusted to reissue the unacknowledged instruction.

Branch Processing

Normally, only adjacent instructions may be dispatched at the same time; the 960CA scheduler issues instructions in parallel but not out-of-order. (Instructions may complete, though, in a different order.) By not skipping instructions that cannot be issued, the scheduler avoids the confusion of keeping track of which instructions have been issued, and eliminates any ambiguity over the meaning of the current IP value.

As a special case, however, control instructions are detected as soon as they enter the quad-word group, even if intervening instructions must be skipped. Branches take two clock cycles to compute the branch destination and retrieve an arbitrary cache location; issuing branch instructions one clock early gives them a "head start" relative to the other execution units.

When the decoder detects the R-x-x-C combination, for example, the REG and CTRL instructions begin executing on the same cycle. During cycle 2 the intervening instructions will be issued; assuming nonconflicting resources and fortuitous cache hits, instructions within the branch-target quad-word group may be issued during cycle 3. As a result, Intel claims most branches fully overlap execution of other instructions, and complete in effectively zero clock cycles.

Early branch detection creates a potential hazard, however. It may not be possible to issue all of intervening instructions—those skipped by the decoder—on the following clock. In the R-x-x-C case, for example, both x's may be of the same instruction type, or a skipped instruction may depend on an unavailable resource. The logic to determine, in advance, which instruction combinations will be eligible to be dispatched one cycle later would be prohibitively complex.

Instead, the 960CA scheduler uses a trick similar to the one used to back out of unacknowledged register operations. The first branch instruction detected within any quad-word group is always issued on every clock cycle. If it turns out that the decision to perform the branch was premature, i.e., if the instructions within the original quad-word group that were skipped cannot all be issued on the following clock cycle, the scheduler will abort the branch within the CTRL pipeline and reissue it on each successive clock.

To further improve branch efficiency, each 960 conditional branch or compare-and-branch instruction contains a branch-prediction bit. Compilers or assembly-language programmers may indicate whether or not the branch is likely to be taken. Prefetch logic takes the state of this bit into account when deciding whether or not to follow a branch path. If the prediction turns out to have been wrong, up to two clocks' worth of spurious instructions along the untaken path can be canceled before they corrupt the processor state.

It's worth noting that the branch-prediction bits are not always needed. Relatively few 960 instructions alter the flags tested by conditional branch instructions. Scoreboard logic keeps track of whether or not condition code bits are valid. If the instructions that precede a conditional branch do not affect the condition codes, the scheduler can determine that the codes are valid before the branch begins. If so, prefetch logic consults the condition code bits directly, and the setting of the branch-prediction bit is irrelevant.

Software Example

To see how these facilities enhance performance, consider the algorithm for checksum verification within TCP/IP data blocks. Two checksum values must be computed. The first is simply the modulo-255 sum of all data bytes within the block. The second is the sum, again modulo-255, of each of the partial sums encountered while computing the first. With 32-bit data words one can simply accumulate each of the running totals and compute modulo-255 equivalents at the end.

A high-level representation of the checksum inner loop appears in Listing 2a; Listing 2b replaces each statement with an equivalent 960 assembly language instruction. These instructions would consume four cycles per iteration in the order shown, but rearranging them as in Table 2 reduces this to three cycles total, or 90 ns per TCP/IP data byte at 33 MHz. The inner loop thus does sustain an execution rate of 2.0 IPC.

This example assumes the data is contained in on-chip RAM, which completes load instructions in a single cycle. By unrolling the inner loop

Listing 2. TCP/IP checksum computation inner loop: (a) high-level representation, (b) assembly-language equivalent

```
loop:  temp=mem[pntr];          loop:  ldob   (g0),g4
       sum1=sum1+temp;                 addo   g4,g2,g2
       sum2=sum2+sum1;                 addo   g2,g3,g3
       pntr=pntr+1;                    lda    1(g0),g0
       count=count-1;                  subc   1,g1,g1
       if (not done) goto loop;        be.t   loop
              (a)                             (b)
```

Table 2.   Reordered TCP/IP Loop

Instruction			Cycle 1	Cycle 2	Cycle 3
loop:	subc	1,g1,g1	REG		
	ldob	(g0),g4	MEM		
	addo	g4,g2,g2		REG	
	lda	1(g0),g0		MEM	
	addo	g2,g3,g3			REG
	be.t	loop		CTRL	

and staggering data loads as shown in Table 3, the 960CA can retrieve data from external system memory, even allowing one wait state per byte, while reducing checksum computation time to only 75 ns per byte.

Performance Caveats

Intel's marketing literature and technical presentations trumpet the fact that the 960CA is the first microprocessor that can sustain execution rates *"up to two instructions per clock within optimized program loops"* (italics added). While this is certainly true, it's worth noting why the disclaimers are needed.

Actually, 960CA performance is guaranteed never to exceed 2 IPC: when three instructions are dispatched at once, only the fourth instruction from the same quad-word group can be dispatched on the following cycle. Achieving peak performance requires at least some optimization, since random instruction sequences and existing binary code are unlikely to

Table 3.   Unrolled TCP/IP Loop with Staggered Loads

Instruction			Cycle 1	Cycle 2	Cycle 3	Cycle 4	Cycle 5
loop:	addo	g4,g2,g2	REG				
	ldob	(g0),g4	MEM				
	addo	g2,g3,g3		REG			
	lda	1(g0),g0		MEM			
	addo	g5,g2,g2			REG		
	ldob	(g0),g5			MEM		
	cmpdeci	0,g1,g1				REG	
	lda	1(g0),g0				MEM	
	addo	g2,g3,g3					REG
	bl.t	loop				CTRL	

exactly match the optimum dispatch patterns. Finally, rates above 1 IPC are possible only within program loops, since multiple instruction words may be decoded in parallel only when being retrieved from the on-chip instruction cache.

While the instruction cache decouples loop performance from external memory speed, system memory becomes a bottleneck for straight-line code execution. Sequential, uncached programs can proceed at best at a rate of four instructions for every six clock cycles, even with zero wait-state memory. This also applies to code that is called repeatedly but intermittently, including extended interrupt service routines and OS routines.

Embedded systems that might use the 960CA generally have DRAM- and EPROM-based main memory systems, in which case straight-line code performance falls to about 0.5 IPC. Ironically, the 4:1 disparity in performance between loops and nonloops gets worse as CPU frequencies increase: loop throughput will scale linearly, but external memories will likely require additional wait states. The net result is that the overall throughput of real 960CA-based systems is likely to vary wildly according to the nature of the application.

Conclusion

Future 960 family members will undoubtedly take steps to further increase performance and remedy the bus interface bottleneck. By adding more EUs, looking farther ahead in the instruction stream, and detecting a wider variety of instruction patterns, it should be possible to sustain more than 2 IPC. At 1 Kbyte, the 960CA instruction cache is small. Increasing the cache size should be straightforward, as would modifying the system interface logic. A 64-bit system bus and improved prefetch-miss detection would make it possible to sustain performance levels close to 2 IPC, even for external, straight-line programs.

30

Intel 960SA and 960SB

Michael Slater

Intel has introduced the 960SA and 960SB low-end members of the 960 family. The SA and SB are essentially the same as the 960KA and KB, respectively, but have a 16-bit data bus with an easier-to-use interface. Both chips have the same integer unit with four on-chip register sets and 512-byte instruction cache. The SB version also has an on-chip floating-point unit. (For now, the SA and SB are the same die; eventually, Intel is likely to design an optimized version of the SA that removes the floating-point logic.)

To create the SA and SB, Intel redesigned the KA/KB chip to eliminate the "secret" MMU, extra microcode, and other circuits that were remnants of the chip's origin at the now-defunct BiiN, and moved from a 1.5-micron to a 1-micron process. The die size reduction (the 960SB is only 270 mils square), combined with a lower-pin-count plastic package, have reduced Intel's costs significantly. The 960SA and SB are available in 10-and 16-MHz versions. While the KA and KB are available at 20 and 25 MHz, however, the SA and SB are limited to 16 MHz because of power dissipation limits in the plastic package.

The 960SA and SB performance is claimed to be about 70% that of the K-series parts, and is rated by Intel (at 16 MHz) at 5 VAX MIPS and 0.5 MFLOPS (for the SB). This may make them the slowest RISC processors yet, as well as the cheapest. Their performance puts them into the same class as the 68020, but at a somewhat lower price. In the future, Intel plans to develop more highly integrated versions with on-chip peripherals, which would compete directly against Motorola's 68300 family. For now, Motorola has the edge in integration, while Intel has the edge in price.

The most interesting aspect of the SA and SB chips is that they bring a very wide range of price/performance to the 960 architecture. At the same time as the SA/SB introduction, Intel announced a 40-MHz version of the superscalar 960CA. This chip provides high integer performance, rated by Intel at 35 VAX MIPS, at a modest price (for its performance level) and with on-chip DMA controllers and programmable bus interface logic. This completes a spectrum of code-compatible parts ranging from the 960SA, to the KA, and then to the CA, for ever-increasing integer performance at clock rates from 10 to 40 MHz. The floating-point spectrum lacks a high end, however—the line ends after the 1-MFLOP 960KB. The missing device is what would naturally be called the 960CB.

P12 Shown, But Not Quite Announced

The closest thing to a 960CB is the 960MM, which Intel has shown off but not quite announced. The 960MM is an impressive chip. With a 620 × 680 mil die that contains over 1.5 million transistors, it is the largest microprocessor chip yet shown and is claimed to be the highest-performance CMOS microprocessor ever built. This is the chip formerly known by the code name P12.

The 960MM adds to the 960CA design a high-performance floating-point unit and a dedicated 64-bit data bus for cache memory or high-speed RAM. Intel claims the 960MM achieves a performance level of 50 VAX MIPS and 22 MFLOPS at 33 MHz. The VAX MIPS rating is of unspecified derivation; the MFLOPS rating is for single-precision SAXPY, which is a best-case benchmark since the 960MM can maintain its peak two instructions per clock rate while executing this loop.

Oddly, Intel isn't announcing the 960MM. Intel representatives talk about the embedded market not being ready for a device at this performance level. The chip was developed for military avionics customers, and is presumably being supplied to those customers—probably at a price tag of many thousands of dollars per chip. Why is Intel not announcing the chip as a commercial product? It is odd indeed for a semiconductor vendor to decide their product is too advanced for their customers; the usual approach is to make it available and let the customers decide if they want it.

Several factors may come into play here. Intel does not have a full set of development tools ready for the chip, and probably doesn't want to add another very complex device to the burden of the already overwhelmed applications and support staff. Yield probably isn't too good on this monster chip, which doesn't matter much at mil-spec prices but might make it difficult to come up with commercial prices that wouldn't provoke laughter. Finally, Intel's i860 group would probably rather see the chip suppressed, since it might confuse some designers looking for a high-performance floating-point engine.

Intel will provide a PC-add-in evaluation card that includes the 960MM with 4 Mbytes of DRAM and 1 Mbyte of SRAM.

VII

AMD 29000

31

AMD 29000 Architecture

Brian Case

In preceding chapters we've presented descriptions of various RISC processors, including the 88000, 80960, and SPARC. The 29000 was announced well before any of these processors, yet is as fast as any. Furthermore, it is relatively inexpensive, and is designed to work well with lower-cost noncached memory systems. This chapter describes the architecture of the 29000, primarily from a software point of view. Following chapters will present the hardware perspective and explore various memory architectures that can be used.

The 29000 is the first member of AMD's high-performance RISC microprocessor family. The architecture of the 29000 puts it squarely in the RISC camp. However, the implementation and the bus structure set the chip apart because the chip was designed to achieve high performance in embedded applications without caches. Of course, cached systems can be built for general-purpose applications like UNIX workstations.

Programmer's Model

The programmer's model for the 29000 is simple but unconventional. In particular:

- There is a very large register file, all of whose registers are simultaneously addressable.
- 128 of the registers are addressed relative to an internal "stack pointer;" this provides a very fast, software-definable procedure call mechanism.

- There is only one memory addressing mode, register indirect.
- Information about the relationship between two operands is communicated by the status of the MSB in any general-purpose register instead of by a single set of condition codes. (The conventional V, N, Z, and C condition codes are available in the special ALU status register.)

In many other respects, the 29000 is a conventional RISC machine:

- All instructions are four bytes long and there are only a few instruction formats.
- All instructions flow through the pipeline in the same way.
- Nearly all instructions can be executed in a single cycle.
- Only load and store instructions reference external memory.
- Low-level parallelism is exposed for optimization in the form of delayed branches, overlapped load and store, and integer/floating-point concurrency.

Register File

The 29000 register file contains a total of 192 general-purpose registers (see Figure 1). The total is distributed among two logically (but not physically) separate files:

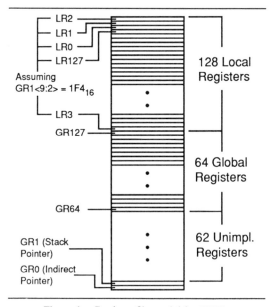

Figure 1. Register file model for 29000

- Global registers: 64 registers with fixed names; the MSB cleared in an 8-bit register field specifies "global" while the remaining seven bits select one of the globals.
- Local registers: 128 registers with relative names; the MSB set in an 8-bit register field specifies "local" and the physical register address (into the local file) is calculated by taking the 7-bit logical register name from the 8-bit register field, adding the 32-bit internal stack pointer [held in global register one (GR1)], and truncating the sum to seven bits.

An implementation of the 29000 architecture may have up to 128 global registers, but, due to die size limitations, only 64 globals are implemented on the first chips. In assembly language, the implemented globals have names GR64 to GR127; the locals have names LR0 to LR127, as Figure 1 shows. Notice that an implementation may have more than 128 local registers, but the local file must be a power-of-two in size and only 128 locals are directly addressable at one time.

The internal stack pointer has the name GR1 even though it is not meant to be used as a general-purpose register. It can be thought of as "pointing into" the local register file since it specifies which of the 128 physical registers LR0 actually names. All other local registers are offset from LR0, wrapping around from top to bottom of the local register file if necessary (e.g., LR2 to LR3 in Figure 1).

GR1 is implemented as a full 32-bit register since it must be used to reference memory for register file overflow and underflow; however, only seven bits (GR1 bits 2–9) actually affect the local register file addressing. The two least-significant bits of GR1 are ignored since the internal stack pointer value is a byte address while register-file addresses are four-byte word addresses.

GR0 is the *indirect pointer;* the indirect pointer allows the register file to be addressed indirectly as if it were simply a bank of RAM. There are three separate indirect pointers, one for each of the three register fields in arithmetic/logical instructions. When an instruction's register field specifies GR0, the corresponding indirect pointer value addresses the register file, and the selected register is then used as a source or destination instead of GR0. This mechanism can be used to pass parameters very efficiently to short subroutines such as integer multiply and to handle traps more efficiently. Special instructions allow the three GR0 registers to be initialized.

Registers can be protected from user-mode access with a resolution of 16 registers per bank. This protection feature can be used to reserve some global registers for exclusive use by the operating system.

Special Registers

The special registers in the 29000 are used to hold non-general-purpose processor state. Information such as processor status, processor configuration, memory-reference restart state, indirect pointer values, register bank protection and condition codes are kept in special registers. Some special registers can only be accessed in supervisor mode.

A value in a special register can be read into a general-purpose register or a value in a general-purpose register can be written into a special register. No direct access between special registers and external memory is possible.

The Translation Look-aside Buffer (TLB) entries form yet another register space in the 29000. Again, information can only be transferred between TLB entries and general-purpose registers. Each of the 64 entries in the TLB has two associated 32-bit special registers.

Memory Addressing

The 29000 architecture defines only load- and store-register instructions for accessing external memory, coprocessors, and I/O devices. The only addressing mode available is register indirect; i.e., the value in a general-purpose register is used, unmodified, as a 32-bit memory pointer. The lack of "powerful" addressing modes may seem crippling at first. However, since the local register file implements a stack-pointer-plus-offset addressing mode, many memory references that would have required an addressing mode go directly to the register file instead. This is evidenced by the fact that traces of 29000 programs show roughly half the number of memory references as exhibited by 32-register architectures such as MIPS' R2000 and Motorola's 88000.

The 29000 has an on-chip MMU, so addresses leaving the chip are physical addresses. The TLB in the MMU has a total of 64 virtual-to-physical address translations. The TLB is two-way-set associative with least-recently used (LRU) replacement. A TLB miss simply causes a trap to a supervisor trap handler; this allows the system to implement any virtual memory scheme. The MMU supports four page sizes in hardware: 1K, 2K, 4K and 8K bytes.

Instruction Set

The instruction set of the 29000 is very simple and regular (see Table 1). All arithmetic and logical operations are defined as three-register-address

Table 1. Instruction Set Summary for 29000

Integer Arithmetic
Add
Add, signed
Add, unsigned
Add, w/carry
Add, w/carry, signed
Add, w/carry, unsigned
Sub
Sub, signed
Sub, unsigned
Sub, w/carry
Sub, w/carry, signed
Sub, w/carry unsigned
Sub reverse
Sub reverse, signed
Sub reverse, unsigned
Sub reverse, w/carry
Sub reverse, w/carry, signed
Sub reverse, w/carry, unsigned
Multiply, unsigned
Multiply, signed
Multiply step, signed
Multiply last step
Multiply step, unsigned
Divide, signed
Divide, unsigned
Divide first step, unsigned
Divide step, unsigned
Divide last step, unsigned
Complete remainder, unsigned

Integer Compare
Compare equal
Compare not equal
Compare less than
Compare less than, unsigned
Compare less equal
Compare less equal, unsigned
Compare greater than
Compare greater than, un-
  signed
Compare greater equal
Compare greater equal,
  unsigned
Compare bytes

**Integer Assert (compare &
trap)**
Assert equal
Assert not equal
Assert less than
Assert less than, unsigned
Assert less equal
Assert less equal, unsigned
Assert greater than
Assert greater than, unsigned
Assert greater equal
Assert greater equal, unsigned

Logical
And   Nand   And-not
Or   Nor
Xor   Xnor

Shift
Shift left logical
Shift right logical
Shift right arithmetic
Extract (uses funnel shifter)

Data Movement
Load   Store
Load & lock bus
Store & lock bus
Load & set (test & set)
Load multiple   Store multiple
Extract byte   Extract halfword
Extract halfword, signed
Insert byte   Insert halfword
Move from special register
Move to special register
Move to special register, imme-
  diate
Move from TLB register
Move to TLB register

Constant
Set lower 16 bits of register,
  zeros to upper 16 bits
Set upper 16 bits of register,
  lower 16-bits unmodified
Set lower 16-bits of register,
  ones to upper 16 bits

Floating Point
Single add   Double add
Single sub   Double sub

Shift (cont.)
Single multiply Double multiply
Single divide   Double divide
Single equal compare
Double equal compare
Single greater equal compare
Double greater equal compare
Single greater than compare
Double greater than compare
Convert, general purpose

Delayed Branch
Call relative (branch and save
  return address)
Call indirect
Jump unconditional
Jump unconditional, indirect
Jump true
Jump true, indirect
Jump false
Jump false, indirect
Jump false and decrement

Miscellaneous, System
Count leading zeros (prioritize)
Set indirect pointers A, B, & C
Emulate (set indirect pointers A
  and B and trap)
Invalidate BTC
Return from interrupt
Return from interrupt and invali-
  date BTC
Halt

operations: Any three of the 192 registers, two sources and a destination, may be specified in a single instruction. Most instructions allow the second source operand field to specify either a register or a zero-extended, 8-bit constant.

Integer addition and subtraction instructions are provided in versions that ignore overflow and versions that trap on overflow. Trapping on signed, two's-complement, or unsigned overflow can be specified. The Carry condition-code bit can be included for implementing multiprecision arithmetic. Integer subtract instructions are provided in "reverse" form to allow "constant minus register" to be implemented in one instruction.

Instructions for atomic integer multiply and divide are defined but simply cause traps in the first implementation. Full multiply and divide can be built from the provided one-bit-at-a-time multiply and divide step instructions.

The logical operations AND, OR, XOR, XNOR, ANDNOT [a AND (NOT b)], NAND, and NOR are provided. The ANDNOT operation is very useful for constructing arbitrary bit-field operations.

Logical left-shift and logical and arithmetic right-shift operations are defined. Since the second source operand may be either a register name or an 8-bit constant, shifting can be done by either a variable or constant amount. More sophisticated shift, rotate, and field operations can be implemented with the funnel-shifter. The funnel shifter concatenates two 32-bit values and extracts a 32-bit value at a bit boundary specified by the value in the FC special register.

Compare instructions create a Boolean value in the MSB of the destination register. The full set of less-than, less-equal, greater-than, greater-equal, equal-to, and not-equal are provided both in two's-complement and unsigned versions. If the tested relationship holds, then the MSB of the destination register is set, otherwise the MSB is cleared.

Branch instructions are available in either PC-relative or register-indirect forms. A 16-bit word offset (equivalent to an 18-bit byte offset) is provided for all PC-relative branches. The call instruction saves the return PC value in any general-purpose register. Conditional branches decide whether or not to branch based on the status of the MSB in the general-purpose register named in the instruction. Both "jump-false" (MSB clear) and "jump-true" (MSB set) versions are available.

The assert instructions are very similar to the compares. The same set of operations is provided, but the assert instructions cause a trap if the asserted condition does not hold. The 8-bit field used for the destination register in compare instructions specifies a trap vector for asserts.

A special compare instruction compares the four pairs of corresponding bytes in two 32-bit operands for equality. If any of the four pairs are equal, then the MSB in the destination register is set to true. This instruction plus the funnel-shifter can be used to implement fast versions of the C library strcpy and strcmp functions.

The load and store instructions specify two registers, one for an address and one for data. The remaining 8-bit field specifies control information such as memory or I/O space. Three of the bits directly drive three pins on the bus interface. These three user bits have predefined meanings, such as the size of a memory operand, but can be used for miscellaneous control purposes if desired.

Load- and store-multiple instructions allow up to 192 registers to be transferred to or from memory with one instruction. These instructions can also invoke burst mode on the data bus, if the system implements it. In burst mode, the data bus transfers 32-bit words as fast as one per clock cycle, for a maximum data-bus bandwidth of 100 MBytes/s at 25 MHz.

Floating-point instructions are defined in the architecture but simply cause traps in the current implementation. The trap handler can then either emulate the instruction or issue the proper sequence of operations to the 29027 floating-point accelerator. For the current version of the 29000, direct manipulation of the 29027 yields the highest performance by eliminating trap overhead.

A forthcoming 29000 implementation with high-performance on-chip floating-point will support only the defined, atomic instructions. Therefore, code will have to be changed if direct manipulation of the 29027 is used.

Instructions for performing such system functions as invalidating the on-chip cache and performing interrupt return are also provided.

Procedure Call Mechanism

The stack-pointer-plus-offset addressing mode implemented by the local register file allows a very fast procedure call mechanism to be implemented. This mechanism is very similar to SPARC's "register windows" but is more flexible since the "window" size and amount of overlap are variable.

Basically, the mechanism works by having a procedure or function allocate, when it is called, as many registers as it needs for its own locals and the maximum number of out-going parameters. The allocation is done by decrementing the internal stack pointer, GR1, by the appropriate amount. Before a procedure calls another procedure, it calculates parameter values directly into the out-going parameter area. The called procedure allocates its registers (by decrementing GR1 again) and checks to make sure that enough free registers exist in the local file. If insufficient space exists, a trap is taken and some of the "oldest" register values are spilled to external memory to make room.

Before the called procedure returns, it deallocates its registers by incrementing GR1 and uses a value passed by its caller to make sure that all of the context of its caller is resident in the register file. If only part of the context is resident, a trap is taken to fill the vacant part.

Thus, the local register file is a circular buffer (this is why it must be a power-of-two in size), and memory is referenced on its behalf only when consecutive calls or returns cause the stack to grow or shrink by more than 128 words. This happens on less than 5% of calls and returns.

Note that as effective as this procedure call mechanism is, the architecture does not force its use. If desired, the register file can be viewed by software as a simple, flat pool of 192 registers. Or, the bank protection feature can be combined with the internal stack pointer to create many small process contexts.

Branching

Branches give rise to two kinds of latency in program execution: pipeline latency, which is the time it takes the processor to generate the address of the branch destination, and memory latency, which is the initial access time of the instruction memory. Most high-bandwidth memories, including video RAMs, static column RAMs, and caches, have an initial latency that must elapse before the full bandwidth is available.

All 29000 branches are delayed branches in which the instruction that immediately follows the branch is executed regardless of whether or not the branch itself is actually taken. Implementing delayed branches allows the 29000 to recover pipeline latency.

The Branch Target Cache (BTC) is implemented to cover the latency of the external instruction memory. The BTC is two-way-set associative and consists of 32 four-instruction entries. The first time a branch is taken, the instructions at the branch destination are fetched into the CPU and the BTC simultaneously. If the same branch target is used again while still resident in the BTC, the first four instructions at the branch destination are supplied to the CPU pipeline directly from the BTC.

At the same time, the branch destination address plus four (16 bytes) is sent to the external instruction memory; the destination address plus four is the address of the fifth instruction at the branch destination. Thus, during the access time of the external instruction memory, the CPU continues to execute instructions. By the time the four BTC instructions are consumed by the pipeline, the external instruction memory is ready with the fifth and succeeding instructions and can supply them at one per cycle.

32

AMD 29000 Bus Structure

Brian Case
Tim Olson

In the preceding chapter we saw how the architecture of the 29000 is based on a large register file and a simple instruction set. In this chapter we look at the bus structure of the 29000 and how it supports different memory configurations for a range of cost and performance levels.

The Problem

The great promise of RISC architectures is the execution of one instruction per clock cycle. However, this means that, somehow, a new instruction must be made available on every cycle. For a RISC microprocessor running at 25 MHz, this means that the instruction bandwidth alone is 100 Mbytes/second.

The first thing that RISC architects and computer system designers realize is that the burden of providing the required instruction bandwidth eventually falls on the external memory system. It seems that each RISC implementation takes a different approach to memory system design. The 29000 somewhat relaxes the burden on external memory systems by adding a separate instruction bus.

But a memory system that can deliver the required bandwidth might still have a problem meeting the latency demands of a RISC processor. To help match the processor with the memory, the 29000's on-chip branch-target cache (BTC) can hide up to four cycles of instruction memory latency.

Bus Structure

The external interface of the 29000 consists of three 32-bit buses and a collection of control lines. The three buses are the input-only instruction bus, the output-only address bus, and the bidirectional data bus. Three access protocols are available on the data and instruction buses (see Figure 1):

- Simple: The 29000 holds the address bus valid for the entire duration of the transaction. Even though the timing constraints can be severe at high clock rates, a transaction as short as one clock cycle is possible.
- Pipelined: The 29000 holds the address bus valid until the external device or memory signals that it has latched the address. The 29000 is then free to output another address. Only one pending transaction is allowed.
- Burst: The 29000 sends one address, which is latched by the external device or memory. Subsequent transitions of the instruction or data READY signal will transfer data or instructions without using the address bus. The addresses for these transactions are formed by incrementing the previous address by four. Burst transactions continue until either the 29000 or the external device or memory chooses to terminate the burst.

All three protocols allow single-cycle completion.

The separate instruction bus combined with the burst protocol gives the 29000 a modified Harvard architecture: it can simultaneously fetch instructions and data. The separate bus also prevents unpredictable data accesses from interrupting the instruction stream. A dedicated instruction address bus is not needed because of the burst-mode protocol. After one instruction address is transmitted, burst mode can take over, freeing

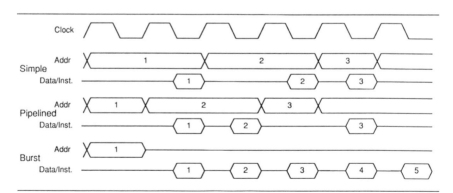

Figure 1. Timing protocols for the 29000's instruction and data buses

the address bus, until the next change of program flow is generated by a branch.

The 29000 has an on-chip translation-look-aside buffer (TLB) that caches 64 translations in a two-way set-associative structure. The TLB translates both instruction and data addresses so the memory system can deal directly with physical, rather than virtual, addresses. This is especially important for low-cost systems where the protection and relocation advantages of virtual-to-physical translation are desired but the expense and access-time impact of an external MMU are prohibitive.

Split Memory System

Figure 2 shows the simplest type of memory system. This configuration gives the highest bandwidth and parallelism for the lowest cost. Cost can be reduced even further by eliminating the latch and counter in front of the instruction memory, although performance will suffer if the memory isn't fast enough.

Using this configuration, casting the instruction memory in ROM makes the most sense for small, embedded applications. However, ROM chips fast enough to keep up with the processor are not readily available (although bipolar ROMs could be used if the program is small enough). One solution is to interleave two or four banks of ROM and let the BTC hide the latency. This is feasible if the program is so large that it would require multiple banks of ROM anyway. Perhaps ROMs with on-chip interleaving will be available someday.

One of the advantages of this system is that the instruction and data memories need not be made from the same technology. For example, the McCray NuBus card from YARC Systems (Westlake Village, California)

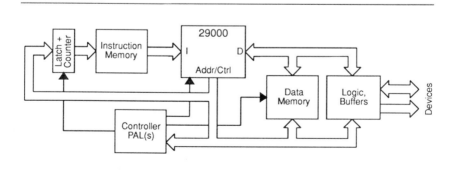

Figure 2. Simple 29000 system with separate instruction and data memory

uses static column DRAM (SCRAM) for instructions and high-speed static RAM for data. This is an especially efficient configuration because SCRAMs have a built-in address latch.

Another possibility is to interleave two or four banks of RAM to get the required bandwidth. This is especially feasible with medium-speed static RAMs since more than one bank is probably necessary anyway just to get the needed capacity.

The problem with using RAM instead of ROM for instructions in this configuration is that the 29000 has no way to load its own programs. However, some systems can safely assume that an external host will be able to address both the instruction and data RAM. For example, the YARC card relies on its host, a Mac II, to load its instruction memory.

Combined Memory

Video system designers have solved some of the problems of high-bandwidth requirements by convincing memory vendors to produce the ubiquitous Video DRAM (VRAM). VRAM is much like static column DRAM in that it has an on-chip address register, but the VRAM adds an up-counter function to that register and a second, completely separate data port.

A VRAM works by latching an entire row of bits in its "serial shift register." After the row is latched, each succeeding transition of the serial shift clock makes the next bit(s) of the row available at the serial data port. Most VRAMs specify a maximum serial shift clock speed of at least 25 MHz; some will be in the 40-MHz range.

VRAMs are a natural match to the 29000 because:

- They have two ports, a serial port and a random-access port, which can connect directly to the 29000's instruction and data buses, respectively.
- The "latch address and shift out until a new address" mode of VRAMs directly matches the "send me sequential instructions until the next branch" burst mode of the 29000.
- The "by-four" organization of most VRAMs means that a minimum system can be built with eight chips.
- The BTC is nearly a perfect match to the initial latency of a serial shift register load operation. Thus, a VRAM system can run 29000 loops at or near full speed.
- The large register file leads to fewer loads and stores; this mitigates the negative effect of the slow random-access port of VRAMs.

Figure 3 shows a VRAM system block diagram. AMD has built a 29000 IBM-PC card with a VRAM memory system for evaluation purposes.

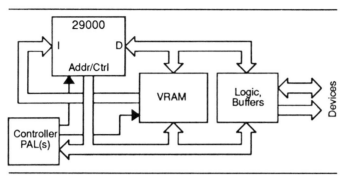

Figure 3. Video-RAM system

Figure 4 shows a second combined memory system, this time built entirely from SCRAMs. This configuration has lower performance than either the VRAM or split memory systems because the instruction and data buses are tied together (parallelism is lost). However, like the VRAM system, it has the advantage that the 29000 can load its own programs.

Split Caches

Of course, the 29000 can also be configured with a cached memory system, and performance is typically highest with caches. Unfortunately, system cost is usually highest as well.

The AMD 29062 8-Kbyte integrated cache chip interfaces directly with the 29000 and has a separate "back-end" multiplexed bus that connects to the main memory system. The multiplexed bus supports high-speed burst

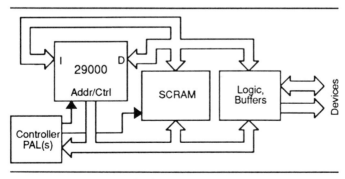

Figure 4. Static-column RAM system

transfers to keep from degrading system performance on cache misses. Figure 5 shows a 29000 system using integrated caches.

Another option is to build the caches using discrete components. Cache tag-buffer RAMs, such as the Fujitsu MB81C51, are a good starting point. This chip implements the tag store RAM, comparators, and multiplexing needed for one-, two-, or four-way set associative operation and comes in 25- and 30-ns speed grades. The data store RAM and reload logic must be implemented externally.

Floating Point

The 29027 is the 29000's companion floating-point accelerator. It operates as an autonomous, slave coprocessor and connects directly to the 29000's address and data buses. The 29027 is a combinatorial floating-point ALU as opposed to the complete, microprogrammed floating-point processors available for most traditional microprocessors. Thus, complex operations, including division, are implemented by a sequence of operations programmed by the 29000. Any of the system designs presented here can incorporate the 29027 if high-performance floating-point capability is required.

The three "user" bits in the control field of load and store instructions address and control some of the 29027 operations. Thus, the address and data buses can be used together (with data on both buses) to send a double-precision operand to the 29027 in one clock cycle.

Cycle Time versus Performance

Since the memory subsystem is such a large part of the total system cost, it makes sense to pay attention to trade-offs possible between processor

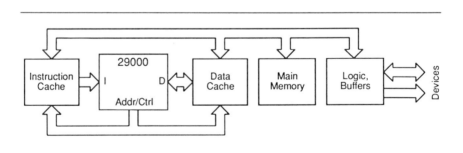

Figure 5. System using integrated caches

clock speed, system cost, and system performance. The interactions can be subtle, and different applications require different solutions.

For a system that spends most of its time waiting on data memory, performance can be improved by exploiting the 29000's ability to complete a memory transaction in a single cycle, even if it means lowering the processor clock rate. A 16-MHz system that completes a data access in one cycle might be faster than a 20-MHz system, or even a 25-MHz system, that requires two or three cycles.

As another example, consider the choice between a 30-MHz system and a 20-MHz system, both using VRAM. If the application executes a fairly large number of instructions between branches, then the 30-MHz system will probably win out, since the initial latency of the VRAM is amortized over a large number of instructions. However, if only a small number of instructions are executed between branches, the 20-MHz system might win because it will waste fewer cycles waiting for the serial shift register in the VRAM to reload.

This points to a general technique for improving performance when instruction memory, such as VRAM, has a single-cycle burst but multiple-cycle latency: "straighten" the code to eliminate taken branches. The technique of loop unrolling (using in-line code instead of iterative loops) is especially useful.

Simulation and prototyping are the keys to designing an appropriate system. It may turn out that a system running at a slower clock rate will be able to use cheaper memory while still delivering acceptable performance. Of course, there is no substitute for fast memory in some applications.

Performance Comparison

A look at Table 1 gives a feeling for the relative performance of 29000 systems built with the memory systems described above. A simulation of the Dhrystone 1.1 benchmark (compiled with the MetaWare C compiler) was done for each of the memory systems. To get a meaningful comparison of the results, you need to know several parameters for each system:

- The 29000 clock rate
- Instruction and data memory parameters: cycles for first (i.e. random) access and cycle for subsequent burst accesses

For example, for the VRAM system running at 25 MHz, the first instruction access takes four cycles with subsequent instruction burst accesses requiring only one cycle; and every data access takes four cycles (i.e, no data burst mode is supported).

Table 1. Relative Performance for Various Memory Configurations

Parameter	Memory System			
	Split (YARC)	Comb. SCRAM	Comb. VRAM	Split Cache
System clock	25 MHz	16 MHz	25 MHz	25 MHz
Instr. first	2–5 cy.	3 cy.	4 cy.	2 cy.
Instr. burst	1 cy.	1 cy.	1 cy.	1 cy.
Data first	2 cy.	3 cy.	4 cy.	2 cy.
Data burst	2 cy.	1 cy.	4 cy.	1 cy.
Dhrystones	31000	12680	24331	35653

The YARC board's SCRAM instruction memory requires two or three cycles for the first instruction fetch, depending on whether the address is even or odd, and five cycles if a page boundary is crossed.

The cache parameters are for AMD's integrated cache chips (one each for data and instructions). The Dhrystone value for this configuration is slightly pessimistic because the simulation did not take into account the cache chip's prefetch capability.

33

AMD 29050

Brian Case

The first real update to AMD's 29000 family is the 29050. This chip significantly increases the level of integration available from AMD by adding high-performance, on-chip floating point and doubling the size of the branch target cache (BTC). The chip contains numerous additional architectural and implementation changes to wring a little extra performance from the integer pipeline without resorting to superscalar or super-pipelined techniques.

The 29050 is composed of 428,000 transistors, as compared to 210,000 for the 29000. The chip is fabricated in an 0.8-micron process and has a die size of 480 × 542 mils.

In some sense, the 29050 implementation only brings the 29000 family into parity with current offerings in other RISC families, such as the 88000 and the 860, which have had on-chip floating point from the beginning. On the other hand, from the point of view of embedded control, which is the 29000's raison d'être, AMD is breaking new RISC ground. (Intel's 960KB has on-chip floating-point hardware, but does not come close to the performance of the 29050.) The 29050 is pin-compatible with the 29000, so existing designs can be upgraded with no hardware changes.

Many of the 29050's new features have been added to improve performance, but a number of functional enhancements have also been incorporated. For performance, the 29050 includes a parallel, pipelined floating-point unit, a larger BTC, a physical address cache (PAC), an early address generator (EAG), instruction forwarding logic, and a four-port register file with 64-bit ports. New functional features include a third operating mode called Monitor Mode (to allow debugging of supervisor code), the ability to set two instruction-address breakpoints, a region-mapping unit (RMU), a condition-code accumulator (CCA), new instructions, and new special registers.

Floating Point

The most prominent new feature of the 29050 is its on-chip floating-point unit. The new hardware directly implements all the floating-point instructions (add, subtract, multiply, divide, compare, convert, and square root) that were defined as part of the 29000 instruction set but implemented in the companion 29027 floating-point accelerator. In earlier family members, 29000 system designers with a need for high-performance floating point had two choices: directly manipulate the companion 29027, or use the floating-point instructions coupled with trap handlers. The trap handlers could then either emulate the instructions in software or manipulate the 29027. This put the designer in a Catch-22 since directly manipulating the 29027 would sacrifice object-code compatibility with the 29050, but using the traps sacrificed considerable performance. Most designers probably opted to manipulate the 29027 directly. Fortunately, in embedded applications, modifying the source code for a next-generation design isn't usually a major problem.

Figure 1 shows a block diagram of the 29050's execution units. As the diagram implies, many instructions can conceptually be executing concurrently. In practice, the sustained parallelism will be limited by the fact that the basic pipeline of the machine can only decode one instruction per cycle. This is why it does not make sense for the register file to have more read ports or to have a separate floating-point register file.

Figure 2 shows a block diagram of the floating-point hardware. Through use of the new multiply-accumulate instructions, an add and a multiply can proceed concurrently. The units are pipelined to allow initiation of a new add, subtract, or multiply every cycle for single-precision. For double-precision multiply, a new operation can be issued only every four cycles. Table 1 summarizes the latencies and issue rates. In IEEE-compatible mode, denormal operands or results can add several additional cycles of latency.

Like Intel's i860, the 29050 FPU uses dedicated accumulators. These registers are included to speed up common multiply-accumulate applications without requiring additional read ports from the general register file. The 29050 also offers an independent divide/square-root unit that operates in parallel with the other units, so other calculations can proceed while these relatively slow operations are in progress.

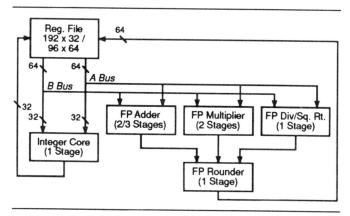

Figure 1. The execution units of the 29050

The floating-point hardware can operate in two basic modes according to the state of the FF bit in the floating-point environment special register: complete IEEE compliance mode and ''fast floating-point'' mode. In fast-float mode, the processing of denormalized numbers is disabled. Implementing denormalized numbers per the IEEE standard can take extra cycles in some cases thereby reducing performance. Fast-float mode is available for applications that will not benefit from denormalized numbers

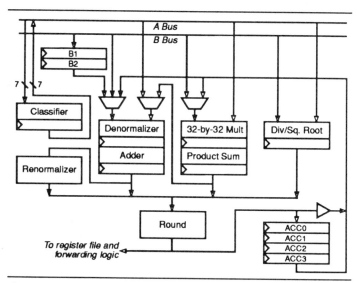

Figure 2. The FP hardware uses dedicated accumulator registers when operating in multiply/accumulate mode. All data paths are 64 bits wide except as noted.

Table 1. Floating-point Performance in Clock Cycles

Operation	Latency		Issue Rate	
	SP	DP	SP	DP
Add/Subtract	3-4	3-4	1	1
Multiply	3	6	1	4
Divide	11	18	10	17
Multiply/ Accumulate	6	9	1	4
Square Root	28	57	27	56

but will benefit from more performance. The composite floating-point instructions that perform multiply-accumulate-type functions always operate in fast-float mode regardless of the FF bit.

The FPU in the 29050 also executes the integer multiply instruction. An integer multiply takes three cycles; an integer divide takes 26 cycles.

Instruction Fetch Performance

The 29050 incorporates two performance enhancements to reduce lost cycles due to branches: a larger branch target cache, and instruction forwarding.

The 29000's BTC can cache up to four instructions at the 32 most-recently used branch targets. The four-instruction depth of each entry is a good match to DRAM and VRAM memories but is wastefully deep for external SRAM memory. In addition, the 32-entry cache has a typical hit rate of only about 60%. For the 29050, the BTC has been doubled in size and can be configured for an entry depth of either four or two instructions. Thus, for DRAM memory systems, the hit rate will be improved to about 80% simply because of the size increase. For designs with SRAM instruction memory (or an external cache), the BTC hit rate can be increased even further by using two-instruction entries, which effectively doubles the number of BTC entries to 128.

The depth of BTC entries is set by the state of the CO (cache organization) bit in the processor configuration register. Regardless of organization, the BTC remains two-way set associative, as in the original 29000.

The second instruction-fetch performance enhancement is instruction forwarding. In the 29000, when an instruction is fetched from external memory, it must pass through an instruction latch and a prefetch buffer before arriving at the instruction register. Thus, whenever the 29000 pipeline needs an instruction from external memory, the processor may have to wait while the instructions flow through the latch and prefetch buffer. Instructions were routed in this way to save the area required to route another 32-bit bus on the chip. In the 29050, instructions bypass the latch and prefetch buffer saving one cycle in certain cases (such as when there is a miss in the BTC).

Accelerating Load Instructions

A source of performance degradation in any processor is memory references. Loads are typically twice as frequent as stores and nearly always create a data dependency, so they are a natural place to look for performance improvement. One way to improve performance without requiring faster external memory is to present the memory address on the pins earlier. In the 29050, early address generation and the physical address cache attempt to put load addresses on the address bus one cycle earlier than in the 29000.

Many load and store instructions are preceded by either an add instruction or a const/consth instruction pair because 29000 load and store instructions have only the register-indirect addressing mode. (The const instruction loads the low half of the register, and consth loads the high half.) These address-calculation instructions will be in the execute stage, which contains the TLB, on the cycle before a load will need to use the TLB.

The early address generator (EAG) is a dedicated adder that duplicates the function of the ALU for address calculation instructions. Since it is a simple adder instead of a full-function ALU, it is faster, and its output is fed directly to the TLB. Since the TLB is guaranteed not to be needed for add and const/consth instructions, the TLB can always be accessed for instructions that are likely to generate a load address. If the translation is not actually needed, it is just discarded.

So, when an address calculation instruction precedes a load instruction that uses the calculated address, the 29050 hardware has automatically translated the address one cycle early. In turn, the physical address can be used to drive the address bus one cycle early.

In effect, the memory access time is reduced by one cycle for loads that can make use of early address generation. For two-cycle external data memory (SRAM or an external cache) this is a factor of two improvement. For slower memory, the improvement is less dramatic.

For loads that are not preceded by an address computation, early address generation is not effective. To help get the memory address out early for these loads, the 29050 has a physical address cache (PAC). The PAC is a four-entry, direct-mapped cache. It is like a small TLB but is conceptually in the decode stage, as shown in Figure 3. The PAC is indexed by the least two significant bits of the register specified as the address in a load instruction. Each PAC entry contains a register number, a valid bit, and a 32-bit physical address.

A hit in the PAC occurs when the load address register number matches the register number in the selected PAC entry. On a hit, the physical address for the load is forwarded directly to the memory address register that drives the address bus, presenting the address to the memory one cycle earlier.

When a load is in the decode stage and the PAC misses, the selected PAC entry is updated with the address register number and physical address of the load. If a regular instruction, say an add, updates the value of a register cached in the PAC, the corresponding PAC entry is updated with the translation of the new address. The PAC is effective when, for example, the address of a variable is passed to a subroutine.

Debugging Features

A couple of new features in the 29050 make debugging a little easier. Two instruction address breakpoint registers have been added. Each breakpoint has two associated special registers: one for the instruction address and one for breakpoint control.

Breakpoint control is configurable in a number of ways. A bit in the control register determines whether the breakpoint causes a trap or a pulse on an external pin. Another bit determines whether or not the breakpoint will occur when address translation is enabled. If so, an eight-bit field specifies which process identifier will trigger the breakpoints. Thus, a breakpoint can be set for a specific process while a multitasking operating system is running.

In addition to the user and supervisor modes of the 29000, the 29050 implements "monitor mode." Monitor mode allows the processor to take a trap while in supervisor mode without corrupting the supervisor state. Normally, when traps are enabled, traps and interrupts vector to a routine specific to the trap or interrupt. When traps are disabled, usually in supervisor mode, and a trap occurs, the 29050 enters monitor mode and vectors to the WARN trap handler regardless of the kind of trap that occurred. The new "reason vector number" special register holds the number of the trap that was taken. Three new special "shadow PC" registers keep track of the PC values for the interrupted supervisor code. Together with instruction address breakpoints, monitor mode allows easier debugging of real-time operating system kernels.

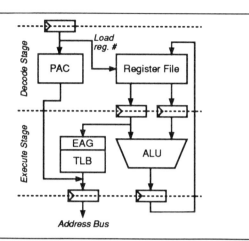

Figure 3. The PAC can send a load address to the address bus one cycle early by bypassing the TLB. The EAG/TLB can translate an address one cycle early when a load is preceded by an address computation instruction.

Region Mapping

The MMU of the 29050 extends the capability of the 29000 with two region mapping units (RMUs). The RMUs allow a large, contiguous area of memory to be given a virtual-to-physical address translation without "polluting" the main TLB with many page translations.

The RMUs are similar to facilities provided by MMUs for other microprocessor families. RMUs are useful for such things as video frame buffers and sparse I/O spaces. Each RMU has two associated special registers: an address register and a control register. The address register contains a 16-bit virtual base address and a 16-bit physical base address. The number of bits of the base addresses that participate in translation is determined by the region-size field in the control register. The region-size field can encode 16 different sizes ranging from 64 Kbytes to 2 Gbytes.

The control register also contains the other bits associated with any TLB entry: user and supervisor access permissions, a task identifier, and other miscellaneous information.

Condition-Code Accumulator

The 29050 implements "condition-code" accumulation to allow the concatenation of the results of several operations into a single "condition-code accumulator'' (CCA). (The 29000 architecture doesn't use traditional condition codes; the CCA accumulates the single-bit results from compare instructions.) Whenever an integer ALU instruction specifies global register gr3 as a destination, the CCA is shifted left one bit and the most-significant bit of the ALU result (which is the one-bit result of a compare instruction) is placed in the least-significant bit of the CCA. After several results have been accumulated, the contents of the CCA can be read by specifying global register gr2 as a source in an integer instruction. The CCA is a peculiar feature that does not appear to be especially useful.

New Instructions

Two new integer instructions have been added: orn (or, not) and consthz. Consthz forms a 32-bit constant where the upper 16 bits are specified in the instruction and the lower 16 bits are cleared. This instruction is useful primarily for forming small floating-point constants. Using the standard 29000 instruction set, forming such a constant takes two instructions, a const followed by a consth.

Six new floating-point instructions, as shown in Table 2, have been added to take advantage of the parallelism available between the adder and the multiplier. The FMAC and DMAC ''multiply-accumulate'' instructions are useful for matrix-multiply applications. The FMSM and DMSM ''multiply-sum'' instructions are useful for Gaussian elimination.

Conclusion

The 29050 significantly expands the range of the 29000 family. By today's standards, it implements high-performance floating point in a conservative number of transistors. At the same time, several implementation tweaks slightly improve integer performance.

The 29050 provides exceptional floating-point performance. At clock rates of 20, 25, 33, and 40 MHz, AMD rates the 29050 at 17, 20, 27, and 32 MIPS (of unspecified derivation). Peak performance at 40 MHz is 40 integer MIPS and 80 MFLOPS. AMD claims sustained performance of 34 MFLOPS at 40 MHz for [4 × 4] × [4 × 1] graphics transforms. Whetstone performance at 40 MHz is 22.7 double-precision MWhets and 30.7 single-precision.

For a range of integer-only programs running on a 29050 with SRAM memory, AMD claims a 5–17% performance improvement over an equivalent 29000 system. For a DRAM memory system, the improvement is less compelling, ranging from 3% to 9%.

Table 2. New Floating-point Instructions

Instruction	Operation
FMAC/DMAC	ACC(n) = SRCA × SRCB + ACC(n)
FMSM/DMSM	DEST = SRCA × ACC(0) + SRCB
MFACC	DEST = ACC(n)
MTACC	ACC(n) = SRCA

The 29050's closest competitor is Intel's i860, which is substantially more expensive. Intel's 960 family, which is positioned more directly against the 29000 family, doesn't yet have an implementation that approaches the floating-point performance of the 29050. While the 29050 won't change the 29000's position in cost-sensitive embedded applications or in applications where floating-point is not needed, it will make the 29000 family competitive for high-end graphics systems and printers. AMD will presumably now direct its development efforts toward providing a low-cost, high-integration member of the family to fend off competition from IDT's new R305x parts and similar devices expected soon from other vendors.

34

PA-RISC

Brian Case

All other things being equal, a computer instruction set whose instructions are more semantically rich (i.e., do more work per instruction) can be better than an instruction set whose instructions do less. This was part of the reasoning that led to CISC architectures. It was thought that processors with semantically richer instructions would require fewer instruction fetches, have more compact programs, have better cache hit ratios, and would therefore execute programs faster. Unfortunately for CISCs, all other things are not equal; semantically rich instruction sets make pipelining difficult and are not the best interface for optimizing compilers, and RISC programs are not enough bigger to significantly reduce cache performance.

Nonetheless, it is worth wondering how rich an instruction set can be without reducing the benefits of the RISC design philosophy. It appears that the architects of the PA-RISC (Precision Architecture RISC, formerly HP PA for Hewlett Packard Precision Architecture, which we'll simply call PA) were wondering the same thing when they designed the instruction set.

Precision Architecture is far from new. HP introduced the first PA machines in 1985, using a TTL implementation of the processor. Since then HP has produced several implementations in NMOS and CMOS. The architecture has been used in both commercial and technical computers, primarily multiuser systems. With its new HP 9000 Series 700 workstations, HP is introducing the first revision to the architecture: PA-RISC

1.1, which includes enhancements designed to improve performance in technical applications.

In many ways, PA is a classic RISC architecture. It has fixed-size instructions, reasonably consistent instruction formats (e.g., register numbers are found in the same places), a load-store architecture (only loads and stores reference memory), a fairly small number of addressing modes, 32 general-purpose registers with register zero always reading as zero, and instruction semantics that permit hardwired implementation (no microcode) and reasonably easy pipelining.

Instruction Formats and Addressing Modes

Figure 1 shows just a sampling of some of the important instruction formats. (In the PA reference manual, the instruction format summary takes four pages.) Due to the large number of formats, there are many variations in field positions, but this probably does not create significant instruction decoding problems.

The convoluted instruction formats reflect a desire for maximum utilization of available instruction bits. Many architects would probably balk at having a noncontiguous displacement field, but there is nothing fundamentally wrong with it. HP's architects assert that the formats were optimized for the hardware structure, and not for aesthetics.

Figure 2 shows the available memory addressing mechanisms. Each load or store instruction provides only a subset of the modes, so to get a particular mode means first picking the right basic instruction.

A PA virtual address consists of a 32-bit linear *offset* and a *space identifier* of 16, 24, or 32 bits. The space identifier is concatenated with the offset to form the virtual address. HP uses the term "space" instead of segment because the spaces are disjoint (nonoverlapping), but they have all the limitations associated with segments. While PA can support 64-bit virtual addressing, linear addresses are limited to 32 bits.

The space ID is supplied from one of eight space registers; the space register number is either implicitly or explicitly selected by the sreg field in the instruction format. The offset may be

- Base register
- Base plus long (14-bit) displacement
- Base plus short (5-bit) displacement
- Base plus optionally shifted index

The base register optionally can be modified by the index or the offset. Base register modification implements a generalized pre-decrement/post-increment facility. If the offset is the base, the mode is like post-increment.

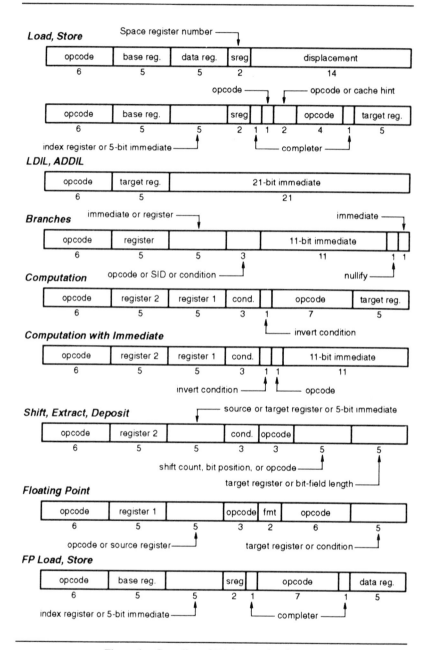

Figure 1. Sampling of PA instruction formats

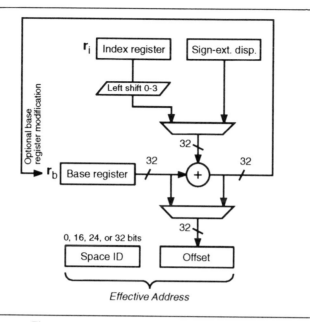

Figure 2. Memory address calculations for PA

If the offset is the result of the addressing computation, the mode is like pre-decrement. Most other RISCs don't provide any form of pre-decrement or post-increment addressing.

There is a tremendous amount of asymmetry in the availability of addressing modes. For example, if a program needs to load a byte and wants to use a base-register-modifying addressing mode, only a 5-bit displacement is available, while for words, 5-bit and 14-bit displacements are available. Indexed addressing is available only for loads, and not for stores.

Instruction Set

Table 1 lists the PA 1.1 instructions by group. Loads and stores for 32-bit words, 16-bit halfwords, and 8-bit bytes are provided. Floating-point loads and stores can move 32 or 64 bits at a time. Only zero-extended (unsigned) loads are provided for halfwords and bytes. Thus, to load a byte and sign extend it to the full width of a register requires an additional EXTRS instruction. Other RISCs have load signed and unsigned versions for bytes and halfwords. HP chose not to implement sign-extended loads because

Table 1.   PA 1.1 Instruction Set

Memory-Reference		Computation	
LDW	Load word	ADD	Add
LDH	Load halfword	ADDL	Add, logical
LDB	Load byte	ADDO	Add, trap on overflow
STW	Store word	ADDC	Add with carry
STH	Store halfword	ADDCO	Add with carry, trap on overflow
STB	Store byte	SH1ADD	Shift one and add
LDWM	Load word and modify	SH1ADDL	Shift one and add, logical
STWM	Store word and modify	SH1ADDO	Shift one and add, trap on overflow
LDWX	Load word, indexed	SH2ADD	Shift two and add
LDHX	Load halfword, indexed	SH2ADDL	Shift two and add, logical
LDBX	Load byte, indexed	SH2ADDO	Shift two and add, trap on overflow
LDWAX	Load word, absolute, indexed	SH3ADD	Shift three and add
LDCWX	Load and clear word, indexed	SH3ADDL	Shift three and add, logical
LDWS	Load word, short displacement	SH3ADDO	Shift three and add, trap on overflow
LDHS	Load halfword, short displacement	SUB	Subtract
LDBS	Load byte, short displacement	SUBO	Subtract, trap on overflow
LDWAS	Load word, absolute, short displacement	SUBB	Subtract with borrow
LDCWS	Load and clear word, short displacememt	SUBBO	Subtract with borrow, trap on overflow
STWS	Store word, short displacement	SUBT	Subtract, trap on condition
STHS	Store halfword, short displacement	SUBTO	Subtract, trap on condition or overflow
STBS	Store byte, short displacement	DS	Divide step
STWAS	Store word, absolute, short displacement	COMCLR	Compare and clear
STBYS	Store bytes, short displacement	OR	Inclusive OR
		XOR	Exclusive OR
Constant		AND	AND
LDO	Load offset	ANDCM	AND complement
LDIL	Load immediate left	UXOR	Unit exclusive OR
ADDIL	Add immediate left	UADDCM	Unit add complement
		UADDCMT	Unit add complement, trap on condition
Branch		DCOR	Decimal correct
BL	Branch and link	IDCOR	Intermediate decimal correct
GATE	Gateway	ADDI	Add to immediate
BLR	Branch and link, register	ADDIO	Add to immediate, trap on overflow
BV	Branch, vectored	ADDIT	Add to immediate, trap on condition
BE	Branch, external	ADDITO	Add to immed., trap on cond. or over.
BLE	Branch and link, external	SUBI	Subtract from immediate
MOVB	Move and branch	SUBIO	Subtract from immediate, trap on overflow
MOVIB	Move immediate and branch	COMICLR	Compare immediate and clear
COMBT	Compare and branch if true	VSHD	Variable shift double
COMBF	Compare and branch if false	SHD	Shift double (static)
COMIBT	Compare immediate and branch if true	VEXTRU	Variable extract, unsigned
COMIBF	Compare immediate and branch if false	VEXTRS	Variable extract, signed
ADDBT	Add and branch if true	EXTRU	Extract, unsigned (static)
ADDBF	Add and branch if false	EXTRS	Extract, signed (static)
ADDIBT	Add immediate and branch if true	VDEP	Variable deposit
ADDIBF	Add immediate and branch if false	DEP	Deposit (static)
BVB	Branch on variable bit	VDEPI	Variable deposit immediate
BB	Branch on (static) bit	DEPI	Deposit immediate (static)
		ZVDEP	Zero and variable deposit
		ZDEP	Zero and deposit (static)
		ZVDEPI	Zero and variable deposit immediate
		ZDEPI	Zero and deposit immediate (static)

(continues)

they require a large fan-out from the sign bit and thus negatively impact a critical speed path.

The definition of PA was at least partly guided by technical talent recruited from IBM. The IBM influence is evident in the architecture's close coupling between the processor and the first-level caches. Six instructions are available to synchronize and flush caches and cache entries.

Table 1. (*Continued*)

System		Floating Point	
BREAK	Break	FLDWX	FP load word, indexed
RFI	Return from interruption	FLDDX	FP load doubleword, indexed
RFIR	Return from interruption and restore	FSTWX	FP store word, indexed
SSM	Set system mask	FSTDX	FP store doubleword, indexed
RSM	Reset system mask	FLDWS	FP load word, short displacement
MTSM	Move to system mask	FLDDS	FP load doubleword, short displacement
LDSID	Load space identifier	FSTWS	FP store word, short displacement
MTSP	Move to space register	FSTDS	FP store doubleword, short displacement
MTCTL	Move to control register	COPR,0,0	FP identify
MFSP	Move from space register	FCPY	FP copy
MFCTL	Move from control register	FABS	FP absolute value
SYNC	Synchronize caches	FSQRT	FP square root
PROBER	Probe read access	FRND	FP round to integer
PROBERI	Probe read access immediate	FCNVFF	FP convert from FP to FP
PROBEW	Probe write access	FCNVXF	FP convert from fixed to FP
PROBEWI	Probe write access immediate	FCNVFX	FP convert from FP to fixed
LPA	Load physical address	FCNVFXT	FP convert from FP to fixed and truncate
PDTLB	Purge dataTLB	FCMP	FP compare
PITLB	Purge instruction TLB	FTEST	FP test
PDTLBE	Purge data TLB entry	FADD	FP add
PITLBE	Purge instruction TLB entry	FSUB	FP subtract
IDTLBA	Insert data TLB address	FMPY	FP multiply
IITLBA	Insert instruction TLB address	FDIV	FP divide
IDTLBP	Insert data TLB protection	XMPYU	Fixed multiply, unsigned
IITLBP	Insert Instruction TLB protection	FMPYADD	FP multiply and add
PDC	Purge data cache	FMPYSUB	FP multiply and subtract
FDC	Flush data cache		
FIC	Flush instruction cache		
FDCE	Flush data cache entry		
FICE	Flush instruction cache entry		
DIAG	Diagnose		
Coprocessor			
SPOP0	Special operation zero	CSTWX	Coprocessor store word, indexed
SPOP1	Special operation one	CSTDX	Coprocessor store doubleword, indexed
SPOP2	Special operation two	CLDWS	Coprocessor load word, short displacement
SPOP3	Special operation three	CLDDS	Coprocessor load double word, short disp.
COPR	Coprocessor operation	CSTWS	Coprocessor store word, short disp.
CLDWX	Coprocessor load word, indexed	CSTDS	Coprocessor store doubleword, short disp.
CLDDX	Coprocessor load doubleword, indexed		

In addition, a new cache-control hint is available in PA 1.1 for store instructions. Normally, when a store causes a cache line to be allocated in a copy-back cache, the entire cache line must first be moved in from memory so it will be valid if the store instruction modifies only part of it. A hinted store to an address that is cache-line aligned need not cause a cache-line move-in on a cache miss. Also, a store instruction that specifies the hint may complete without waiting for the cache coherency check to complete on the central (shared-memory) bus. These two features can result in certain programming constructs executing significantly faster because out-of-order execution is allowed and some cache misses will not require memory references.

The instructions used to form constants are considered part of the load group. The LDO instruction is essentially an add-immediate instruction with a larger offset. LDIL is a primitive for building up large constants; it places its 21-bit immediate data into the most-significant 21 bits of the destination register. ADDIL can be used to help perform a load or store with a 32-bit displacement. This instruction shifts its 21-bit immediate data left by 11 bits, adds it to the specified source register, and places the result in register GR1. Thus, GR1 is slightly special in PA.

Computation Instructions

PA has a very large number of instructions that perform computations between registers. The add and subtract instructions are available in several varieties: setting the carry/borrow bits or not, trapping on overflow or not, with carry/borrow or not, and using 11-bit immediate data or a register. The subtract-immediate is unique in that it performs the operation "immediate-minus-register." Register-minus-immediate is available as register-plus-negative-immediate.

PA has four logical instructions: AND, OR, XOR, and ANDCM (src1 AND complement-src2). The UADDCM (unit-add-complement) can perform the NOT operation when the src1 register is R0. Surprisingly, there are no immediate forms of the logicals; only register-to-register forms are available. The "deposit" instruction, described later, allows bit fields to be set or cleared using immediate data.

PA is unique among RISCs in its support for BCD arithmetic. This reflects PA's heritage as an architecture for commercial computing; COBOL programs use BCD extensively. The BCD support consists of a few instructions and eight carry bits, one for each 4-bit "unit." Three instructions form the core of the BCD support: UADDCM (unit add complement), IDCOR (intermediate decimal correct), and DCOR (decimal correct). To perform BCD addition, UADDCM is used to pre-bias the first operand (UADDCMT can be used to check for validity at the same time), then the ADD/IDCOR instruction pairs sum each additional operand, and finally an ADD/DCOR pair sums the final operand and corrects the result. Just nine instructions are required to sum four 8-digit BCD numbers.

Another unit instruction, UXOR, was added to speed certain COBOL operations and also happens to boost the architecture's Dhrystone performance. The condition field of UXOR (as well as the other unit instructions described above) can encode the conditions SBZ (some bytes zero) and NBZ (no bytes zero). One way to speed up C-language string subroutines, which consume a disproportionate amount of execution time in the Dhrystone benchmark, is with an instruction that detects the end of a string. Any instruction that senses a zero byte anywhere in a 32-bit word will do the trick. In PA, this is done using UXOR with the NBZ condition to conditionally skip a branch instruction.

PA has a powerful set of shift and bit-field instructions. Instructions are available to treat two source registers as a single 64-bit operand and shift it up to 31 bits right (keeping only the low 32 bits); to extract a signed or unsigned bit field from a source register and right-justify it into a target register; and to deposit (merge) a right-justified bit field from a source register into any position in a target. The deposit instructions can optionally clear the target first, and they are available in versions that deposit part or all of a 5-bit immediate constant. The only drawback of these instructions is that the versions with dynamic bit-field starting positions get the position information from the Shift Amount special register. Thus, a separate MTCTL instruction must be used to set up the shift amount. Using a dedicated register eliminates the need for another read port for the register file.

Integer multiplication and division are performed either with a sequence of primitives or by using the floating-point unit. Whereas SPARC has a multiply step but no divide step, presumably because division is much less frequent than multiplication in real programs, PA has a divide step but no multiply step.

PA 1.1 adds an integer multiply instruction that is implemented in the floating-point unit and operates on the floating-point register file. The XMPYU instruction operates on two 32-bit unsigned numbers and produces a 64-bit result.

PA has some unique computation instructions that are useful for speeding up the most common kind of integer multiply: multiplication of a register by a constant. Early RISC advocates pointed out that this kind of multiply is probably better implemented with a tailored sequence of simple shift and add instructions than with a general multiply instruction or a call to a multiply subroutine. PA goes one step further by supplying composite shift-and-add instructions that combine two steps of the algorithm into one instruction. These instructions shift one source register left by one, two, or three bits, add a second source register, and store the result in a third target register.

Listing 1 compares a multiplication coded in a standard RISC instruction set to one coded using PA shift-and-add instructions. This multiplication is implemented with three fewer instructions in PA.

Flow Control Instructions

All PA branches are delayed. To increase the likelihood that a useful instruction can be placed in the delay slot, all branches have a nullify bit that determines the treatment of the delayed instruction. For unconditional branches, the nullify bit simply cancels the execution of the delayed

Listing 1. (a) Multiplication using typical RISC instruction set; (b) multiplication using PA shift-and-add instructions

```
; compute r2 = r1 * 11          ; compute r2 = r1 * 11
    add      r2,r1,0                sh1add   r1,r1,r2
    shleft   r3,r1,1                sh3add   r1,r2,r2
    add      r2,r2,r3
    shleft   r3,r1,3
    add      r2,r2,r3
           (a)                              ( b)
```

instruction. For conditional branches, the delayed instruction is canceled if the branch is backward and fails, or is forward and succeeds. This behavior, which is designed to maximize the opportunities to fill delay slots, is similar to "annulling" branches in SPARC or "branch likely" in MIPS-II. PA's nullifying branches have the additional feature of treating forward and backward branches differently.

PA has an unusual conditional-branch architecture. Most other RISCs have either a fairly traditional condition-code model, such as SPARC and ARM, or a "relationship-as-data" model (compare instructions that generate Booleans in registers), such as MIPS, 29000, and 88000. PA has neither; instead, it uses composite compare-and-branch instructions to effect major conditional control flow changes and skip-like instructions to effect minor changes in control flow. These features reduce the number of branch instructions required and increase code density.

Most RISCs have delayed branches to keep the pipeline full while the target of a taken branch is being fetched. This is necessary because branches are typically executed in the decode stage of a fetch/decode/execute pipeline. Most RISCs eschew general compare-and-branch instructions, such as those in PA, because they cannot be executed until the execute stage of the pipeline. To keep the pipeline full during these instructions would require two delay slots. Since PA does not have two delay slots, a one-cycle stall may be required after a compare-and-branch instruction. The current implementation avoids this stall in most cases by using static branch prediction; the stall is required only if the branch is incorrectly predicted.

Most PA computation instructions have a field that encodes a condition. The condition is often used to determine whether or not to nullify the execution of the immediately following instruction. This gives the architecture a set of general "compute-and-skip" instructions, which make use of the same logic that implements the nullifying branches.

The condition encodes a relationship between the two source operands, and the relationship defined depends on the operation being performed. For example, condition=1 encodes "op1 equal to op2" for subtraction but "op1 equal to −op2" for addition. While the conditions for the subtract instruction are obviously useful, it is less clear that the add conditions are applicable in real situations; they are included because they fall out naturally from the same logic.

In addition, PA is unique in that most branches perform an additional function such as a register-to-register move or a register-to-register add. For example, it is possible to unconditionally branch and move one register to another or move a small (5-bit) constant to a register. It is also possible to add two registers or a register plus a constant and branch conditionally based on the outcome of the addition (although the addition overwrites one of the source registers). These composite instructions exploit available hardware parallelism by making use of two disjoint data paths at the same time.

Floating Point

Like most other RISCs, the floating-point architecture of PA defines a separate register file, a set of FP loads and stores, and a set of FP operations. PA 1.1 increases the FP register file from 16 to 32 double-precision registers and also adds the ability to access them as 64 single-precision registers. This is double the number of FP registers provided by other RISCs. Some modern compiler optimizations will be able to take advantage of the extra registers and potentially get faster program execution. Load and store double-word instructions are provided to move 64-bit values between the FP register file and memory with a single instruction.

Like all modern processors, the FP model fully supports the IEEE 754 standard. Like SPARC and unlike MIPS, PA supports single-, double-, and quad-precision FP number formats (MIPS has only single and double, and, so far, no SPARC designs actually implement quad).

PA 1.1 adds two composite FP operations: multiply/add and multiply/subtract. These instructions are directly applicable to scientific applications programs, DSP algorithms, and certain SPEC benchmarks. They were added to PA as a result of Apollo's experience with the DN10000 "Prism" architecture.

Control flow changes based on comparisons between floating-point values are effected by executing an FCMP instruction, followed by an FTEST instruction, followed by an unconditional branch instruction. The FCMP tests for a specified relationship while the FTEST nullifies its immediate successor if the result of the FCMP was TRUE. Thus, the branch will execute or be nullified based on the outcome of the FCMP. This method requires one more instruction than other RISCs, which provide conditional branches that directly test the FP conditions.

Memory Management and Protection

PA defines a memory-management architecture in four different levels: 0, 1, 1.5, and 2. The differences between the levels lie primarily in the support for virtual memory. Level 0 supports only physical addressing while the other three support virtual-to-physical address translation. Page size is fixed at 4 Kbytes in PA 1.1, increased from 2 Kbytes in PA 1.0.

As with all modern architectures, the virtual memory address translation is supported with TLBs. The architecture permits implementations to have either hardware or software TLB reload; the current implementation uses software reload. PA 1.1 adds four block translation entries for instructions and four for data, each of which can map a region from 128 Kbytes to 16 Mbytes for frame buffers and large code or data areas.

PA 1.1 adds an optional context-switching enhancement: general registers 1, 8, 9, 16, 17, 24, and 25 are automatically saved into seven "shadow registers" when the processor recognizes an interrupt. The general registers are restored from the shadow copies by an RFIR instruction. This facility was added primarily to speed TLB miss handling, but it can be used by any interrupt service routine as long as nested routines do not attempt to use it.

Unlike most other RISC architectures, which have only user and supervisor privilege levels, PA provides four levels (called simply 0, 1, 2, and 3 with 0 being the most privileged). Base-relative (register-plus-register) unconditional branches may effect a decrease in privilege-level. Only the GATE instruction may promote a program to higher privilege levels. The new level is determined by the type field located in the TLB entry for the page from which the GATE instruction is fetched.

Rich RISC

PA is an extremely rich architecture. Although simply counting instructions can be misleading, it is clear that PA has significantly more basic instructions than other mainstream RISCs. In addition, many of the basic instructions combine two basic operations into one powerful instruction. Compare-and-branch, move-and-branch, add-and-branch, loads and stores with base register modification, shift-and-add, compare-and-clear, multiply-and-add, and multiply-and-subtract all perform in one instruction operations that would require at least two instructions on other RISCs. These instructions enable PA to exploit some of the concurrency that would otherwise require a superscalar implementation. Other instructions, such as the extract and deposit group and the unit (BCD) instructions, provide powerful primitives.

Unfortunately, this power comes at a price. For example, the PA register file potentially needs an extra write port for the loads with base register modification. Since these loads need to write back both the loaded value and the modified base register value, two write ports are required (or these instructions could be made to take two cycles).

While the number of instructions is more or less irrelevant to the "RISCyness" of an architecture, it is still true that more instructions can lead to larger and possibly slower instruction decode logic and more headaches for designers who must build a faithful implementation. HP contends that the larger instruction decoder is not necessarily slower, and that in any case, instruction decoding is not the critical-speed path.

Despite the large, rich instruction set there is considerable quirkiness. For example, many addressing modes are unavailable for stores and more addressing modes are available for words than for bytes or halfwords. HP's design decisions were based on traditional RISC principles of optimizing for fast, simple hardware and the most common instruction usage. The quirkiness of the instruction set is perhaps due to a greater than usual willingness to sacrifice aesthetics in the instruction set to more naturally fit the capabilities of the hardware. All instruction set designs require trade-offs, and HP's architects made a somewhat different set of decisions than other RISC designers.

PA is a powerful architecture for a wide range of applications. The wide range of applicability was one of the guiding principles during the design of the architecture, since HP has an installed base of computers in environments ranging from financial houses to factory floors. There is no question that the rich architecture can lead to more compact, efficient programs compared to other RISCs. While, at first glance, it may seem that this very richness would lead to slower implementations, HP's latest implementations show that this is not necessarily the case.

35

PA Workstations

Michael Slater

Hewlett-Packard has revealed its first line of low-cost Precision Architecture workstations, previously known by the code-name "Snakes," as the HP Apollo 9000 series 700. The new workstations provide an astonishing level of performance: 55.5 SPECmarks for the entry-level model 720 and 72.2 SPECmarks for the higher-end models 730 and 750. These figures require some qualification, as explained later in this article, but it is clear that HP's new machines provide performance unmatched by any existing workstations. The impressive performance offered by these workstations may enable HP to become a significant player in the RISC workstation market despite its very late entry.

HP was one of the RISC pioneers with its Precision Architecture, known as Spectrum during its development in the mid-80s and now called PA-RISC. For the past several years, HP has built a substantial business selling multiuser systems based on this architecture, which has largely replaced HP's old HP3000 architecture. These PA systems have also been available in workstation configurations. The new Series 700 is the first workstation-focused PA implementation and provides much higher performance at a lower price than previous Series 800 Models. Until now, HP has addressed mainstream workstation applications with its 68000-family line.

The new workstations are based on a processor chip designed and fabricated by HP, a floating-point coprocessor jointly designed by HP and Texas Instruments and fabricated by TI, and support chips designed and fabricated by HP. At this point, HP is the only company shipping PA systems, and PA chips are not available on the open market. In a bid to make PA an open architecture, HP has licensed PA to Samsung, Hitachi, and Sequoia Systems, and it is selling PA processor chips and software to all three licensees. Hitachi's efforts are aimed at very high performance (over 100 MIPS per processor), while Samsung's goal is low cost. Samsung will make PA systems but has not committed to selling chips. Hitachi will make systems and has stated its intent to sell chips for embedded control applications. Sequoia Systems will make fault-tolerant PA systems.

All of the workstations come standard with 16 Mbytes of error-correcting RAM, as compared to 8 Mbytes for the base configuration of most competitive models. The least-expensive system, the 50-MHz Model 720, is in a diskless configuration with a 19-inch grayscale monitor. An EISA interface is available using an optional adapter. The 66-MHz Model 730 adds one EISA slot and a 200-Mbyte disk. Both of these models are desktop units and include 128 Kbytes of instruction cache and 256 Kbytes of data cache. The top-of-the-line Model 750 is a deskside unit with twice the instruction cache, four EISA slots, a 19-inch color monitor, and a 660-Mbyte disk.

Several different graphics accelerators can be added to any of the models. The low-end graphics systems, the GRX (grayscale) and CRX (color) use an "intelligent frame buffer" that provides scan-conversion hardware for 2-D and 3-D wireframe applications. These systems provide exceptional X-Window performance, beating competitive systems by more than a factor of three. The basic 2-D and 3-D solid-modeling accelerator is the PVRX, which uses a single 33-MHz i860. For high-end 3-D applications, the TVRX uses either two or four 40-MHz i860 processors. It dramatically boosts the system price, as well as graphics performance.

This chapter focuses on the hardware design, processor implementation, and performance of the Series 700 workstations.

System Hardware Design

Figure 1 shows a block diagram of a PA workstation. The processor is composed of the HP-fabricated CPU, TI-fabricated floating-point unit (FPU), and standard SRAMs for the cache memory. Both the CPU and the FPU have a 64-bit path to the data cache and a 32-bit path to the instruction cache. Cache RAM speed required is 15 ns at 50 MHz or 12 ns at 66 MHz. The FPU maintains a copy of the CPU's pipeline and directly executes floating-point instructions from the fetched instruction stream; the CPU does not need to pass the instruction to the FPU. The wide path to the data cache allows double-precision floating-point operands to be read in a single cycle.

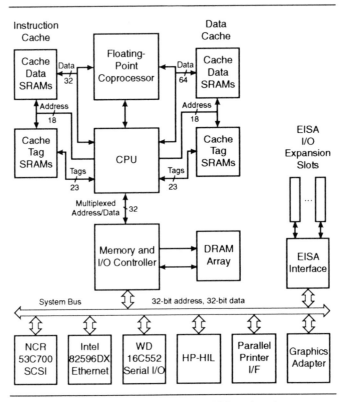

Figure 1. Block diagram of HP's PA-RISC workstations

To support the high-frequency operation, a differential ECL-level signal is used for the clock input, which runs at twice the processor clock rate. All other signals use standard CMOS levels. The system interface from the CPU operates at the full processor clock rate, but this interface connects only to the memory and I/O controller, which is a custom chip fabricated by HP. In other system implementations, the CPU can be used with other bus and memory interface chips. PC trace lengths are used for delays to fine-tune the cache timing.

The memory and I/O controller provides an interface to the proprietary system bus, which has separate address and data lines and runs at one-half the CPU's clock rate. HP does not intend for other vendors to build hardware that connects to this bus.

The memory controller is designed to work with 80-ns DRAMs. By interleaving two DRAM banks, the memory system can stream words at a rate of one per clock after an initial access latency. The memory controller includes a prefetch buffer that holds the equivalent of one cache line. Whenever a cache miss occurs, the data requested is passed to the CPU and then the prefetch buffer is filled with next sequential 8-word memory block. If the processor requests data that is in the prefetch buffer, it is transferred to the CPU at the maximum bus rate. While the transfer is occurring, the prefetch buffer is refilled from the next 8-word block.

The memory controller includes several functions to speed graphics operations. A block move instruction, which is not formally part of the architecture and is used only by HP's graphics libraries, triggers logic in the memory controller to perform a block move to the frame buffer without processor intervention. The memory controller also includes logic to perform Z-buffer compares and to aid in color interpolation.

The 53C700 SCSI interface and 82596DX Ethernet interface chips both include on-chip DMA controllers. An I/O interface ASIC provides decoding and control logic, and also includes a DMA controller for the parallel port. The HP-HIL (Hewlett-Packard Human Interface Link) is the interface for keyboards, mice, and other slow-speed I/O devices, and is similar in concept to the Apple Desktop Bus (ADB). This interface has been used for many years in other HP products.

The Model 730 bundles this interface in the base system, and the Model 750 uses a different system board design that includes the EISA interface on the same board as the processor. The EISA interface uses Intel's EISA PC chip set to provide the bus protocol support and considerable additional logic to interface to HP's system bus. EISA assumes the opposite byte ordering as PA, and the interface blindly swaps bytes within a word. This makes the byte order correct for byte-sequential data, but software must reverse the byte order when writing 16- or 32-bit words to EISA devices.

The clumsiness and high chip count of the EISA interface are a stark contrast to the otherwise streamlined system design, and this is one area where Sun (with the SBus) and DEC (with the Turbochannel) have superior technical solutions. HP believes that it was worth paying the price to have a standard interface bus for which a large number of I/O boards are available.

Figure 2 shows a photograph of the boards used in Models 720 and 730. For the Model 750, these functions are combined into one board.

Processor Implementation

The processor chip includes 577,000 transistors on a 304,000 mil^2 die and is packaged in a 408-pin PGA. It uses a 1-micron, three-layer-metal CMOS process (HP's CMOS26) and is a fully static design. The FPU uses an

Figure 2. Board set used in the model 720 and 730 workstations. The board on the left includes the CPU, FPU, IO/Memory controller, cache memory, system bus interface, and up to 64 Mbytes of DRAM. The board on the right provides all the system I/O, including the Ethernet interface, serial ports, parallel port, and SCSI interface. The board on the top is the EISA bus adapter. The graphics adapter is not shown.

0.8-micron, two-layer-metal CMOS process (TI's EPIC-2), includes 640,000 transistors on a 262,000 mil^2 die, and is packaged in a 207-pin PGA.

This 577,000-transistor size is very large for a processor without on-chip caches. The large TLBs use up a significant number of transistors, but even so, 374,000 of the transistors are devoted to logic, which is far more than other RISC integer units. A basic MIPS or SPARC integer unit, for example, is well under 100,000 transistors. The increased transistor count is due to the complexity of the architecture, an emphasis on high-speed, rather than dense, circuit design, and inclusion of a write-back cache controller.

The processor uses a five-stage pipeline:

- I-Cache Read (IR)
- Operand Read (OR)
- Execute (EX)
- D-Cache Read (DR)
- Register Write (RW)

There are two clock phases in each stage, and some operations cross the boundary between stages. Instruction cache reads, for example, start in the IR stage but complete in the middle of the OR stage; the actual operand read occurs in the second half of the OR stage. The MIPS R3000 uses a similar technique.

Static branch prediction eliminates most pipeline stalls due to branches. Forward conditional branches are predicted untaken and backward branches are predicted taken. A one-cycle stall occurs only when the prediction is incorrect.

The processor does not include write buffers, so successive store operations stall the pipeline for two clock cycles. If there are two instructions between stores, the pipeline does not stall; if there is only one instruction, the pipeline stalls for one clock cycle.

Separate fully associative TLBs with 96 entries each are provided for instructions and data. The virtual address consists of a 32-bit offset and a 16-bit segment number, and the physical address is 32 bits. The replacement algorithm uses only one bit per entry, as compared to eight for least-recently used (LRU), and HP claims the performance is close to that of LRU. The first entry whose bit is 0 is chosen for replacement, and this bit is then set to 1. When all the bits are set to 1, the first entry is replaced and all the other bits are cleared.

Both caches are virtually indexed and physically tagged, are direct-mapped, and have a 32-byte line size. The indexes are hashed to reduce the likelihood of thrashing due to the direct-mapped design. The data cache uses a copy-back memory update policy. "Private" and "dirty" bits are maintained for each cache line, and cache coherency support is provided in hardware.

The cache fill mechanism always fills from the start of a line; it does not implement "critical word first." Once the word requested by the processor is read from memory, however, it and all subsequent words in the line are passed directly to the processor as requested without waiting for the entire line to be fetched.

Performance

Without their exceptional performance level, it would be difficult for HP to gain attention for yet another RISC workstation. Much of the performance comes from raw clock speed: the low-end system runs at 50 MHz and the higher-end systems run at 66 MHz. These are the fastest clock rates of any CMOS microprocessor-based systems shipping today. Even MIPS's RC6280 ECL-based system operates at only 60 MHz.

HP's ability to achieve these high clock rates is due to a variety of factors. Chief among them are HP's high-performance semiconductor technology and circuit design techniques. While the instruction-set architecture contributes to the performance, it isn't apparent that it contributes to the high clock speed. In part, it is simply a matter of priorities; HP treated high clock rates as a key goal and did what it took to get there.

Controlling the design of the entire system, including the VLSI chips and the circuit boards, certainly helped. HP's chip designers worked closely with the system design team. HP says that the resulting design is well-specified for easy implementation by other teams; for example, minimum and maximum trace lengths are specified for critical traces. HP may also be willing to accept lower yields on its chips than a merchant semiconductor vendor could tolerate, though the company claims that yields are good at 66 MHz and that the processor chip is not the speed limiting part.

The performance of the systems is much more impressive on some programs than on others. Table 1 shows the SPEC benchmark ratings for HP's new machines as compared to high-end workstations using other RISC architectures. Looking at the individual SPEC benchmarks, it becomes clear that the overall SPECmark rating is strongly influenced by the floating-point performance; while the composite SPECmark at 50 MHz is 55.5, the integer-only SPECmark is a still-impressive, but much lower, 39.0. Furthermore, the floating-point SPECmark of 70.2 is boosted by incredible performance on one benchmark: matrix300.

The outstanding performance on this benchmark is largely due to compiler optimizations. This is illustrated by Table 2, which shows the SPECmark ratings for the currently available HP compilers as compared to those available in June 1991. The performance figures in Table 1, as well as those used in HP's press announcements, are based on these future compilers. HP's performance brief lists numbers with the current compilers as well. While HP will surely encounter much criticism from its competitors for quoting performance figures based on future compilers, these are not speculative numbers. HP says that all results are measured and that the compilers are currently in the quality assurance process. It remains to be seen to what degree other architectures will get similar gains by implementing similar optimizations.

Table 2 shows that the new compilers don't do much for most of the integer programs, but have a tremendous effect on the matrix300 benchmark—a speedup of about 6.5 times. Both current and future compilers use the multiply-and-add instructions, so these are not the source of the improvement. HP says the improvement comes primarily from an optimization technique called blocking, in which the algorithm operates on blocks of the array, performing all operations on each block before moving on to the next block, rather than moving through the entire array multiple

Table 1. SPEC Benchmark Results

Architecture		PA-RISC	PA-RISC	RS/6000	SPARC	MIPS	88000	68040	486	i860
Clock Rate (MHz)		50	66	30	40	33	33	25	33	40
Integer	gcc	35.2	46.5	21.0	19.6	25.9	18.3	13.8	18.8	15.1
	espresso	42.5	55.2	24.9	19.0	26.3	23.0	13.4	17.1	22.3
	li	38.1	50.3	23.7	23.2	32.1	23.9	15.5	23.3	21.7
	eqntott	40.6	52.6	26.7	21.5	24.7	20.7	9.8	14.8	18.9
Floating-Point	spice2g6	46.9	60.9	33.2	16.8	21.0	14.8	13.1	12.0	18.1
	doduc	48.6	64.0	33.1	18.4	27.1	12.2	8.1	7.7	18.8
	nasa7	58.0	73.7	43.4	27.4	29.6	17.5	12.1	7.8	57.6
	matrix300	210.0	273.3	26.5	28.1	21.7	21.5	11.5	12.8	28.1
	fpppp	81.4	107.0	65.8	23.7	33.8	15.3	13.4	10.2	25.7
	tomcatv	52.9	67.4	91.0	17.8	25.8	14.9	9.1	6.3	43.8
Geometric Means	SPECmark	55.5	72.2	34.7	21.2	26.5	17.8	11.8	12.1	24.7
	Integer-Only	39.0	51.0	24.0	20.8	27.1	21.4	12.9	18.2	19.3
	FP-Only	70.2	91.0	44.3	21.6	26.1	15.8	11.0	9.2	29.2

These represent the highest clock rates currently available in systems, except for IBM's 41.6-MHz RS/6000 Model 550, which was excluded because it is not in the same price class. Note PA results are for June 1991 compiler release. The systems are the HP 9000 Model 720, HP 9000 Model 730, IBM RS/6000 Model 540, Sun SPARCstation 2, MIPS RC3360, Motorola Delta Series Model 8612, HP 425s, and Alacron AL860. All machines except i860 have external cache.

Table 2. SPEC Benchmark Results at 50 MHz Using Current Compilers (HP-UX 8.01) Compared to Compilers and Optimizing FORTRAN Preprocessor Available in June 1991 (HP-UX 8.05)

	Benchmark	Current Compilers	June '91 Compilers	Improvement
Integer	gcc	35.2	35.2	0%
	espresso	42.5	42.5	0%
	li	38.1	38.1	0%
	eqntott	37.0	40.6	9.7%
Floating-Point	spice2g6	46.9	46.9	0%
	doduc	48.6	48.6	0%
	nasa7	44.3	58.0	30.9%
	matrix300	27.9	210.0	653%
	fppp	81.4	81.4	0%
	tomcatv	50.3	52.9	5.2%
Geometric Means	SPECmark	43.5	55.5	27.6%
	Integer	38.1	39.0	2.4%
	FP	47.5	70.2	47.8%

times. This dramatically reduces the number of cache and TLB misses. The FORTRAN preprocessor also recognizes vector operations and calls optimized library routines.

These optimizations are "legal" within the SPEC guidelines, and, for users with applications similar to matrix300, the performance of the HP workstations should be truly amazing. For users with primarily integer programs, on the other hand, performance is still very good, but the composite SPECmark number overstates the performance that will be achieved. Even with floating-point applications, the performance will vary dramatically depending on whether the application is susceptible to the optimizations used in matrix300. Taking the matrix300 benchmark out of the set, the floating-point SPECmark drops nearly 20% to 56.4.

The dramatic variation in performance from one SPEC benchmark to another demonstrates once again that buyers must look at programs typical of their application in evaluating performance; even looking at the average of the floating-point subset of the SPEC benchmarks can be misleading. On the other hand, HP's large caches and graphics instructions will boost performance in many real-world environments. The SPEC benchmarks don't reflect graphics performance and most fit in smaller caches, so they don't show the benefit of these features.

To see how much of the performance is due to the clock rate and how much is due to other factors, it is useful to look at SPECmark per MHz values, as shown in Figure 3. When normalized for clock rate, the PA-RISC workstations have average performance characteristics similar to

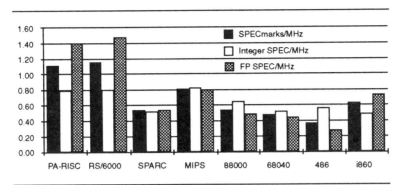

Figure 3. SPECmark/MHz for current implementations of various architectures

IBM's superscalar RS/6000. This is quite impressive, in that HP achieves this performance without superscalar instruction issue. Furthermore, IBM's machines primarily operate at a 25- to 30-MHz clock rate, with the high-end machine at 41.6 MHz—less than two-thirds the clock rate of HP's high-end model. As with the RS/6000, the inclusion of instructions that produce both a floating-point ALU operation and a multiplication is responsible for some of the high floating-point performance.

For integer programs, the performance normalized for clock rate is quite similar to that provided by MIPS, the 88000, and the RS/6000. This shows that there is no magic in the architecture for integer programs; the performance is due entirely to clock rate. Note that while Figure 3 eliminates the influence of clock rate, it does not take out other implementation-dependent aspects and is in no way a "pure" evaluation of the instruction set architecture. For example, current SPARC implementations don't have separate instruction and data caches, which reduces their performance.

The 50-MHz HP system is rated at 17.17 double-precision Linpack MFLOPS and 22.89 single-precision, with the future compilers. With the current compilers, the rating is 13.7 MFLOPS for single or double. Double-precision Whetstone performance goes from 32,680 KWhets with the current compilers to 48,310 KWhets with the new compilers. Dhrystone ratings are 100,000 for Dhrystone 1.1 and 87,000 for version 2.0; these figures do not change with the new compilers.

Conclusions

HP has created a new line of workstations that are poised to make PA-RISC a serious contender in the Unix workstation market. By providing outstanding performance, HP has a real chance to rise above the noise level and generate considerable interest despite its very late entry. In addition to performance, HP has a tremendous asset: the largest base of 68000-family workstation customers. While HP says that it will support the 68000 family as long as its customers want it, it is clear that performance-oriented users will be sorely tempted to switch to PA, and HP is going to make this switch as easy as possible.

Availability of software will be a key issue. HP claims that more than 2600 applications are available for its earlier PA machines, and all these applications are supposed to run unchanged on the new models. Recompilation and/or relinking will be required, however, to gain the full floating-point and graphics performance. HP is also conducting an aggressive porting campaign to encourage developers to port from HP's 68000-family workstations to the new PA line.

For the moment, even the low end of the PA line is much more expensive than the 68000-family line. This is not likely to last, however—HP has made it clear that it plans to use PA in a wide range of products. The initial products were designed to gain attention with stellar performance, and there are many opportunities for cost reduction through higher integration.

HP's design approach differs from that of other processor vendors in that it avoided complex techniques, such as superscalar and superpipelined designs, and eschewed on-chip caches and floating-point hardware. Instead, HP focused on high clock rates and large caches. The implementation style is quite similar to the MIPS R3000/3010, but with separate instruction and data cache buses and a wider data cache interface. HP also boosted the system performance by taking into account the entire system design, rather than just the CPU. HP is developing superscalar implementations that will boost performance further; its designers don't think superpipelining is necessary.

While PA is far behind SPARC and MIPS in building a RISC workstation base, there is still a good chance for PA to become a major player. HP should be able to build a considerable installed base of PA workstations simply by marketing them to its existing customers. Assuming that competitive PA-RISC chips become available from Samsung and Hitachi, PA could become an attractive alternative for other workstation vendors. Unfortunately, nearly every good candidate has already chosen an architecture. Nevertheless, HP's potent PA-RISC push makes it clear that today's leading architectures have a serious new contender to worry about.

Index